T0188674

**Especially For:**

..............................................

**From:**

..............................................

**Date:**

..............................................

# 3-Minute
## *Daily*
## *Devotions*
### for
### Teen Girls

**BARBOUR**
PUBLISHING

## Day 1
# The Race

*Do you not know that in a race all the runners run, but only one gets the prize? Run in such a way as to get the prize. Everyone who competes in the games goes into strict training. They do it to get a crown that will not last, but we do it to get a crown that will last forever.*

1 CORINTHIANS 9:24–25 NIV

Have you ever trained for something—a race or performance or big game or competition? When it gets close to the event, your thoughts and actions are consumed with preparing for it. You train as hard as you can so that you can do as well as you can, right? You should have the same diligence and self-discipline about your walk with God.

It's the start of a new year. It's kind of like a starting line in a race. You have the whole year ahead of you, full of opportunity. Maybe you've made some resolutions about how you want to live this year. It's very important that your resolutions include taking your walk with God more seriously. Commit to spending time in the Bible, praying, and memorizing scripture. Run the spiritual race this year like you want to win. Train yourself to be a better follower of God.

If you've ever won a prize, you know how good it feels to get that award. In life, you are training to receive a crown in heaven that will never rust, never get lost, and never break. Keep your eyes focused on Christ and on the prize of an eternity in heaven with Him.

*Lord, help me train well this year to follow You more closely.*

## Day 2
# Light

*You, LORD, keep my lamp burning; my God turns my darkness into light.*
PSALM 18:28 NIV

Do you ever feel like the future seems very dark? Or maybe something is happening in your life right now that makes you feel like you are lost in darkness. It's the start of a new year, and you have no idea what this year will hold. Imagine being out in the woods in the dark—isn't it so comforting to have a flashlight to turn on so that you can follow the path out of the dark? Similarly, when you put your trust in God, He will light your path and show you the way that you should go.

If you're confused about what you should be doing in some area of your life, ask God for advice and help. Ask Him to light the path in front of you so that you know the next step that you should take. Ask to be shown His will for your life.

A flashlight beam only lights up the area several feet in front of you. In the same way, God won't reveal to you your entire future. But He will show you the next step you should take. He will light up the path that is right in front of you. So seek Him and take the next step in faith, confident that you are never alone in the darkness. You have a light by your side that is more magnificent and brighter than any other light in the universe.

*Lord, thank You that You light up the uncertain darkness around me. Thank You that I am never alone in the dark.*

## *Day 3*
# **Eternal Rock**

*Trust in the L*ORD *forever, for the L*ORD*,*
*the L*ORD *himself, is the Rock eternal.*
ISAIAH 26:4 NIV

Have you ever seen a mountain up close? Maybe you live near mountains or have visited an area that has them. They are so huge and impressive that they seem completely indestructible. It's easy to feel very small when standing at the base of a mountain.

When Isaiah, who wrote this verse, says that God is your Rock, he isn't talking about a piece of gravel or a stone you can throw. He is saying that God is like one of those mountains. It is crazy to think that the mountains that you see today have been around from the beginning of the world. But God is even older than the mountains, and He will last infinitely longer than they will. You could never push down a mountain by leaning on it. In the same way, when you are feeling weak or afraid, you can lean on God, and He will hold you up. He is stronger and even more indestructible than the biggest mountain.

Trust in God. He will always be there for you. He is stronger than anything and anyone on this earth, so He can give you strength and help you through anything you are struggling with. He is bigger than any problems you are having. Next time you are feeling weak or afraid, turn to your strong and eternal Rock.

*Lord, You are my Rock. You will never be destroyed.*
*You are far stronger than anything on earth. You will*
*always be there for me when I call on You.*

## *Day* 4
# When I Am Afraid

*When I am afraid, I put my trust in you. In God, whose word I praise—*
*in God I trust and am not afraid. What can mere mortals do to me?*
PSALM 56:3–4 NIV

There are a lot of things in this world that can cause us fear. Maybe you have fear about the future or the health of yourself or your family. Maybe you feel afraid when you're alone or have to do something outside of your comfort zone. Or maybe you're fearful when you hear the news about the things that are happening in the rest of the world.

Whenever you feel afraid, put your trust in God. Think about this— God created the world. He is the one who is in charge of what happens in your life and in the lives of everyone on this earth. He is all-powerful and all-knowing. And on top of all that, He loves you and will be right there with you through everything in your life. Even when there is no one else around, He is there with you. He will never leave you or forget about you. And He will always listen when you pray to Him. Can you think of anyone better to trust?

*Thank You, Lord, that You are the perfect one to trust. When I trust in You, I truly have nothing to fear, because I know that You love me, You are in control of my life, and You will never leave me.*

## Day 5
# Work Hard

*Whatever you do, work at it with all your heart,*
*as working for the Lord, not for human masters, since you*
*know that you will receive an inheritance from the Lord*
*as a reward. It is the Lord Christ you are serving.*
COLOSSIANS 3:23–24 NIV

Whatever you do, you are supposed to work at it with all your heart. This means that you shouldn't do a bad job just so you can get it done. You shouldn't complain while working but rather do the work assigned to you with a cheerful heart. But it's not always easy to have a good attitude and good work ethic, right? Imagine if Jesus was the one who assigned you a paper in school. Or imagine if He was the one telling you to do your chores or clean up after yourself. Would your attitude about the work change? You would want to do your very best to please Him, wouldn't you?

In all of life, it is the Lord whom you are serving. Even the small things that you do, like homework or cleaning the bathroom, can glorify God. So try to do everything with a willing attitude the first time you're asked. Bring glory to God by working in such a way that He is pleased. He cares about what you do. He watches over and delights in you. He notices when you do the small things well. So work wholeheartedly for Him.

*Lord, forgive me when I have a bad attitude about the things*
*I'm supposed to do. Help me remember that You are watching*
*and that You are the one that I am working for.*

## Day 6
# God's Word

*"Keep this Book of the Law always on your lips; meditate on it day and night, so that you may be careful to do everything written in it. Then you will be prosperous and successful."*

Joshua 1:8 niv

In this verse, God commands Joshua to make God's Word an essential part of his life. This command is also for you. God wants you to read the Bible, meditate on it, memorize it, and make it a daily part of your routine to spend time in it. You should know the Bible better than any other book because it's through the Bible that you get to know God better and learn how to live in a way that pleases Him.

God also gives a promise in this verse. If you do spend time in God's Word, He promises that you will be prosperous and successful. This doesn't mean that spending time in God's Word is your ticket to being rich and famous. But you will be blessed and rewarded in ways that you may never have imagined. By reading and knowing the Bible, you will have a close relationship with God—you will know Him just like you know one of your best friends. Can you think of anything more successful than knowing the Creator of the universe as a close friend? So make the commitment now to spend time getting to know Him through His Word.

*Lord, thank You that You have given me the Bible as a way to get to know You better. Help me be consistent and diligent in reading it.*

## Day 7

# Refuge & Strength

*God is our refuge and strength, an ever-present help in*
*trouble. Therefore we will not fear, though the earth give*
*way and the mountains fall into the heart of the sea.*

PSALM 46:1–2 NIV

Imagine what it would look like for the mountains to fall into the ocean. That's a pretty scary image. But even if something as frightening as that were to happen, this verse tells you that you have no reason to fear. Even if the whole earth would change, you have no reason to fear. Why? Because God is your refuge and your strength.

A refuge is somewhere that you can run and take shelter to escape from something that is trying to harm you. God is your refuge, so run to Him when you're scared, worried, or lonely. He will comfort and protect you and give you the strength you need to continue. He already knows how you're feeling, so there is no reason to hide from Him. You can trust Him fully with any secrets or fears that you have. Talk to Him and let Him be your refuge and strength.

This verse says that God is "an ever-present help in trouble." What does that mean? It means that He is always right there for you. You don't have to wait for Him to finish talking to someone else. You don't have to worry that He doesn't hear you because He's busy. He is always listening and always there to help as soon as you call on Him.

*Lord, thank You that You are my refuge and*
*strength that I can run to at any time.*

*Day 8*

# The Same

*Jesus Christ is the same yesterday and today and forever.*
HEBREWS 13:8 NIV

Why does it matter that Jesus has not and will not change? Think about your life—has any circumstance changed recently? Maybe a friend or family member has changed and become someone different from who you thought they were. Maybe you've noticed that you have changed. Chances are that something has changed in your life. Change can be scary. It can make the future seem very uncertain and dark. In this life, anything and anyone can change, *except* God.

God is the only one who has always been and will always be the same. He loves you today, and He will love you through every day in your future. *That will not change.* He is the most powerful person in the universe. *That will not change.* He is in sovereign control of what happens in your life and the lives of those around you. *That will not change.* He has a plan and a purpose for you. *That will not change.*

In a world that is very uncertain and changeable, isn't it comforting to know that God will always be the same? You can trust Him fully because you can be absolutely certain that He will never go away and will never leave you or stop loving you.

*Lord, thank You that You will never change. Some changes have been very hard in my life, but I know that I can trust You—that You will be the same and will always be there for me through any changes that happen in my life in the future.*

## Day 9

# Greater Than, Less Than

*"He must become greater; I must become less."*
JOHN 3:30 NIV

Do you have this same attitude that John the Baptist had? John was very aware of how great Jesus was and how small he was. He wanted nothing more than for Christ to be exalted more and more. Meanwhile, he wanted to become less. John was not concerned about his own glory or fame; he only wanted Jesus to be known and glorified.

We live in a world where people are obsessed with themselves. It seems that everyone wants to make sure that they are noticed and praised. Social media sites where people constantly post pictures and comments about themselves especially promote this. You may notice that you are being influenced by the world's self-centered attitude as well.

As a child of God, you are not called to promote and glorify yourself. Your life should be lived in such a way that you reflect and proclaim God's glory, not your own. Do the people around you think that God is great because of the way you live your life? Does your life revolve around God and others, or does it revolve around you? It's not easy to learn to honor God and others more than yourself. But we were created to reflect God's glory and lovingly serve others. When you live this way, you will find that you have so much more joy and peace because you are living for something greater than yourself.

. . . . . . . . . . . . . . . . . . . . . . . . . . . . . . . . . . . . . . . . . . . . . . . . . . . . . . .

*Lord, I pray that You would become greater in
my life and that I would become less.*

## Day 10

# No Unwholesome Word

*Do not let any unwholesome talk come out of your mouths,*
*but only what is helpful for building others up according*
*to their needs, that it may benefit those who listen.*
EPHESIANS 4:29 NIV

What is unwholesome talk? It's not just a swear word or rude talk, it's any talk that is not uplifting. The author of this verse is telling you that you shouldn't gossip, speak badly of someone else, or complain about a circumstance that you don't like. The words that come out of your mouth should be ones that build others up and promote grace. You may be thinking that this verse gives an impossible command—everyone gossips and complains and says rude things under their breath. Think about how much you will stand out as a good example of someone who follows God if you don't engage in these activities.

Not only will you stand out as a child of God, but you will have a happier, more fulfilling life. Your thoughts would be so much freer if you rid yourself of all the negative comments that come up every day in your heart and mind. The people around you will flourish as well when you begin to encourage rather than tear down, give grace rather than condemn. Pray that God would help you follow the command in this verse, and then watch as He transforms your thoughts and life.

*Lord, forgive me for all the unwholesome words that I have*
*thought and spoken. Cleanse my heart and mind now, and help*
*me only speak words that will benefit those who hear.*

## Day 11
# For You

*The LORD is with me; I will not be afraid.*
*What can mere mortals do to me?*
PSALM 118:6 NIV

What is your view of God? Do you think that He is for you? Maybe at times when things aren't going well, you think that He's against you. Or maybe you think He just doesn't really know you or care about you.

As this verse says, God is with you. He is *for* you. He is on your side. He desires the very best for you. He is working every day to make you more like Himself. He created you in His image and loves you in a way that you cannot possibly understand. He sent His only Son to die for the sins that you should have died for.

Really think about the fact that God is for you. If you don't already believe this, then it will radically change your life to start believing it now. Since He is for you, that means everything in your life is for your good and His glory. God will use even the worst circumstance in your life to draw you closer to Him. When you're going through a hard time, be encouraged that one day you will be able to look back and see how God used this circumstance for good.

Remember as you go through your day today that the all-powerful God who created the universe is *on your side*. You truly do not have anything to fear.

*Lord, help me believe that You are with me and for me.*
*Thank You that You love me deeply and that You are*
*always working for my good and Your glory.*

## Day 12
# Good Thoughts

*Finally, brothers and sisters, whatever is true,*
*whatever is noble, whatever is right, whatever is pure,*
*whatever is lovely, whatever is admirable—if anything is*
*excellent or praiseworthy—think about such things.*
PHILIPPIANS 4:8 NIV

This is a challenging verse. Do you only think about things that are true, noble, right, pure, lovely, admirable, excellent, and praiseworthy? Or are your thoughts filled with gossip, inappropriate language, rude words, and worthless things? With cell phones, computers, TV shows, and social media right at your fingertips all the time, you are most likely flooded with images and words that do not match the descriptions in this verse.

Be very careful what you let yourself watch, read, and dwell on. Those things will take root in your heart and mind and will begin to greatly influence your thoughts. Be wise about what you spend your time on. If you find that a particular show or website is making you think in ways that are not pleasing to God, cut that out of your life. It is much better for you to lose some entertainment than to let your mind be changed by things that are not true, right, and pure.

If your thoughts are focused on things that are not true and lovely, then very soon your words and actions will not be true and lovely either. So start now and work on focusing your thoughts on things that will point you to God—things that are described in this verse. See how that will change your life.

*Lord, don't let me think about worthless things,*
*but instead, may my thoughts please You.*

## Day 13

# God's Image

*So God created mankind in his own image, in the image of
God he created them; male and female he created them.*

GENESIS 1:27 NIV

Humans are created in God's image. This means that every human has
value and worth. So if someone is making you feel like you are worthless or
have no value, know that those things aren't true. You are highly valuable
to God. You're so valuable that He made you like Him, in His image.
Even more than that, He sent His Son to die for *you.* He would not do
that for someone that He did not deeply love and care for. So don't listen
to people that try to make you feel unloved or unworthy.

Everyone that was created in God's image has worth. That means
that the kid that no one wants to talk to at school is valuable to God.
That means that the new family that just moved into the neighborhood
is valuable to God. That means that someone who doesn't look or dress
or talk like you is valuable to God. If they are valuable to God, then you
should treat them as valuable too. If someone needs a friend, reach out
to them. Let them know they have worth and value. Don't participate in
talk that hurts someone else. Instead, use your words to build them up
and love them as God would love them.

*Lord, help me always remember that I am valuable and loved
by You. Help me show Your love to other people as well.*

## *Day 14*
# Confidence

*I lift up my eyes to the mountains—where does my help come from? My help comes from the LORD, the Maker of heaven and earth. He will not let your foot slip—he who watches over you will not slumber; indeed, he who watches over Israel will neither slumber nor sleep.*

PSALM 121:1–4 NIV

Where do you place your confidence? Do you place it in your own skills, intelligence, or abilities? Do you place it in the status of your family? Do you place it in your social standing or circle of friends? Do you place it in the safety of your house or your neighborhood?

Your confidence should be placed solely in the Lord. He is the one, the only one, who can keep you safe and give you help. The earthly things that you place your trust in may someday fail you—so place your trust in the Maker of heaven and earth. He will never fail you, and He will forever guard and protect you.

He does not sleep or grow tired. Whenever you pray to Him, He is alert and ready to help. He won't forget about you or get tired of you praying to Him. In fact, He wants you to pray to Him all the time. So bring your fears, joys, desires, disappointments, and requests to Him. You won't catch Him at a bad time.

Place your confidence in Him. You will not be disappointed.

*Lord, my help comes from You, not from anything else on this earth. Forgive me when I put my confidence in earthly things that cannot help or protect me. Thank You for constantly watching over me.*

# Day 15
# Child of God

*See what great love the Father has lavished on us, that we should be called children of God! And that is what we are!*
1 JOHN 3:1 NIV

How do you think God sees you? Does He see you as a casual acquaintance? As an employee? As someone that He knows from a distance? The truth is, He sees you as one of His children. You are part of His family. He loves you, protects you, cares for you, and wants the best for you.

This is amazing that you are called a child of God. He is the all-powerful God who created everything. He is completely self-sustaining and does not need anything from anyone. You are just a small speck in the whole scheme of eternity. You are one of billions of people on the earth. How is it possible that God would even notice you? And yet He has done more than merely notice you. He has adopted you into His family. What an amazing love that He would choose to take you and make you one of His own. Once you have accepted Christ into your life, you will never stop being one of God's children. It is a position and a heavenly status that you will hold into eternity. God will forever love and protect you as one of His family. Nothing *can* and nothing *will* change that.

*Lord, I am amazed by the love that You have bestowed on me—that You would adopt me to be one of Your children. Thank You that I am and always will be a part of Your family.*

# Day 16
# Save Me

*But when he saw the wind, he was afraid and, beginning to sink,*
*cried out, "Lord, save me!" Immediately Jesus reached out his hand*
*and caught him. "You of little faith," he said, "why did you doubt?"*
MATTHEW 14:30–31 NIV

In this passage, Jesus was walking on water toward His disciples who were in a boat in the middle of a windy sea. Peter asked to come out to Jesus on the water. Jesus told him to come. So Peter started walking on the water toward Jesus. But when he saw the wind and the waves, he became afraid and started to sink.

Does this ever happen to you—you get so overwhelmed by the difficult or frightening things in life that you start to feel like you're sinking under the waves of your struggles? Sometimes it is easy to lose faith during difficult times in life. You get so distracted by everything around you that you forget to keep your eyes focused on Jesus. But when this happens and you feel like you're sinking, call out for God to save you as Peter did. He will be there to reach out and pull you up from the waves and will walk with you to safety. He will not leave you to drown in your struggles. So reach out to Him and have faith that He will save you.

*Lord, keep me from getting distracted by all the overwhelming*
*things in my life. May I keep my eyes focused on You*
*and reach out to You in the difficult times of life.*

## *Day 17*
# Outward Appearance

*"The LORD does not look at the things people look at. People look at the outward appearance, but the LORD looks at the heart."*
1 SAMUEL 16:7 NIV

Self-image is a powerful thing. The way you think that you look can affect the way you live your life and the friends you make. It can also affect your perception of your self-worth. But your outward appearance does not matter to God. So if you find yourself wishing that you could be prettier or have clearer skin or a better smile, just remember—God does not look at those things. Your worth and value are not affected by your appearance. God does not choose how much to love you based on the way you look.

On the other hand, if you find yourself feeling prideful about the way you look, remember that your looks don't change your standing before God. When it comes to Him, you can't get by on your looks. He pays attention to what's inside. He desires that your heart and mind be beautiful and perfect rather than your outward appearance.

Though some days it may not feel like it, God's opinion of you matters way more than anyone else's opinion. He is the one who is in charge of your life and your eternity. He is the all-powerful God of the universe. Of course His opinion matters the most. And He is the one who will love you even on your worst days. The fact that God loves you makes you the most valuable thing on earth.

*Lord, help me be more concerned about how my heart is rather than how I look on the outside.*

## Day 18
# Seek Justice

*Learn to do right; seek justice. Defend the oppressed. Take up
the cause of the fatherless; plead the case of the widow.*
ISAIAH 1:17 NIV

Martin Luther King Jr. was a man who stood up for what was right. He was a brave and courageous man who was not afraid or ashamed to speak out against the evil and injustice of his time. He was able to have amazing perseverance and courage because he knew that God backed him up. He knew that God hates injustice and oppression even more than he did. The Bible is filled with verses that talk about God's love for the orphan, the widow, and anyone who is oppressed, mistreated, or forgotten.

In this world, the rich, famous, strong, and beautiful are often the ones who we give our attention to. But that is not how God operates. He is not impressed by worldly standing. He doesn't look at skin color, bank accounts, or popularity. When Jesus was on earth, He reached out to the poor and outcast, condemned the prejudice of the well-to-do, and healed the sick and weak. As followers of God, you are called to do what is right, seek justice, and stand up for those who are oppressed and needy . . .even when it's unpopular.

*Lord, You are a God of justice. Help me always do right,
seek justice, and stand up for the oppressed and needy.*

## Day 19
# Saved Forever

*"My sheep listen to my voice; I know them, and they*
*follow me. I give them eternal life, and they shall never*
*perish; no one will snatch them out of my hand."*
JOHN 10:27–28 NIV

When you received Christ into your heart, you became one of His flock of sheep. He is your Good Shepherd. This means that He cares for you, protects you, and leads and guides you. He knows you by name.

If you have prayed to receive Christ, you have already been given eternal life. You can have confidence that this life on earth is only the beginning. You will spend an eternity in unspeakable joy with your Good Shepherd in heaven. In these verses Jesus promises that you will never perish. You do not have to fear death. Death is only a doorway into the rest of your life. You will not perish—you will pass into glory.

Jesus also promises that no one will be able to snatch you out of His hand. There is no need to fear losing your salvation. There is nothing that you or anyone else can do to cause you to be separated from God. You will forever be part of His flock and His family. You don't have to live up to some standard in order to earn your salvation. He has freely given it. Be thankful that your future in heaven is already secured.

*Lord, thank You that I am one of Your sheep. And thank You that*
*absolutely nothing will ever be able to take me out of Your hand.*

## Day 20
# The Rising Sun

*Because of the LORD's great love we are not consumed, for his compassions never fail. They are new every morning; great is your faithfulness.*
LAMENTATIONS 3:22–23 NIV

Do you ever doubt that the sun will come up in the morning? Of course not. You probably don't even think about whether or not the sun will rise because you just *know* that it will. It always has. Your trust in the rising of the sun is so complete that you don't have to waste any time thinking about it.

You can have the same attitude about God's love. It is just as (and even more) faithful than the rising of the sun. His love will never cease, and it will never fail you. It will never grow old or dim. You can put just as much trust in His love and faithfulness as you put in the rising of the sun.

Take a moment to think back through your life and consider all the times that you have seen God's love and faithfulness in your life. It is good to remember and maybe even record those times so that if you ever go through a period in your life where you doubt God's love for you, you can look back on all the times that He has displayed how faithful He is. When the sun comes up in the morning, let it remind you that God's love is shining on you fresh and new as well.

*Lord, Your love is as faithful as the rising of the sun.*
*Help me never doubt that You love me.*

## Day 21
# Boast in God

*"Let not the wise boast of their wisdom or the strong boast of their strength or the rich boast of their riches, but let the one who boasts boast about this: that they have the understanding to know me, that I am the LORD, who exercises kindness, justice and righteousness on earth, for in these I delight," declares the LORD.*

JEREMIAH 9:23–24 NIV

Let's look at these verses in terms that might make more sense in your life: Don't be proud because you're good at sports. Don't be proud because you're pretty or popular. Don't be proud because of your good grades. Don't be proud because of your family's wealth. These verses are saying that even though these are not bad things, they are not something that you should be prideful about or base your self-worth on. Even though it's good to work hard, your earthly accomplishments are worthless compared to the incredible worth of knowing God.

Your greatest goal in life should be to know God. The thing that should cause you the most pride in life is the fact that you have the opportunity to know God. This is not an arrogant pride but rather a humble pride that causes you to be thankful that God allows you to know Him. How amazing would it be if the thing that stood out about you the most was the way in which you know and walk closely with God. Work to be defined not by your athletic or intellectual ability but by your relationship with your heavenly Father.

*Lord, help me know You better since that is more valuable than anything else on earth.*

## Day 22
# Hold My Hand

*Yet I am always with you; you hold me by my right hand. You guide me with your counsel, and afterward you will take me into glory.*
PSALM 73:23–24 NIV

When you were younger, you probably were told to hold someone's hand while crossing the street or when walking through a busy area. Back then you held someone's hand for safety reasons. But even now that you're older, holding someone's hand is still comforting and gives you a sense of belonging. The author of this verse says that God has taken hold of his hand. Obviously, this is not literal. But the author is saying that God's presence is as close and comforting to him as if God were actually holding his hand.

God is that close to you as well. He is there to hold your hand when you need extra courage, when you're feeling sad or lonely, or when you just need to be comforted. Holding hands is something you would only do with someone that you're close to and belong to in some way. God offers to hold your hand because you belong to Him—He loves you and wants to be connected with you. Isn't that amazing? The God of the universe wants to be connected to *you* and walk through life with *you*.

He will never stop holding your hand. Even through death (when no one else can walk with you), God will be right there beside you and will welcome you home into heaven. So hold even tighter to His hand and know that He walks with you.

*Lord, thank You that You are holding on tightly to me.*

## Day 23

# Be an Example

*Don't let anyone look down on you because you are*
*young, but set an example for the believers in speech,*
*in conduct, in love, in faith and in purity.*

1 TIMOTHY 4:12 NIV

Paul, who wrote this verse, is encouraging Timothy to not let anyone look down on him because he's young. By saying this, he's not telling Timothy to ignore the advice or correction of those older than him. And he's certainly not saying that Timothy should arrogantly puff himself up with an "I'm better than you" attitude. Instead, Paul is encouraging Timothy to live in such a way that no one has anything negative to say about him. Challenge yourself to do the same.

Try to be someone that is an example of how a follower of Christ should be. Don't let your young age be an excuse to act immaturely or inappropriately. Instead, speak, act, and love in such a way that you glorify God. Look for ways to serve. Immerse yourself in God's Word. Find people that need to be loved. Use your words to encourage instead of tear down. Glorify and acknowledge God in all that you do—whether it be doing homework, having fun with friends, or just relaxing. And don't give anyone a reason to think negatively of you or look down on you.

. . . . . . . . . . . . . . . . . . . . . . . . . . . . . . . . . . . . . . . . . . . . . . . . . . . . . . . . . . . . .

*Lord, even though I'm young, help me live my life in such a way that I'm*
*a good example of someone who follows You closely and brings You glory.*

## Day 24

# Strong Foundation

*"They are like a man building a house, who dug down deep and laid the foundation on rock. When a flood came, the torrent struck that house but could not shake it, because it was well built."*

LUKE 6:48 NIV

You have probably seen pictures or videos of houses that have been swept away by a flood. Or maybe you've experienced a flood in person. It's scary to see something that once stood so solid and strong get destroyed by a powerful wave. You do not want to be like one of those houses. You should have such a firm foundation that no amount of battering from waves can knock you down. It is inevitable that you will have struggles and storms in your life. Now is the time to start building a strong foundation to prepare for those hardships.

How do you build a solid foundation? Start by committing yourself to reading the Bible and praying every day. Set aside a time to do it and stick to it. Challenge yourself to memorize scripture and to spend time meditating on it. Be faithful to go to church and other events that get you in contact with God's Word and other believers. Work hard now to get to know God and place Him at the center of your life—then when trials come, you will not be shaken because you will be grounded firmly on the unshakable Rock of Christ. The only foundation that will survive the violent storms of life is one that is built on this Rock.

*Lord, help me build a foundation now that will survive any storm that life brings me.*

# Praise Him

*Let everything that has breath praise the LORD. Praise the LORD.*
PSALM 150:6 NIV

Do you ever wonder why you should read the Bible? Or why you have to go to church? Or why God tells you to worship Him? Maybe you think that it's kind of arrogant of God that He tells you to worship Him. You certainly aren't supposed to tell people to worship you, right? Well, God wants you to worship and praise Him because it is good for *you*.

Have you ever seen something that almost takes your breath away it's so beautiful—like the Grand Canyon, a mountain range, a spectacular sunset, or an intricate flower? Think about that feeling you get after seeing something so beautiful. Don't you feel exhilarated and amazed? Maybe you want to share whatever you saw with someone else.

Does the mountain or sunset or flower need you to look at it? Does it feel better because you thought it was beautiful? Of course not! It's the same way with God. He doesn't *need* your praise. He doesn't *need* you to go to church or learn more about Him by reading your Bible. He tells you to do these things because *you* will benefit from it. You will feel better and be more fulfilled when you worship and praise Him. He is a beautiful and awesome God that deserves your praise—so praise Him, being thankful that He has allowed you the opportunity to know Him and be loved by Him.

*Lord, I praise You because You are beautiful, powerful, and glorious. I praise You because You have chosen to love me.*

## Day 26
# On His Hand

*"See, I have engraved you on the palms of my
hands; your walls are ever before me."*
Isaiah 49:16 niv

Do you ever write things on your hand with a pen? Why do you do that? Probably because you don't want to forget whatever it is you've written. You can't miss seeing something that's written on your hand. It's right there in front of you, constantly reminding you of what you wrote.

This verse says that God has engraved you on the palms of His hands. He has put you in such a conspicuous place that He can't possibly forget about you. No matter what He does, He is reminded of you. The word *engrave* implies that something has been written in a permanent manner. Unlike ink from a pen that will eventually wash or rub away, you will never fade from God's attention. As you go through your day today or tomorrow, think about the fact that God is thinking of you every moment of the day. You are constantly on His mind. The Almighty God loves you enough to think about you all the time—knowing that just might change how your day goes.

How wonderful would it be if your thoughts were constantly turned to Him as well?

*Lord, I am in awe that You think about me all the time.
Help me think about You just as often.*

## *Day 27*
# **Peaceful Sleep**

*In peace I will lie down and sleep, for you alone,*
*Lord, make me dwell in safety.*
PSALM 4:8 NIV

Do your thoughts ever keep you awake at night? Maybe you're worried about something in the future or something that you wish you had done differently in the past. Maybe you struggle to keep fear from entering into your mind and keeping you from sleep. But because you are a child of God, you can lie down and sleep in peace.

God offers you a peace that is unlike anything else on earth. If you are in Christ, you know that you are saved and will spend eternity in heaven. You know that in this life you are cared for by God. He loves you and will not let anyone take you from His hands. He will hold you up when you fall and comfort you in the dark times. You do not even have to fear death because Christ has already conquered death and will walk with you through even that most feared experience. The all-powerful God is on your side and knows exactly what will happen in your future. If you can really grasp and believe these truths, you will recognize that you have no need to worry or fear. You will have a depth of peace that nothing can shake.

* * * * * * * * * * * * * * * * * * * * * * * * * * * * * * * * * * * * * * * * * * * * * * * * * * * * *

*Lord, thank You that I can lie down and sleep in perfect*
*peace because of what You have done for me.*

## Day 28
# Life Is Short

*"Show me, Lord, my life's end and the number*
*of my days; let me know how fleeting my life is."*
PSALM 39:4 NIV

This verse brings up a somewhat uncomfortable truth: life is short. Sometimes we try to ignore that fact, or we just get so caught up in the everyday happenings of our life that we forget that we won't be here for long. But the author of this verse is asking God to remind him of how short his life is. Why? So that he will live his life to the fullest without wasting the time he has been given.

You may think that you're too young to be thinking about the end of life on earth. And while you shouldn't obsess over those thoughts, ask God to let you see how precious each day is. Ask Him to show you what your purpose is here on earth so that you can make the most of it. Since life is short, ask yourself the question, "What can I do here that will have a lasting impact?"

Anything that you do for Christ and His kingdom will last into eternity. The impact that you have on other people will also last. So invest in those around you, recognizing that you will spend eternity with your fellow believers. And also, don't sweat the small stuff. Don't get so caught up in the details and stress of life that you lose the big picture—life on this earth is just a speck of dust compared to the eternity you get to spend in heaven.

*Lord, let me know how fleeting my life is.*

## Day 29

# God Loves You

*This is love: not that we loved God, but that he loved us
and sent his Son as an atoning sacrifice for our sins.*

1 John 4:10 NIV

God loves you. Do you know that? Do you believe that? Do you *really* believe that? The Almighty God who created and sustains the entire universe loves you and knows you by name. That is amazing! His love for you is not just a casual love. He doesn't love you because He has to or because He wants you to do something for Him. He loves you enough that He sent His Son to die in your place. Your sins would have condemned you to death. But instead of letting you die for your sins, God decided to send His Son to die for you. That is remarkable love. It is impossible to understand how deeply He loves you.

Maybe you have been hurt in the past because someone didn't love you the way that they should have. Maybe they didn't care for you or left you feeling abandoned. Or maybe right now you're struggling because you are feeling unloved or unlovable. But no matter what the circumstance, you can be confident that God has, does, and always will love you. And, unlike the love that you may receive on this earth, His love is perfect and unfailing. So go to Him when you feel lonely, scared, or abandoned. He will always be there to care for and protect you.

*Lord, You loved me enough to send Your Son to die for
me. I can't possibly understand how much You love me,
and I can't possibly be grateful enough for it.*

# By Grace

*For it is by grace you have been saved, through faith—*
*and this is not from yourselves, it is the gift of God—*
*not by works, so that no one can boast.*

EPHESIANS 2:8–9 NIV

You have been saved by grace. This means that you did nothing to earn your salvation. It means that God chose you to be one of His children simply because He decided to have mercy on you. You have no right to feel arrogant about your salvation. It is a gift that was bought with the precious blood of Christ. This is a debt that you could never possibly pay back. So be humbled by it and forever grateful for the grace that God chose to give you.

Since you cannot earn your salvation, this also means that you have no need to feel guilty. You do not have to live up to some standard to keep your salvation. It was given as a gift that you can't lose. So if you make mistakes or feel like you have failed God, don't let guilt have any power over you. Your mistakes and failures do not affect your standing before God. Live in the forgiveness and grace that Christ purchased for you with His life. Let your thankfulness for the gift of salvation spur you on to love God more and follow Him more closely.

. . . . . . . . . . . . . . . . . . . . . . . . . . . . . . . . . . . . . . . . . . . . . . . . . . . . . .

*Lord, thank You for Your overwhelming gift of grace.*
*Thank You that I cannot earn and cannot lose my salvation.*

## Day 31
# Your Name

*But now, this is what the LORD says—he who created you,*
*Jacob, he who formed you, Israel: "Do not fear, for I have*
*redeemed you; I have summoned you by name; you are mine."*
ISAIAH 43:1 NIV

✦

What does it mean when someone knows your name? It means that they
know who you are. They have interacted with you enough to be able to
remember your name. Someone that doesn't know or care about you
would not know your name.

God knows your name. Really think about that—that is pretty
amazing. There are billions of people on this earth. In the whole scheme
of history, you are just a small speck of dust among a lot of other specks
of dust. And yet God knows your name. You are infinitely more important to Him than a speck of dust. He knows your thoughts, what you
like and don't like, your greatest fears and your greatest desires. In fact,
He knows you better than anyone else. Isn't that incredible that you are
known that well *by God*?

In this verse, God tells you not to fear. Think about it—what is there
to fear when you know that the all-powerful God knows you by name
and loves you? You belong to Him and are safe under His protection.

* * *

*Lord, You know me so well—better even than I know myself.*
*Thank You that even though there are billions of people on*
*the earth, you know me personally and love me deeply.*

## Day 32
# Community

*As iron sharpens iron, so one person sharpens another.*
PROVERBS 27:17 NIV

Sometimes we pretend to be excited that God made us unique and original, but believing we are different actually gives us a sick feeling in the pit of our stomach. How can we applaud originality when we are desperate for friendship and rapport? How do we find the courage to explore unique talents when we are afraid they will exclude us from the people around us?

The Bible has a lot to say about friends:

- A friend loves at all times. PROVERBS 17:17 NIV

- The pleasantness of a friend springs from their heartfelt advice. PROVERBS 27:9 NIV

- Do not be misled: "Bad company corrupts good character." 1 CORINTHIANS 15:33 NIV

- "Do to others as you would have them do to you." LUKE 6:31 NIV

Choose your friends wisely. . .deliberately. No one has five hundred friends like their Facebook profile claims. True friendship is with one or two who hear your heart, offer their shoulder, and carry your concerns to Jesus. A friend will be honest with you and allow you to be honest with them. A friend will listen, laugh, and tell you to grow up when you need it! A friend will remind you to keep priorities straight and that stretching limits isn't cool. You will do the same for them.

*Father, teach me to be a friend—Thank You for Your example.*

## Day 33

# Be Careful What You See

*I will not look with approval on anything that is vile.*
PSALM 101:3 NIV

How many times have you heard it? "I know there are a few dirty words and a bad scene or two, but it was really a great movie!" The reply is usually something like, "Oh, that won't affect me."

Seeing or hearing what we consider a "little" sin DOES have consequences. It will weaken your conscience and can alter your feelings and thoughts. You don't think so? Advertising agencies all over the world will contradict you! Why else would companies spend huge amounts of money, knowing that a television ad will run only thirty seconds during an hour-long program? Why would a company pay thousands of dollars for a billboard that is seen for only a split second by a traveller driving on a busy highway? *We are affected by what we see.*

In Genesis, Satan tempted Eve to think about the fruit God had forbidden: "When the woman saw that the fruit of the tree was good for food and pleasing to the eye, and also desirable for gaining wisdom, she took some and ate it" (3:6 NIV).

A look became a temptation, which resulted in a wrong decision—sin. Guard your heart by guarding your eyes. No "small peeks." Keep your eyes fixed on Jesus. He loves you.

. . . . . . . . . . . . . . . . . . . . . . . . . . . . . . . . . . . . . . . . . . . . . . . . . . . . . . . . . .

*Father, help me understand purity from*
*Your perspective—with no compromise.*

## Day 34
# Knowing Him

*"Be still, and know that I am God."*
Psalm 46:10 niv

What can you tell me about George Washington? What about Abraham Lincoln? I will wait while you think for a moment. Now, I understand that you know *about* them, but how well do you *know them*? (Yes. Trick question.)

For years my closest friend was my grandmother. As she aged, she felt bad about not being able to participate in things she had always loved. She felt it made her less interesting and even less lovable. Actually, we grew closer because we spent so much unhurried time together.

Do you see the difference? You can know *about* someone, but you don't *know* him or her without quality time together.

Now that you understand the difference, consider this: You know *about* the Father. But do you *know Him*? Do you talk with Him as problems come to mind? Do you ask His opinion on friends or issues? Do you thank Him? Are you His friend? He tells us in John 15:14–15: "You are my friends if you do what I command. I no longer call you servants. . . . Instead, I have called you friends" (niv).

Jesus wants to be your best friend. Slow down and spend time with Him. Read the Bible, talk to Him (pray), and then quietly listen.

He loves you.

* * *

*Father, I want to be Your friend. I want to listen.*
*Teach me how to hear and understand Your Word.*

## Day 35
# Masterpiece

*For we are God's masterpiece. He has created us anew in Christ*
*Jesus, so we can do the good things he planned for us long ago.*
EPHESIANS 2:10 NLT

The baby was born prematurely, requiring shots of adrenaline into her
chest to prompt the tiny heart to find its rhythm. The minutes of oxygen
deprivation caused the baby's body to grow unevenly. Slightly different-
sized hands, feet, and legs were unnoticed by most people. Pain, however,
began to restrict the little girl's activities.

As she grew, she felt like her body was a mistake. Clothes would
not fit correctly, and shoe shopping was almost impossible. Even one of
her brothers had teased, "When God created everything, He said it was
good. . .except for you. After creating you, He said, 'Oh, that will do.'"

To escape pain, the girl with the tomboy tendencies began to avoid
sports and lean toward the guitar. Amazingly, she discovered her hands
and arms were "made" for guitar. Her left hand, because of its increased
size and span, could handle chords not easily achieved by others. Music
and leading worship became her passion.

What she had seen as defects, God had planned for a purpose. What
she had deemed restrictions, God had used to direct her to her purpose.

. . . . . . . . . . . . . . . . . . . . . . . . . . . . . . . . . . . . . . . . . . . . . . . . . . . . . . .

*Father, help me see myself from Your perspective—*
*that "flaws" have function and my pain has purpose.*
*Help me understand how much You love me.*

## Day 36
# Off the Leash

*"You must love the LORD your God and always obey his*
*requirements, decrees, regulations, and commands."*
DEUTERONOMY 11:1 NLT

The dog managed to slip his neck out of his collar and run. Carrie called him back, but he pretended not to hear. The dog ran in and out of the woods and through multiple neighbors' yards. He absolutely refused to go to the house. Carrie was suddenly ashamed watching the dog, realizing she was watching her own stubbornness.

The dog knew what his master wanted but refused to be obedient. He never strayed too far—stayed close to his home—but knew that when he surrendered, he would be on a leash.

Carrie knew that she too wanted the security of her Master—Jesus—without the restraints of obedience. She knew she stayed close enough to appease her conscience but enjoyed feeling like she could make her own decisions and maintain some level of independence. She had secretly begun to resent what she believed to be unnecessary limitations. She wanted to choose her friends, her clothes, and her curfew!

The dog ran for hours, but Carrie loved him too much to close the door until he was inside. She realized neither her parents nor the Lord had closed the door on her either. She also realized that her partial obedience wasn't obedience at all.

. . . . . . . . . . . . . . . . . . . . . . . . . . . . . . . . . . . . . . . . . . . . . . . . . . . . .

*Father, I know You say I cannot be lukewarm. I cannot be mediocre.*
*Forgive me. I want to be 100 percent devoted to You and Your will.*

## Day 37
# Not Fair!

*"From everyone who has been given much, much will be demanded; and from the one who has been entrusted with much, much more will be asked."*

LUKE 12:48 NIV

Our Father wants us to become like Christ. He wants us to learn to love, to serve, and to forgive. He teaches us through experiences that play out like school grades—the more we grow, the harder the next lesson; anything failed has to be retaken. Then, the more we learn, the more responsibility He requires. Lesson. Test. Repeat. . .

We must work to "grow up" and take responsibility. We must try to be diligent in our improvements. Yet we often feel surrounded by people whose lives seem easier. We are even required to show mercy and patience to people who do not seem to be working or progressing at the same pace as we are. Sometimes life doesn't seem fair!

We must remember that it is our job to love and God's job to judge. We are simply responsible for our own work and attitude. The more we know, the more we are required to do; and the more we have, the more we are required to give. Got it?

*Father, help me remember that I can never repay You for what You have done for me, and I will never give back to You as much as You have already given to me. Forgive me for judging others. I want to show as much mercy to other people as You show to me.*

*Day 38*

# Rock Solid Part 1

*"For who is God besides the LORD? And who is the Rock except our God?"*

2 SAMUEL 22:32 NIV

How about a lesson on rocks? I know it sounds pretty boring, but stick with me for a minute.

I don't mean a pebble—nothing small or cutesy—I mean a rock large enough for a cave to be carved in its side. Torrential rains, high winds, or a bone-chilling blizzard would not change it. It would not move. It would be secure and steady. It could not burn. It could not leak or blow away. It would be immovable and dependable.

The point? Several times in scripture our God compares Himself to a rock. He does not change. His promises are true. He is always dependable. He can be trusted. He is all-powerful. He is never panicked. He wants to be your Father. He loves you.

> *For I am convinced that neither death nor life, neither angels nor demons, neither the present nor the future, nor any powers, neither height nor depth, nor anything else in all creation, will be able to separate us from the love of God that is in Christ Jesus our Lord.*
> ROMANS 8:38–39 NIV

Remember. He loves you. That will not change. It's etched in stone.

. . . . . . . . . . . . . . . . . . . . . . . . . . . . . . . . . . . . . . . . . . . . . . . . . . . . . . .

*Father, help me understand the height, depth, and width of Your love for me. Help me open my heart to Your love and never doubt it.*

## Day 39
# Rock Solid Part 2

*"You must be holy because I am holy."*
1 PETER 1:16 NLT

When we accept Jesus as our Savior, we take on the name "Christian." In the same way that we favor our human mother and father, we should also begin more and more to look like our heavenly Father. People should look at us and see the resemblance.

Think about it this way: We are prone to adjust our personality according to our surroundings. We might act differently at church than we would with people we want to impress at school. We might treat teachers differently than we would treat our parents.

But God does not change. His personality and promises remain the same. Therefore, we should not change either. We should be firm in our beliefs. We should be immovable in our morals. We should not waver, wobble, or waffle. He is not evil—we should have nothing in us that appears to be evil. He loves—we should love. He is good—we should be good. He does not compromise—we should not compromise.

Our standards, morals, and principles should not change. They should not shift. They should not be variable. They must be rock solid—set in stone.

. . . . . . . . . . . . . . . . . . . . . . . . . . . . . . . . . . . . . . . . . . . . . . . . . . . . . . . . . . . .

*Father, forgive me for my tendency to compromise in an effort to fit in with others. Please give me the courage to stand firm. I want people to look at me and see You.*

## Day 40
# As I Have Loved You

*"A new command I give you: Love one another.*
*As I have loved you, so you must love one another."*
JOHN 13:34 NIV

What do we know about God's love and the characteristics it produces?

- Love never fails. 1 CORINTHIANS 13:8 NIV

- "I have loved you with an everlasting love."
  JEREMIAH 31:3 NIV

- [His compassions] are new every morning.
  LAMENTATIONS 3:23 NIV

- He is patient with you. 2 PETER 3:9 NIV

- He does not treat us as our sins deserve.
  PSALM 103:10 NIV

- . . .and the list goes on and on.

Do you feel secure knowing that He loves you completely and that forgiveness is always available? Think about it for a moment. Feel it.

Time to be honest: Do you depend on mercy for your own actions yet want justice for someone who has hurt you? Do you find your own bad attitudes justifiable but believe others deserve punishment?

Am I willing to forgive and love others in the same way that God loves me?

*Father, I don't always feel loving toward people who hurt me.*
*Help me see others as Your children. Help me think with Your mind*
*and love with Your heart. Would You love them through me?*

## Day 41

# First Things First

*"'Love the Lord your God with all your heart and with all your soul and with all your strength and with all your mind'; and, 'Love your neighbor as yourself.'"*

LUKE 10:27 NIV

Sunday school teachers say you should love the Lord. Grandmothers tell you to love others. But do you skip the end of the verse? Go back and read closely. *"Love your neighbor as yourself."*

Do you love yourself? How well do you love yourself? Are you as kind to the girl who looks back at you from the mirror as you are to your best friend? Are you as patient with yourself as you are with a little old lady at church? Are you as gentle with yourself as you are with a small child who is lost at the mall?

Why not? You are God's child. He loves you. He treasures you. You are created in His image. From the moment you accept Christ as your Savior, His Spirit lives in you! Say this aloud: "God loves me. He treasures me. He adores me. He wants me to feel His love—to accept His love. Then I can pass it on to people around me."

Does that seem like a strange concept? Well, you know that haughty girl who makes you feel self-conscious? Or the loud boy that tries to be the center of attention? They are all insecure in the deepest part of their hearts—desperate to be accepted. Yes. We are all the same—desperate to be loved.

*Father, please fill me with Your love. Fill me up to overflowing.*
*Let it spill out on the thirsty people around me.*

## Day 42
# Prove It!

*Don't suppress the Spirit, and don't stifle those who have a word from the Master. On the other hand, don't be gullible. Check out everything, and keep only what's good. Throw out anything tainted with evil.*
1 THESSALONIANS 5:19–22 MSG

Through Bible stories, small children learn very basic truths—that God loves, forgives, and protects people in difficult situations. They learn about Jesus.

Fast-forward a few years, and we learn a new skill. . .reading. Once we learn to read, our responsibility for learning God's Word totally changes! Anytime you hear a preacher or a teacher discuss a topic that is different from how you have understood it, go to the Bible. Google it. Read everything you can about the subject. Do NOT accept anything into your beliefs, your faith, your *theology*, unless it is proven in scripture.

People are teaching some WEIRD stuff! A lot of it is altered from the Bible. On the other hand, our God has said and done some REALLY strange things! Awesome things! Wild things! We have the responsibility and the privilege to study His Word and to know Him as our God, our King, our Creator, our Abba. Are you wondering what *Abba* means? It's in the Bible. It means "Papa." He loves us and calls us His children. The Bible also says He sings over us. Can you imagine the Creator of the universe calling your name and singing to you? You have so much to learn! He loves you!

. . . . . . . . . . . . . . . . . . . . . . . . . . . . . . . . . . . . . . . . . . . . . . . . . . . . . . . . . .

***Father, as I read the Bible, help me know You!***

## Day 43
# Wedding Plans

*The LORD God said, "It is not good for the man to be alone. I will make a helper suitable for him."*
GENESIS 2:18 NIV

Every girl dreams of her "Big Day."

Of her gown overlaid with lace...

Of whispered vows, a diamond ring...

The sweet love on her chosen's face...

Have you begun wedding planning? Do you dream about candlelight flickering in a church as you whisper promises that will take a lifetime to fulfill? Hold on a second. I am not talking about dreaming, but real preparation.

Starting today, pray for your future husband. He is probably close to your age and going through a lot of the same insecurities that you experience. Pray for his salvation—that he will be hungry to study the Bible and learn God's truths. Pray that he has Christian friends who will help him live a strong, moral life. Pray that he will stay pure and not fall into any sort of immorality or addiction. Pray that he will apply himself in school so he can provide for your family. Pray that he will learn a good work ethic but also learn to laugh and play. Pray that he has mentors to teach him strength and kindness. Pray for his parents to protect him and love him. Pray for him to be protected from evil.

Pray for him every day, beginning today, for the rest of your life.

*Father, I pray protection and blessing on my future husband. Please give him a hunger for wisdom and purity and a hunger to follow You.*

## Day 44
# The Gift Is You

*Run from anything that stimulates youthful lusts.*
*Instead, pursue righteous living, faithfulness, love, and peace.*
2 TIMOTHY 2:22 NLT

One day you will probably stand face-to-face with the man you love. You will take vows of "for better or worse, in sickness and in health. . ." You will have opened a multitude of wedding gifts, and people will ask you, "What is your favorite gift?" hoping it will be the one they gave you.

I have not met your future husband. I have no clue about his height, weight, skin tone, musical preference, or facial hair. But I do know one thing about that man. I know what HIS favorite gift will be—it's a no-brainer. His favorite gift will be you! You heard right. You. Don't you think he deserves the very best YOU that you can offer him?

Pretend for a minute. . . IF you begin a journal for your future husband. IF every time you hold someone's hand, give or accept a hug or a kiss—any time you give anything of yourself away—you write a note about it. IF you plan on giving him the journal the day you marry him. . . *What would you want written in it?* Wouldn't you want to hand him a book with completely clean pages? Wouldn't you want to tell him that he had always been worth the wait?

. . . . . . . . . . . . . . . . . . . . . . . . . . . . . . . . . . . . . . . . . . . . . . . . . . . .

*Father, please help me remain completely pure. I need Your*
*gift of self-control to strengthen me at all times. I want to*
*stand before my husband as a spotless and pure bride.*

## Day 45

# God Hearts You!

*You have searched me, LORD, and you know me. You know when I sit and when I rise; you perceive my thoughts from afar. You discern my going out and my lying down; you are familiar with all my ways. Before a word is on my tongue you, LORD, know it completely. You hem me in behind and before, and you lay your hand upon me.*

PSALM 139:1–5 NIV

Do you know that God loves you? I don't mean just a little. He adores you. He treasures you. Don't believe for one minute that you are an afterthought. He knows where you are, what you are thinking, and what you are about to say before you say it.

He created you with care—every detail before and after your birth:

*You knit me together in my mother's womb. I praise you because I am fearfully and wonderfully made; your works are wonderful. . . . Your eyes saw my unformed body; all the days ordained for me were written in your book before one of them came to be. How precious to me are your thoughts, God! How vast is the sum of them! Were I to count them, they would outnumber the grains of sand.*

PSALM 139:13–14, 16–18 NIV

He created you. He knows you. He loves you. Do you wonder how much? Once you accept Him as your Savior, He calls you His bride!

. . . . . . . . . . . . . . . . . . . . . . . . . . . . . . . . . . . . . . . . . . . . . . . . . . . .

***Father, I want to live a pure life. I want to follow Your commandments and honor You with my life. I want to be Your bride.***

## Day 46
# Knowing It by Heart

*I have hidden your word in my heart that I might not sin against you.*
PSALM 119:11 NIV

The soldiers were introduced as they stepped off the military plane. They were prisoners of war who were being returned to their country and their families.

One was asked how he survived the years of solitary confinement. He said they would wait for the silence of night when a new prisoner was brought into camp. Using Morse code they would ask if he knew any Bible verses. He said they had collected a handful of verses they repeated constantly. He quoted a few quickly. One of them was actually a quote by Benjamin Franklin.

Think about it. We have Bibles lying around everywhere—even Bibles on our computers and smartphones. But do we *know* it? If all Bibles suddenly disappeared, how much of God's Word do you have in your head and heart? Don't say you can't memorize it! You can probably sing dozens of songs and quote more than a dozen commercials right now!

If someone wrote you a love note, *you would read it until you could repeat it!* The Bible is a sixty-six-book love letter from the Father to YOU. Write verses on index cards or sticky notes. Stick one on your bathroom mirror, and have one on your nightstand. If you memorize only one or two weekly, think about how much of God's truth you will have in you within a few years! Begin making it a priority today.

*Father, thank You for Your Word—for Your promises and Your instruction. Plant it deeply in my heart.*

## Day 47

# Sticks and Stones

*The tongue has the power of life and death.*

PROVERBS 18:21 NIV

. . .but words can never harm me.

What a lie! What a terrible, pathetic lie! Words *do* hurt! They shame. They demean. They criticize. They wound. They humiliate. They expose secrets. They crush confidence. They minimize worth. They shatter security. They destroy relationships.

Words can also love. They can build up. They can comfort. They can console. They sympathize. They teach. They encourage. They inspire. They motivate. They nurture. They can heal.

Please, please be very careful with your words! Your words can attract people to you or repel people from you. They also reveal your heart. Have you seen someone mash their finger and been surprised at the words that came flying out of their mouth? Scripture says, "For the mouth speaks what the heart is full of" (Luke 6:45 NIV).

Stated a different way, you are like a tube of toothpaste—whatever is inside of you squirts out when pressure is applied!

Guard your heart. Do not allow someone's words to distort your view of yourself. Ask God to protect your heart from false criticism.

Guard your mouth. Be careful of how your words affect others. Ask God to remind you of Ephesians 4:29: "Watch the way you talk. Let nothing foul or dirty come out of your mouth. Say only what helps, each word a gift" (MSG).

* * * * * * * * * * * * * * * * * * * * * * * * * * * * * * * * * * * * * * * *

*Father, help my words be gifts to others.*

## *Day 48*
# Big Faith

*Without faith it is impossible to please God.*
HEBREWS 11:6 NIV

Does it seem like faith came easily to people in the Bible? Because you know how Bible stories end, do you have a hard time understanding their struggles? Can you imagine the nausea from the rolling, swaying ark, multiplied by the smells of animals? Have you felt Joseph's fear from the bottom of the well as he wondered if he would ever walk on solid ground again? Somehow we miss the depth of trust in Almighty God these people had. Why? Do we not understand how great our God truly is?

Think about it. . . . Our God is the Creator of the universe.

*Who has scooped up the ocean in his two hands, or measured the sky between his thumb and little finger?*
ISAIAH 40:12 MSG

He has power over everything.

*Then Jesus came to them and said, "All authority in heaven and on earth has been given to me."*
MATTHEW 28:18 NIV

He is in control of the biggest, yet He cares for the smallest.

*"Are not two sparrows sold for a penny? Yet not one of them will fall to the ground outside your Father's care."*
MATTHEW 10:29 NIV

He cares about *you.* Trust Him.

*Father, I want my faith to increase because You are the one true God.*

## Day 49

# When It's Boring

*"Obedience is better than sacrifice, and submission
is better than offering the fat of rams."*
1 SAMUEL 15:22 NLT

I never quite understood this verse. I would read it and react like my Boston terrier—head tilted to the side with a confused look on my face. So I decided to dissect it.

I realized the two sentences are parallel. The first part of each sentence refers to God's commands. We are commanded to be obedient. We are commanded to submit. The second part of each sentence (sacrifice and fat of rams) refers to payment for sin. Suddenly I understood. The Lord desires what is better—obedience rather than begging forgiveness for sin.

The Lord is merciful. He always loves. He certainly forgives. But He wants us to bypass sin and its consequences. He wants the best for us through obedience to His commands. He wants us to have a foundation of moral purity. Does it sound boring? Maybe sometimes. But it's always right. Always.

What happens when we choose to ignore God's commands? Just remember that our religious razzle-dazzle does not negate our sin. He sees. He knows. He's willing to forgive. But life would be much better if we would simply choose to obey. . .first.

*Father, forgive me for my willful disobedience.
I confess it. I want to live a life of purity.*

## *Day* 50
# No More Regret

*Don't let anyone look down on you because you are
young, but set an example for the believers in speech,
in conduct, in love, in faith and in purity.*
1 TIMOTHY 4:12 NIV

Remember the last time you had that sick feeling in the pit of your stomach? You know the one—when you regret what you said, what you did, or how you reacted. You wish you could take it all back. You wish it could be undone. You dread the coming punishment. Maybe you had a temper fit or temptation got the best of you. Maybe it was a lie.

Think about it a moment. Our God wants you to never experience that defeat again.

Reread today's scripture. Let's be honest. The synonyms of *purity* can sound pretty boring: *moral, wholesome, decent,* and *spotless.*

Truthfully, a life of purity is anything but simple or boring. It requires strength, self-control, and discipline. How is it even possible? You make *what God says* more important than what you feel or think. You make the decision to stay close to the Lord and be obedient to His commands minute by minute and day by day.

The perks? You can live without that sick regret. You can respect yourself. You will develop a close friendship with Jesus. He loves you, you know.

*Father, teach me Your Word and Your will for me. I commit to
obedience. I want to live my life as an example to other people.*

# His Name!

*The name of the LORD is a fortified tower;*
*the righteous run to it and are safe.*
PROVERBS 18:10 NIV

Remember in kindergarten when the mean boys would call the other students names? Fatso, Beanpole, Dumbo, and Pinocchio were among the favorites. The names were descriptive and, even now, provide a mental image of a child they were pointed toward.

In scripture, God was into name-calling but in a different way. When He wanted to further explain Himself—introduce Himself—to His people, He would use one of His names to explain His character.

When people were sick, He introduced himself as *Jehovah Rapha*, the God who heals. When they were in need, He introduced himself as *Jehovah Jireh*, the God who provides.

Are you facing a HUGE problem? I want to assure you that *El Elyon*, the Most High God, is in control! Do you feel like no one understands you? *El Roi* is the God who sees. He sees every detail, understands, and cares. Feeling alone in the middle of a conflict? *Jehovah Nissi* is your banner. He goes ahead of you!

He is our Creator, our righteousness, our Shepherd, our Savior and friend! He is everything we need! We are never alone. We can always run to Him and be safe.

. . . . . . . . . . . . . . . . . . . . . . . . . . . . . . . . . . . . . . . . . . . . . . . . . . . . . . . . . .

*Father, thank You that You are always with me.*
*Teach me to depend on You more fully.*

# Everyone Is Listening

*Set a guard over my mouth, LORD; keep watch over the door of my lips.*
PSALM 141:3–4 NIV

Just a few years ago, a person could lose control momentarily, make a few rude or crude comments, and within a short amount of time, it was forgotten. No more. YouTube videos and screenshots of Facebook posts or comments on Twitter retain every rant or tantrum permanently!

Obviously, you are reading words I have written. Yet I have a motto: never put anything in writing! Let me explain. Words can easily be twisted and misunderstood. Have you ever written something, hoping that the reader would understand you had typed using your "teasing font" or your "sarcastic font"? The written word carries heavy responsibility.

Some good rules?

- NEVER say anything on social media you would not want read in front of your class at school, your church, AND your parents.

- NEVER say anything about a person you would not say to the person.

- NEVER "like," "share," or "comment" on anything you would not have written.

Finally. . .would you want to read and explain it to Jesus Christ?

Remember, it is called SOCIAL media for a reason! Nothing about it is private. Guard your words. They are powerful.

*Father, let the words of my mouth be acceptable in Your sight.*

## Day 53

# Speak the Truth

*The LORD detests lying lips, but he delights in those who tell the truth.*
PROVERBS 12:22 NLT

The school secretary called the young mother and asked her to pick her son up from school. He had been suspended from riding the school bus. The mom went straight to the principal's office. After hearing the accusations, she motioned for her son to come outside with her. The principal asked her to have a seat and discuss the circumstances. She declined until she had a moment with the child.

The young boy's account was different than the adult's. The mother went into the school office and defended her son. In spite of the principal's attitude, she did not waver. After a few phone calls, the principal admitted the boy's account had been accurate. The suspension was lifted immediately.

How could a mom believe an eight-year-old instead of school officials? Well, *I did it because I knew my son.* He had a reputation for being honest with me. I knew I could trust him.

Be THAT person. Be honest. Stand for truth. Be credible. Do not stretch, bend, fold, or mutilate the truth. Be honest even when you know you were wrong—ESPECIALLY when you know you were wrong. Be honest and offer apologies when necessary. But always tell the truth.

*Father, I want to be known for being a person of my word. Teach me to guard my words.*

*Day 54*

# Small Is Not Insignificant

*For we are God's handiwork, created in Christ Jesus to do*
*good works, which God prepared in advance for us to do.*
Ephesians 2:10 niv

Consider this: just as there was only one Moses, one Joseph, and one Peter, there is only one Billy Graham and one YOU. Don't roll your eyes! I am fully aware of the numbers of people who were influenced by each of these men—three thousand people accepted Jesus as their Savior after one of Peter's sermons! But the real importance of each of these men is not the NUMBERS. Rather, it's in their obedience to do the "good works, which God prepared in advance."

You may not expect to teach in front of thousands—but what about the fifteen who may listen on a Sunday morning. . .or the person at the lunch table who needs encouragement because of problems at home? God is in the small. He cares about the day-to-day. He is interested in the one sheep that is separated from the ninety-nine (see Luke 15:4 and Matthew 18:12).

Do you feel that your life lacks importance because you are not chosen for "greatness"? Check out Galilee, Bethlehem, and Nazareth. They were small towns. Consider having twelve followers and one of them not believing—just a small handful of men. Would you dare call Jesus' life insignificant?

You are important too. You "are [His] handiwork, created in Christ Jesus to do good works, which God prepared in advance." Works assigned to you, entrusted to you. Because He loves you.

. . . . . . . . . . . . . . . . . . . . . . . . . . . . . . . . . . . . . . . . . . . . . . . . . . . . . . . . . .

*Father, show me what You have planned for me.*
*I want to accomplish exactly what You have prepared for me.*

## Day 55

# Limping and Leaning

*Now to him who is able to do immeasurably
more than all we ask or imagine, according
to his power that is at work within us.*

EPHESIANS 3:20 NIV

Life is sometimes hard and confusing. When we roll the problems or fears over and over in our minds, we can become overwhelmed. We feel incompetent to face people and situations.

Instead of focusing on our weakness, we need to focus on God's strength—His power! Think about it. What has His power accomplished? He spoke the world into being. He breathed life into man and woman. He directed Noah to build an ark on dry land. He parted the sea. He instructed Peter to walk on water. He protected Daniel in the lions' den. He fed five thousand with five loaves and two fishes. He raised people from the dead!

The truth is, we spend way too much energy trying to limp around and handle things on our own rather than leaning on the Father, who is able to do "immeasurably more than all we ask or imagine"! Instead of worrying about issues, we should pray. We should ask God for specific direction, wisdom, and strength. Then we should thank Him that He has the answers. He loves us!

*Father, forgive me for trying to be independent. You said we
should come to You as children. Teach me how to lean on You.*

## Day 56
# Evil for Evil

*Do not repay anyone evil for evil.*
ROMANS 12:17 NIV

Maybe she tried to steal your homework. Maybe she tried to steal your reputation. Either way, you have two choices: revenge or forgiveness. You know how you feel, but you want to do what scripture says. First Corinthians 13:4–7 (NIV) spells it out.

You know revenge would be easy and maybe a little gratifying.

*"Love is patient, love is kind. . ."*

You are so glad you are not like her! It would feel good to put her in her place.

*"It does not boast, it is not proud."*

You think it is time she was treated the same way.

*"It does not dishonor others, it is not self-seeking."*

This same thing has happened over and over, and someone needs to stand up to her!

*"It is not easily angered, it keeps no record of wrongs."*

Two can play her game!

*"Love does not delight in evil but rejoices with the truth."*

You are really tired of trying to be nice to her.

*"It always protects, always trusts, always hopes, always perseveres."*

Be honest. Are you glad that God continues to love you? Are you thankful that He willingly forgives you? Are you willing to be used by Him to offer forgiveness to someone else?

*Father, please love and forgive others through me.*

## Day 57

# Christ Alone

*Follow God's example, therefore, as dearly loved children
and walk in the way of love, just as Christ loved us and gave
himself up for us as a fragrant offering and sacrifice to God.*
EPHESIANS 5:1–2 NIV

Life can be confusing! One minute you are treated like a child, but the next minute you are expected to act like an adult. One minute you are told to think for yourself; the next minute you are told you are not old enough to make your own decisions.

What do you do? First: obey your parents.

Second: don't base your actions or decisions on other people's opinions. Do not work to pattern your life after others. Do not try to resemble the clique. Realize that people will sometimes offer poor advice. People make bad decisions. People hurt one another.

Instead, make it your goal to imitate God. Imitate His love, kindness, and goodness. Imitate Jesus. Try to live with complete honesty, purity, and selflessness. Try to act and react in all situations just as you would if Christ was with you—He is, you know.

He sees everything you do. He listens to everything you say. He feels everything you feel. He knows everything you need. He knows your heart. *He loves you.*

*Father, I want to act and react obediently to You. I want to
live my life for You. Please love other people through me.*

## Day 58
# Change

*Jesus Christ is the same yesterday and today and forever.*
HEBREWS 13:8 NIV

The kids laughed at their parents' high school yearbooks. The clothing was ridiculous! Hairstyles were hideous. Makeup was clownish. Everything had changed since they were young. Right? Wrong. The outsides looked different, but everything else was the same—exactly the same.

Kids were worried about not fitting in and having friends. Girls were deciding what they were willing to do to attract a boyfriend. Boys were deciding how to attract the girls. People were sneaking around to smoke, drink, or whatever else. . .ignoring the legal, moral, and physical consequences. Kids were scarring themselves through physical relationships meant only for marriage and wounding themselves emotionally with pornography. The year was different, but the loneliness, guilt, and gnawing hunger to be loved were the same. The pain of compromise was the same. The need to be wanted was the same.

Hear me. Take a deep breath and listen. Jesus loves you. He is not an imaginary friend. He is not "there" if you believe but nonexistent if you ignore Him. He knows you. He sees what you go through. He has always loved you more fully and deeply than you can even love yourself. If you have never accepted His forgiveness—He is offering. If you mess up over and over, He knows and yet never loves you less. You are not alone. Not ever.

*Father, I know my fear of being alone or unloved does not match up with the truth that You are with me and love me. You never change. Forgive my doubt.*

## Day 59

# Contagious Emotion

*The tongue can bring death or life.*
PROVERBS 18:21 NLT

Imagine. Your mom's remark about your outfit as you leave the house makes you a little self-conscious. You run into your best friend, and she pretty much ignores you. A little while later, one of your teachers reprimands you in front of the class. With the one-two-three, you are suddenly overwhelmed with embarrassment, loneliness, and feelings of failure....

The rest of the story? Your mom was upset because she forgot the car payment was due last week. Your friend was preoccupied because she had not studied for a quiz she was about to take. The teacher had been arguing with her husband before coming to school. *None of them meant you any harm.* Their careless words, however, negatively affected your feelings about yourself and, therefore, the way you would approach others around you.

When people are critical of you, weigh their words. Are they correct? Are they meant to help me? Are they covered in love? Use the same filter when you start to speak. Are my words correct? Are they kind? Will they wound? Are they self-serving?

*Father, help me avoid being wounded by careless words, and please help me avoid wounding anyone else. Teach me to be an encourager.*

## Day 60
# Begin Again

*GOD's loyal love couldn't have run out, his merciful love couldn't have dried up. They're created new every morning. How great your faithfulness!*
LAMENTATIONS 3:22–24 MSG

Think back to New Year's Eve. Did you make any resolutions? Have you successfully kept them? (Have you refused junk food, exercised more, made better grades. . . ?)

Sure, academics, health, and other physical and mental resolutions are important, but did you make any spiritual resolutions? (Did you commit to pray more consistently? Worry less? Be more obedient? Read your Bible regularly?)

Tomorrow is a new day! It is also the first day of your future. Why not evaluate where you are now? Why not begin again? We need Christ's mercy every morning. Why not commit or recommit to be closer to Him?

Did you know that you could read the *entire* Bible in one year with only 15–16 minutes a day? Think about your schedule. Could the fifteen minutes replace some television or Facebook or other social media? What would you give up that would be more important than soaking yourself in His Word for fifteen minutes per day?

I challenge you! Begin tomorrow. Commit to His Word!

*Father, I know I need Your mercy every day. I also need You to speak to me through scripture every day. I want to know You more.*

# Beasties in the Sky

*Do not be anxious about anything, but in every situation,*
*by prayer and petition, with thanksgiving, present your requests*
*to God. And the peace of God, which transcends all understanding,*
*will guard your hearts and your minds in Christ Jesus.*

PHILIPPIANS 4:6–7 NIV

One day after school, Ashton went for a walk. There were clouds in the sky, and there were clouds in her heart. She decided to try to find pictures in the clouds to cheer herself up, but everything she saw in the fluffy white shapes looked mean; everything had teeth. A handful of beasties snarled at her from their home above. *Great, that's just what I need*, she thought.

On the way home, she decided to tell God how great He is. She thanked Him for her friends; she thanked Him for her family; she thanked Him for bringing good out of bad, for being in control of her life and loving her.

Suddenly, the clouds in the sky, and those that felt like they were in her heart, changed! Her next look at the sky was different. A cute bunny came into view, and she saw a happy hippo chasing a fish. The whole sky was filled with animals playing. When she started thanking God and praising Him, the weather outside her—and "inside" her—changed.

Do you feel sad today? One way to feel happier and to have more joy is to remind yourself how great God is by telling Him how great He is. Sing Him a song about how much you are thankful for His love and how powerful you know He is. Then the bad weather inside you will change too.

*Lord Jesus, please help me always focus on how amazing and*
*wonderful You are. Help me remember to not only ask You for*
*help but also thank You for the help that You are giving me.*

## Day 62
# It's Okay to Make Mistakes

*You make your saving help my shield, and your right
hand sustains me; your help has made me great.*
PSALM 18:35 NIV

✦

Have you ever seen tiny girls dance? Lots of times they are having so much fun that they don't know if they are messing up. They are just having a fun time twirling, prancing, and skipping.

When you were little, you were just like this. You didn't know that you could make mistakes. You sang, even if you didn't sing perfectly; you danced, even if you missed a step; and you drew pictures, even if they weren't perfect. You didn't worry about messing up.

But when you got a little older, maybe you forgot that it's okay to make mistakes, that being perfect isn't possible, and that before you can learn to do anything really well, you'll sometimes mess up, and that's okay. Think about it. Before babies can walk, they fall down. Before they can talk, they jabber. Why should it be different when we get older? We'll still make mistakes, and it's okay.

Remember, if you worry about doing something perfectly the first time, you may never start. Everyone who does anything great starts out learning and making mistakes. Today, why don't you "dance through life" like a tiny girl who isn't afraid of messing up?

. . . . . . . . . . . . . . . . . . . . . . . . . . . . . . . . . . . . . . . . . . . . . . . . . . . . . . . . .

*Lord, thank You that I am free to make mistakes and that my
mistakes don't define me. I am free to make mistakes because that
is how I learn. Help me remember not to worry about doing things
perfectly so that I will have the courage to try new things that You
bring into my life. Thank You, God, for loving me so much!*

## Day 63
# You Can Do It!

*If God is for us, who can be against us?*
ROMANS 8:31 NIV

Avery wants to play the piano. She is excited about taking lessons, but she isn't excited about what one of the girls at school has been saying to her: "Avery, I don't think you'll be good at the piano." Maybe you have had something like this happen to you. Maybe you want to learn to do something new, but someone has made you wonder if you can do it or if you'll be good at it.

Here is something that will encourage you: all throughout life there will be people who think that you can't do something or will tell you it's not possible. Maybe they will say, "You can't be a chemist. You're not smart enough." "You can't be a singer. You're not pretty enough." "You can't be a teacher. You're not patient enough."

No matter what you want to do, the only one who needs to decide if you can do it is God. He is the one who gives us talents and abilities. He is the one who puts dreams in our hearts.

Sometimes the best way to move toward what you would like to do is to ignore people who may say negative and unkind things and just go for what you want to accomplish instead. As you do, your courage will grow.

Do you have a dream? If it's a plan for you from God, He is the only one who needs to believe you can do it. Live for Him.

. . . . . . . . . . . . . . . . . . . . . . . . . . . . . . . . . . . . . . . . . . . . . . . . . . . . . . . . .

*Lord, thank You that if You have created me for something, I can do it. If You have placed a dream in my heart, I can accomplish it. No one can stop me from doing what You have made me for. That's such great news!*

## Day 64

# Hide-and-Seek and God

*"You will seek me and find me when you seek me with all your heart."*
JEREMIAH 29:13 NIV

Have you ever played hide-and-seek? Did you wait in the hall closet while your heart pounded and you thought, "I hope no one finds me!"

What's really great about God is that He isn't hoping that you won't find Him the way you hope no one will find you during hide-and-seek. Instead, He wants you to discover Him and learn more about Him by praying and reading the Bible. The Bible is the main way that He speaks to people He loves—including you.

God can be found when you seek Him with your whole heart. You don't have to say your prayers a certain way, go to one special church, or wear your hair a particular way. He is most interested in your heart. And when you look for Him with all your heart, you will find Him—guaranteed.

Then when you do find Him, it will be like finding one of your friends who jumps out of a hall closet and shouts, "You found me!" Because God invites you to seek Him and find Him, He is really happy when you do.

. . . . . . . . . . . . . . . . . . . . . . . . . . . . . . . . . . . . . . . . . . . . . . . . . . . . . .

*Lord, it is so awesome that You want me to find You! You aren't going to keep Yourself from me where I can't discover Your thoughts toward me and thoughts that will help me with my life. You have given them freely to me through the Bible. Help me seek You with all my heart.*

## Day 65

# God Sees the "Parade" of Your Life

*"Do not worry about your life, what you will eat or drink; or about your body, what you will wear. Is not life more than food, and the body more than clothes? Look at the birds of the air; they do not sow or reap or store away in barns, and yet your heavenly Father feeds them. Are you not much more valuable than they?"*
MATTHEW 6:25–27 NIV

Every year Allison likes to go to a special parade in her town. She likes to sit on the curb and watch each of the floats pass one by one.

Life is like a parade. The events that happen in our lives happen one by one. We get up. We go to school. We take a test. All of those things don't happen all at once, and we can't see them until they "pass by," just like a float in a parade.

Because this is true, there are times when you might worry because you can't see what's coming. But remember that God is like a helicopter over the "parade" of your life. Because He has made your life, because He doesn't experience time the same way we do, He can see everything that has happened to you and will happen to you. So nothing surprises Him—and He is in control. He will help you for what is coming. He will prepare you for the things ahead. He knows the beginning of your life to the end, and everything in between. You can trust Him because He sees your whole life as if it has already happened. And He loves you.

*You see my entire life, Lord. You made me, and You have known every day what will happen to me before one of my days came to be. Help me always keep this in mind so that I don't worry about the future.*

## *Day 66*
# Let God Guide You

*Trust in the LORD with all your heart and lean not
on your own understanding; in all your ways submit
to him, and he will make your paths straight.*
PROVERBS 3:5–6 NIV

When friends ride a two-seater bicycle, one person rides in front and the other person rides in back. The one in the front can see everything that happens. The person in the back pedals, but she can't see what's ahead like the person in front. She just holds on and helps by pedaling. And she knows that two people can't steer at the same time. If they did, they would crash.

This is how it is with God. It's as if you are on a two-seater bicycle with Him. You are in the back pedaling, going places with Him, doing what He has asked you to do. He knows what's coming and is making the plan on where to go. He is steering. But if you try to take over, you will crash. It's always best to trust God with where you are going.

Some people try to "take over" their life by ignoring God and/or by telling Him what to do. Sometimes they disobey Him. But this will never get them where they are supposed to go in life. The best thing to do is trust Him, listen to Him, and cooperate with His plan, just like you would cooperate if you were on the back of a two-seater bicycle.

. . . . . . . . . . . . . . . . . . . . . . . . . . . . . . . . . . . . . . . . . . . . . . . . . . . . . . . . . . . . . . . . .

*Lord, thank You that I can trust You. You will never take
me somewhere that isn't good for me. And even if I don't
understand where You are going, You will get me where I am
supposed to be. Just help me keep pedaling and obeying.*

## Day 67

# Trouble Can
# Make You Stronger

*"So do not fear, for I am with you; do not be dismayed,*
*for I am your God. I will strengthen you and help you;*
*I will uphold you with my righteous right hand."*

ISAIAH 41:10 NIV

Chloe loved riding horses, but she was afraid too. Every day when she went to her horseback-riding lesson, she was afraid that she would fall. Then one afternoon, it happened. Her horse stumbled, and Chloe wasn't holding tight to the reins. She went tumbling through the air and landed on her behind. But instead of crying, she started to laugh. All of a sudden the thing that she was so terrified of wasn't so scary anymore because she knew that she could handle it.

Life can be kind of like Chloe's experience. You may be afraid of failing, afraid of losing a friend, or afraid of saying something stupid in a group. Sometimes God may allow these things to happen to us so that you realize that what you thought would ruin you, doesn't. He may allow them to happen so that we are no longer being held captive by fear. Instead, you become stronger and more courageous, just like Chloe.

*Lord, I know that You only allow those things into my life*
*that are for my good and Your glory. Help me seek You when*
*challenges come and trust in Your goodness when I feel pain.*

## Day 68

# Hold Your Tongue and Your Text

*Do not be overcome by evil, but overcome evil with good.*
ROMANS 12:21 NIV

Before Facebook and Twitter, before Instagram and Snapchat, before email and computers, if a girl wanted to communicate with her long-distance friend and she couldn't use the telephone at home, she wrote a letter, placed it in an envelope, put a stamp on it, and put it in the mailbox. Then she had to wait for the mailman to come and deliver the letter to her friend, and then she had to wait for an answer.

Now because of social media, texting, and the quick ways people can communicate on the internet, no one has to wait to say anything to anyone. They can just say it right now, and their friend will hear it in seconds.

It is awesome to be able to communicate with someone immediately, but it can also be bad if we don't know how to control our emotions while using social media. Let's imagine someone hurts your feelings and makes you angry by something rude they say about you on Facebook. It's unwise to respond right away from your feelings. It could turn into a big fight, and that won't help anyone. A better thing is to wait until your emotions calm down. Then ask God if you should respond at all, or, if you should respond, what you should say. Our words can create a lot of trouble for us if we don't know how to control them. Ask God to teach you how to be wise and use your words for His glory.

*Lord, when my feelings get hurt, I may want to respond in an unkind way, in a way that does not honor You. Help me remember that my words can make a bad situation worse.*

## Day 69

# Shame vs. Conviction

*If we confess our sins, he is faithful and just and will forgive us our sins and purify us from all unrighteousness.*

1 JOHN 1:9 NIV

Elsa lied and cheated on her test. She didn't get caught, but she knew it was wrong. After she made this bad decision, there was a little thought that came into her mind: *You are a bad person.*

When you sin, make mistakes, or make poor choices, sometimes you will think, *I did a bad thing.* This can be God telling you that what you did wasn't right. It's called conviction. Other times you may experience shame like Elsa did. Shame will always make you think that *you* are bad, not that what you *did* was bad.

When you do something wrong, remember that you may have sinned and you may be guilty, but you are never bad. You are loved by God, and God wants to help you make good choices.

. . . . . . . . . . . . . . . . . . . . . . . . . . . . . . . . . . . . . . . . . . . . . . . . . . . . . . . . . . . . . . . .

*Lord Jesus, thank You that when I confess my sins to You, You will wash me and make me clean. I never have to carry guilt as a punishment and think that I am a bad person. Please help me make the choices You want me to make, but also help me remember that when I do sin, You still love me.*

## *Day 70*
# Compassion Means Stop

*When he saw the crowds, he had compassion on them.*
MATTHEW 9:36 NIV

In eighth grade, Tamara's English teacher asked her to draw a picture to show what the word *compassion* meant. When she looked the word up in the dictionary, she discovered that when someone feels compassion toward another person, they want to help them.

Tamara wasn't sure how to illustrate this, but then she figured it out. She drew a stop sign because a stop sign shows that when you feel compassion toward someone, you want to help them by keeping them from doing anything that would hurt them.

That's the way God is with us. He is compassionate toward those He has made—including you!—so sometimes He will say, "Stop." It's like a mom who hollers at her son not to run out in the street because she doesn't want him to get run over. Sometimes the most compassionate, kind thing anyone can do for us is to tell us to stop.

Keep this in mind when God says no to something that you want, or He uses the adults in your life to tell you to stop doing something. It's because they love you, have compassion for you, and want to protect you.

*Lord, when I feel restricted by rules or chafe at not getting my way, help me stop and reexamine the situation. Help me see the care and compassion behind the rules and be thankful that I have people in my life who love me and want to protect me.*

# When Bullies Ignore Boundaries

*"But I tell you, love your enemies and pray for those who persecute you."*
MATTHEW 5:44 NIV

Every night Mr. White locks the doors to his home. He doesn't want any intruders to break in. If he wants someone to come inside, he opens the door to them or gives them a key. The lock on the door creates a barrier against bad guys.

Bullies are like bad intruders. They bust into your life and space when they aren't invited. They will be pushy with their words and actions. If you tell them to stop, they just keep going, just like an intruder would push right through a locked door.

If you ask someone to stop bothering you, if you tell them you aren't comfortable with what they are doing to you and they ignore what you say, they aren't respecting your boundaries. They are pushing right into your life when you didn't open the door to them.

If this happens to you or someone you know, tell an adult until it is resolved. If one adult isn't helping, tell another one. Remember that you are loved. No bully can take away that truth. And finally, forgive the person who hurt you and pray for God to help them become more kind.

*Lord, please give me courage to stand up for what is right—*
*for myself and for others when I see someone being bullied.*
*Finally, give me the right heart to forgive and to pray for the bully.*

## Day 72

# When You Have a Fight with a Friend

*"Therefore, if you are offering your gift at the altar and there remember that your brother or sister has something against you, leave your gift there in front of the altar. First go and be reconciled to them; then come and offer your gift."*

MATTHEW 5:23–24 NIV

When Sammie heard that she had hurt the feelings of her best friend, Gina, she was upset and ashamed. She didn't think they could ever be friends again. But then she went to church, and her youth pastor gave her some really good advice.

He said the Bible says that if you know someone has something against you, to go to that person to work it out and fix the relationship. So that's exactly what Sammie did. Plus, she did a few other things that her youth pastor shared with her too.

She said. . .

"I'm sorry."

"I was wrong."

"Will you forgive me?"

"Can we be friends again?"

Thankfully, Gina forgave Sammie, and they made up. But there are those times when someone else doesn't want to forgive or make up. If that ever happens to you, remember that God still wants you to do what is right even if the other person won't forgive.

*Lord, please help me always be willing to admit when I am wrong.*

## *Day 73*

# He Cares about Friendship

*Cast all your anxiety on him because he cares for you.*
1 PETER 5:7 NIV

Sarah was lonely. She had moved with her family to another country, and she really wanted to make a good friend. One night she prayed, "Lord, will You please give me a good friend?" A month or so went by, and she didn't meet anyone special.

One Sunday, Sarah went to church with her family, and a girl about her age sat down next to her. That's when she felt God quietly impress on her that this was her new friend. Sarah was excited. After church, she turned to the girl, said hi, and asked her name. Her name was Nicola. What was so amazing is that Nicola's family lived right next to Sarah's. They were best friends for months until it was time for Sarah's family to move. Nicola was sad, so she went to visit Sarah. Sarah had never told Nicola how God had answered her prayer for a friend, but she did that night. They both hugged, and Sarah was reminded that God cares about friendship because He made it.

If you are lonely and you need a friend, pray and ask Jesus to give you one. Then keep your eyes and heart open to people who are around you. You never know when He will answer.

* * * * * * * * * * * * * * * * * * * * * * * * * * * * * * * * * * * * * * * * * * *

*Lord, You tell me to give You all of my cares because You care for me. You care if I am lonely. You care if I need a friend. Lord, thank You for bringing the right friends into my life at the right time.*

## Day 74

# Popcorn Prayers and Longer Ones Too

*"For the eyes of the Lord are on the righteous and his ears are attentive to their prayer, but the face of the Lord is against those who do evil."*

1 PETER 3:12 NIV

Some prayers are like popcorn. We pop them up when we are taking a shower. We pop them up when our mom drives us to school. We pop them up on the bus. We pop them up when we are standing in line for school lunch. No matter how short or how long, God hears our prayers—even popcorn prayers. He wants you to communicate with Him all the time, all throughout the day shooting up popcorn prayers.

One thing to keep in mind as you are growing in your relationship with Jesus is to remember that it's also good to spend time talking with God for longer periods of time. You can do this by finding a quiet spot to sit and read the Bible and pray. You can do this at night before you go to bed. Or you can do it in the morning. But whenever you do, it will help you experience more peace and greater joy because you'll take more time to hear from Him.

. . . . . . . . . . . . . . . . . . . . . . . . . . . . . . . . . . . . . . . . . . . . . . . . . . . . . . . . .

*Lord, I am so thankful that You hear me all the time, every day. I am so glad I can always talk to You no matter where I am. Please teach me also to spend time with You, learning from You in the Bible.*

## Day 75

# You Are Someone Else's Idea

*For you created my inmost being; you knit me*
*together in my mother's womb. I praise you*
*because I am fearfully and wonderfully made;*
*your works are wonderful, I know that full well.*

PSALM 139:13–14 NIV

Here is a really amazing thought: you didn't dream up yourself. You didn't decide where you would be born, who your parents would be, which country you would be born in, the color of your hair, the color of your eyes, or the way you would laugh. You didn't pick your height, or if you are right- or left-handed. You were dreamed up by the Creator of the universe, the same God who made the oceans, mountains, stars, and streams.

When God made you, He made you with the same care that He made hummingbirds and ostriches and the fish in the depths of the sea. And because He made you with such precision, He made you to accomplish certain things. He gifted you for particular purposes to fulfill in His creation.

It's pretty amazing to think that you were made on purpose, for a purpose, by a magnificent Creator.

*Lord, I am fearfully and wonderfully made. How incredible*
*You must be to make so many animals and people—all so*
*unique! Wow! You are so amazing, Lord! Please help me*
*remember that how You have made me is very special.*

# Getting Wisdom Is Like
# Standing on Your Head

*If any of you lacks wisdom, you should ask God, who gives generously
to all without finding fault, and it will be given to you.*

JAMES 1:5 NIV

Shannon used to spend hours standing on her head in the living room at home. Have you ever stood on your head like Shannon? If so, you know that you see the exact same thing as when you are standing up, but your world looks different once you stand on your head.

This is kind of how it is with getting wisdom from God. Wisdom is what helps us understand life, and God gives it to those who ask Him for it. You can be looking at a problem, for example, from one perspective, but it looks totally different when you receive wisdom about it. It's like standing on your head; your world looks totally different in a very good way. Wisdom changes your perspective on your problems.

If you aren't sure what to do about something in your life, ask the Lord to give you wisdom, to give you His perspective. When you do, it'll be like standing on your head. Your problems will look different from God's perspective.

. . . . . . . . . . . . . . . . . . . . . . . . . . . . . . . . . . . . . . . . . . . . . . . . . . . .

*Lord, You are the giver of wisdom. And You promise that You
will give wisdom to anyone who asks for it. Lord, please give me
wisdom for the problems in my life. Thank You for helping me.*

## Day 77

# Love Is Contagious

*We love because he first loved us.*

1 JOHN 4:19 NIV

There are some truths about God that make me want to do a happy dance. One of them is that real love is contagious. You see, since I met my husband, I've caught his love kind of like you catch a cold and spread it around. Because he gives me his love, I find myself giving it back to him—and to others who are around me too. That's the way real love is. It's contagious.

Think about the most loving person you know. When you are around them, I bet they make you light up on the inside, and when you walk away, you feel more tender and loving. Why? Because love is contagious.

Sometimes I forget this truth because I try to love in my own power. I think I have to muster up the ability to be loving all on my own. But that's not true. In fact, none of God's kids have to do that. Why? Because He is the author of love—and His love is definitely contagious! And that definitely makes me do a happy dance. How about you?

God wants to give you the power to love well. You just have to remain in a close relationship with Jesus and ask the Holy Spirit to help you love. If you try to love just on willpower, you will become emotionally exhausted! But when you get the power to love from the one who is love, you will feel exhilarated!

When you are around someone who is loving, you become more loving too because love is contagious! And that's definitely something to dance about.

*Lord, thank You that I can love because You loved me first.*

## Day 78

# Come Find Me

*Look to the LORD and his strength; seek his face always.*
1 CHRONICLES 16:11 NIV

Clark's dog, a border collie named Dixie, loves to play hide-and-seek. Clark can hide anywhere in the house and call out, "Come find me," and Dixie will search down the halls, in the rooms, and up the stairs until she finds Clark. When she reaches him, Dixie looks into his eyes as if to say, "Master, why did you want me to come and find you?"

God is always calling to those He loves, "Come find Me." He invites them to find Him through prayer. He invites them to find Him through reading the Bible. And He never hides where He can't be found, but He always wants His children to search for Him.

Sometimes people don't answer God when He invites them to come find Him because they think He isn't really listening to them or that He won't really speak to them. But both of these things are untrue. The Bible says that God speaks to those He loves, and He listens to those who call on Him.

Will you say "yes" when God says, "Come find Me"?

*Lord, You always want me to come find You the way that Dixie looks for Clark. I am thankful that You hear me and that You are listening when I call. I am so thankful that You care so much for me.*

# Got Fruit?

*But the fruit of the Spirit is love, joy, peace, forbearance,*
*kindness, goodness, faithfulness, gentleness and*
*self-control. Against such things there is no law.*
GALATIANS 5:22–23 NIV

Sam has an apple tree in his backyard. Each year the apple tree blossoms and then produces baskets full of juicy fruit that is delicious to eat.

In the same way that an apple tree produces apples, those who belong to Jesus and are living by God's Spirit produce fruit too. Galatians 5:22-23 says that the fruit of the Spirit is love, joy, peace, patience, kindness, goodness, faithfulness, gentleness, and self-control.

Imagine that the tree in Sam's backyard started producing fruit that was rotten. None of the fruit could be picked. No one could use it. In the same way, we can produce rotten fruit too if we have a bad attitude. Instead of love, we can produce meanness. Instead of joy, we can be cranky. Instead of patience, we can be impatient. If you don't have some of the fruits of the Spirit and you know Jesus, ask Him to show you why you are producing rotten fruit. Then ask Him to help you change so you can produce the right fruit for Him again.

. . . . . . . . . . . . . . . . . . . . . . . . . . . . . . . . . . . . . . . . . . . . . . . . . . . . . . . . .

*Lord, there are days when the fruit isn't very good. I am cranky*
*or irritable, mean or impatient. Sometimes I am unkind or selfish.*
*Help me understand how to change my attitude when I need to so*
*that I can produce the good fruit that comes from Your Holy Spirit.*

## *Day 80*
# Palm Sunday

*For God so loved the world that he gave his one and only Son,*
*that whoever believes in him shall not perish but have eternal life.*
JOHN 3:16 NIV

Palm Sunday is the day when Jesus came riding into Jerusalem on a donkey. All of the Jews in the city waved palm branches in celebration because they believed Jesus had come to be king of their nation. They thought He would be an earthly king who would save them from their enemies. But they didn't understand that Jesus was really the King of heaven, the Christ who had come from heaven to save them from their sins so they could spend eternity with the Lord.

They were totally missing the truth of who Jesus was. They saw Him with their eyes, but they didn't understand what God sent Him to do.

Do you understand what God sent Jesus to do for you? Do you know that God sent Jesus to die on a cross for your sins so that you can be with Jesus forever in heaven and so you can have a relationship with God? Without understanding and believing this truth, you can't go to heaven. It's important for you to know who He is and what He came to do. If you believe Jesus is who He says and that He came to die on the cross for your sins, you may want to pray the prayer below.

*Lord, thank You that You came to die on the cross for my sins so that I can go to heaven and have a relationship with You. I believe that You are God, and I accept Your free gift of salvation. Please forgive me for my sins.*

# You Can't Put It Back in the Tube!

*A perverse person stirs up conflict, and a gossip separates close friends.*
PROVERBS 16:28 NIV

Rosie had a best friend named Abigail—until Rosie said some mean things about Abigail to some of the kids at school. Abigail was really hurt by Rosie's gossip, and even though Rosie went to Abigail and asked for her forgiveness, Abigail didn't trust Rosie like she did before.

This can be a very hard lesson. Once gossip leaks out of our lips, we can't get it back. It's kind of like making a mess with toothpaste. If it squirts out of the tube and makes a mess all over, no matter how much we want to put the toothpaste back in the tube, there's no way for it to happen. The mess has already been made, and things won't ever be the same again.

Sure, friends can forgive each other, but it's best to be careful with what we say so that we aren't sorry for the words we have spoken.

. . . . . . . . . . . . . . . . . . . . . . . . . . . . . . . . . . . . . . . . . . . . . . . . . . . . . . . . . .

*Lord, please help me be careful with my words so that I don't hurt others and make a mess that is very hard to fix. Help me be kind with my mouth, always building others up.*

## Day 82

# A Light to Your Path

*Your word is a lamp for my feet, a light on my path.*
PSALM 119:105 NIV

Molly went camping every year with her family. At night, sometimes she had to leave the tent and walk a few hundred yards to the campground restroom. Her dad always told her, "Make sure you take the flashlight with you so you can see where you are going." One night as she walked along, she noticed that she could only see a few feet in front of her. The light would only shine on the path where she walked and definitely wouldn't light up more than that.

The Bible says that God's Word is like a light to your path. It won't light up the sky or illuminate too far ahead, just like Molly's flashlight. It will give you just enough light for the step you are on. This is good to remember. When you aren't sure what is going to happen in the future and you worry, remember that God will only give you just enough direction and light for the road directly ahead. But He *will* give you light. He will never leave you in the dark.

. . . . . . . . . . . . . . . . . . . . . . . . . . . . . . . . . . . . . . . . . . . . . . . . . . . . . . . .

*Lord, thank You that You light my path. Thank You that I can always trust You to lead me, even if You don't lead me far in advance.*

# Not All the Same on Purpose

*Each of you should use whatever gift you have received to serve others, as faithful stewards of God's grace in its various forms.*

1 PETER 4:10 NIV

One day Madalyn was eating her sandwich during lunch when her friend Emilia sat down by her. "What? You like your peanut butter sandwiches with bananas? Yuck! That's just stupid."

Madalyn frowned. Emilia's words made her feel bad. Next, Aaron came to sit by both of the girls. "Madalyn likes her peanut butter sandwiches with bananas. Blech!" she told Aaron.

"Yeah, blech!" he said. "I like mine sprinkled with M&M's." Both the girls laughed.

Some kids think they all have to like the same thing. They think that you have to be the same to be accepted, that being different isn't okay. But God made everyone different, and He gave everyone different tastes and desires for a reason. Can you imagine if everyone in the world liked to drive the same kind of car, wear the same kind of clothes, and laugh the same way? The world would be totally boring. Can you imagine if everyone liked to build things and no one liked to paint? Nothing would get done if we were all the same.

So the next time someone doesn't appreciate your special differences, remind yourself that God made everyone different for a reason.

* * *

*Lord, thank You so much that I am unique! You made me special! I am so thankful that I am not like everyone else. That means I get to do special things for You in Your kingdom.*

## Day 84

# Your Most Powerful Muscle

*Do not let any unwholesome talk come out of your mouths,*
*but only what is helpful for building others up according*
*to their needs, that it may benefit those who listen.*

EPHESIANS 4:29 NIV

Cade likes to work out at the gym. Five days a week he goes to pump up his muscles because he wants to be a fireman one day. Every day his biceps are getting bigger, and he is able to lift heavier and heavier things. One thing that Cade doesn't know is that his tongue is the most powerful muscle in his whole body. With it, he can encourage someone to overcome an obstacle, pray for them to get well, or praise them for their abilities—or he can use his tongue for bad. With it, he can tear people apart, make them feel bad about themselves, or discourage them from trying.

Do you have a friend who is having a tough time? Maybe they are afraid about an upcoming test or they are discouraged about a friendship. Because you have a most powerful muscle called the tongue just like Cade, you can do amazing things. You can completely change someone's path, just by what you say to them. You can make them feel alive in their heart, just like Proverbs 18:21 says.

Be a change maker. Use your strongest muscle to make a difference for someone today.

. . . . . . . . . . . . . . . . . . . . . . . . . . . . . . . . . . . . . . . . . . . . . . . . . .

*Lord, please help me help those around me feel life in their hearts and not*
*death by what I say. Help me remember that my tongue is amazing and*
*can be used for good or for evil. It's the most powerful muscle I have.*

## Day 85

# Good Change Is Coming

*But those who hope in the LORD will renew their strength.*
*They will soar on wings like eagles; they will run and*
*not grow weary, they will walk and not be faint.*
ISAIAH 40:31 NIV

Becca slid out of bed and groaned. "*Aaaaaagh*. It's going to be a bad day just like yesterday. I doubt things are going to get better."

On Good Friday, the day that Jesus died, the disciples—the men who followed Jesus—didn't think that things would get better either. Jesus was hanging on a cross, and He was their best friend and Lord. They had followed Him for three years while He taught them all about heaven and God's kingdom. Now He was about ready to die, and they didn't know what they were going to do. They were afraid and sad.

But they didn't know that in three days Jesus would rise from the dead to save His people from their sins. They didn't know God was getting ready to do something more amazing than they had ever seen.

Some days are like this. You wake up like Becca and feel discouraged. But remember that God is always at work, and you never know what wonderful things are coming. It may feel dark in your life now, but if you wait, Jesus will change things for you, just like He did for the disciples. Just keep holding on to hope.

. . . . . . . . . . . . . . . . . . . . . . . . . . . . . . . . . . . . . . . . . . . . . . . . . . . .

*Lord, thank You that You are always at work. Thank You that*
*You never leave me alone, even when things seem very dark in my*
*life. You are always moving to bring good change into my life.*

## Day 86

# Wait with Hope

*Wait for the LORD; be strong and take heart and wait for the LORD.*
PSALM 27:14 NIV

Every day John's dog, Molly, waits by the front door. John walks out the door to go to school, and Molly waits by the door until John comes home. Molly waits because she knows that John is coming back. If she didn't believe he was coming home, she wouldn't wait so patiently.

When is the last time you had to wait for something that you really wanted? Did you wait in confident hope like Molly, or did you wait thinking that only bad things were going to happen?

Sometimes we have to wait on God to do something in our lives or to make a change that we have been asking Him for. If we wait in confident hope like Molly, knowing that our Master will help us, then we will have joy when we wait. If we wait and don't believe that God really cares, then waiting will feel like torture.

If you are waiting for something today, dare to believe that God will come to the rescue. When He comes, He may not give you the exact answer you were looking for, but He will show up to give you the answer you need at exactly the right time.

*Lord, please help me wait in confident hope. Help me so that I don't doubt that You will give me an answer. You will never leave me alone without help because You love and care for me.*

*Day 87*

# The True Meaning of Easter

*For the wages of sin is death, but the gift of God
is eternal life in Christ Jesus our Lord.*

ROMANS 6:23 NIV

People often celebrate Easter with bunnies and colored Easter eggs. They hide them in the yard and search for them. They eat chocolate eggs and marshmallow chicks. But some people don't know the real meaning of Easter. Do you?

Do you remember that Jesus died on Good Friday? Easter is the day God raised Him from the dead! This is the day that Christianity is all about. It's about Jesus' resurrection from the dead. Without Easter, there wouldn't be any reason to be a Christian. When Jesus was raised after He died on the cross, the power of death was broken. Now everyone who asks Him into their hearts and who believes in Him is saved from the power of hell. This is great news!

As you celebrate Easter, as you enjoy your chocolate eggs, remember the true meaning of Easter and share the joy of it with a good friend so that they can learn the true meaning of the holiday too.

. . . . . . . . . . . . . . . . . . . . . . . . . . . . . . . . . . . . . . . . . . . . . . . . . . . .

*Thank You for dying on the cross for my sins, Lord.
I am so grateful that I know the true meaning of Easter.
Help me share this truth with someone else today.*

# More Than Looks

*Above all else, guard your heart, for everything you do flows from it.*
PROVERBS 4:23 NIV

✦

Emily looked at herself in the mirror. "Ugh! I hate my hair." She thought about her friend Sarah. Sarah had long, beautiful hair. It looked like silk. "Mine is so boring. It's not shiny, and it's short and sticks out all over!" She stomped her feet in frustration, grabbed a hat, and slammed the door.

On the way to school, her mom asked Emily why she was so grumpy. "I hate how I look."

Emily's mother frowned with compassion and reached for her daughter's arm. "Sweetheart, you are beautiful."

"Mom, you think I'm beautiful because I'm your daughter." Mom smiled. "But other people don't think I am beautiful."

Maybe you feel like Emily. Maybe you don't like your hair, your eyes, your height, or your weight. But don't focus so much on what you look like on the outside that you forget to take care of the most important part of you: your heart. Hairstyles change. People get older. They get taller. They get thinner or fatter. But a person's heart can grow more and more beautiful over time if they let Jesus change it.

Sure, make the most of your hair, but don't neglect your heart. People will always notice it and say how beautiful it is if you take care of it.

· · · · · · · · · · · · · · · · · · · · · · · · · · · · · · · · · · · · · · · · · · · · · · · · · · · · ·

*Lord, thank You for giving me a beautiful heart. Help me to be changed more and more so that my heart looks like Yours.*

# Take the Risk

*It has given me great joy to find some of your children
walking in the truth, just as the Father commanded us.*
2 JOHN 1:4 NIV

A lot of people want to do great things in life, but they don't want to take the chance. "What if I fail? What if I look stupid? What if something happens that ruins my future?" They never get past asking negative what-if questions to asking positive what-if questions like, "What if I succeed? What if I do something greater than I have ever done before? What if it turns out really great?"

They focus so much on the negative that they never think about how fantastic things could be.

Is there something in your life that you want to accomplish? Have you been worried that it might turn out horribly? Do you think that it's something that God is leading you to try? Instead of looking at the negative, try looking at the positive. Take out a piece of paper and make a list of all the good things that could happen as a result of taking the risk to do this new, great thing.

And finally, remember that God is with you. Remember that no matter what happens in your life, He will never leave you, and He is always at work to make a beautiful story out of all that happens in your life—whether good or bad.

*Lord, sometimes I am afraid of making mistakes. Help me focus on the good that You could bring to me if I dare take a risk and trust You.*

## Day 90

# The Most Amazing Love
# Letter Ever Written

*Your statutes are my heritage forever; they are the joy of my heart.*
PSALM 119:111 NIV

In his book *When I'm Longing for God*, Dan Stuecher tells a touching story about a great composer named Beethoven. This music man never got married but was in love with a mystery woman that a lot of smart people have spent years trying to identify. They aren't sure who she was, but they call her Beethoven's "Immortal Beloved."

When he was forty-one years old, Beethoven wrote a letter of affection to her. "Oh God, why must one be separated from her who is so dear," he wrote. "However much you love me—my love for you is even greater." After he died, the letter was found in a bureau belonging to Beethoven, without a date or an address.

Some people have wondered if the lady ever knew how important she was to Beethoven because of this secret, undelivered note. Can you imagine being the one who was supposed to receive the letter and never reading it?

God has written you a love letter. It's called the Bible. It's the most beautiful love letter ever written. Remember to make sure that you don't stuff it in a drawer somewhere and never read it. It will give you joy in your heart, direction for your life, and light for your path. Plus, it has some really great stories in it.

. . . . . . . . . . . . . . . . . . . . . . . . . . . . . . . . . . . . . . . . . . . . . . . . . . . . . . . . . . . .

*Lord, thank You for Your love letter!*
*Help me spend time with You reading it.*

## Day 91

# Notice Your Blessings Now

*The LORD has done it this very day; let us rejoice today and be glad.*
PSALM 118:24 NIV

"I wish I were older," said Amanda. "I wish I were old enough to drive a car, take myself to the grocery store, and I wish that I didn't have to go to bed when my mom tells me! I can't wait to grow up!"

Have you ever felt like Amanda? Are you in a hurry to grow up, for life to change, for things to be different? Most everyone has wished that their life was different at some time or another. They want things to hurry up and change.

One thing to keep in mind is that when we get in a hurry for things to change, we miss out on the great things that are happening *now*. We miss the friends who make us laugh. We miss the fun of exchanging a joke with a teacher. We miss a lot of things that we are taking for granted because we are looking too far into the future.

If you are in a hurry for life to change, take a minute today and notice as many things as you can that God has given you that are awesome right now. Many of those things will pass quickly, and you won't have them ever again. As you grow, your life will change and so will the blessings God gives you. So take note of how He is showing His love to you now.

. . . . . . . . . . . . . . . . . . . . . . . . . . . . . . . . . . . . . . . . . . . . . . . . .

*Lord, thank You for how You are taking care of me and all the blessings You have given me right now. I have so much to be grateful for. Help me resist being in such a hurry to grow up that I miss the good things that You are giving me right now.*

## Day 92
# Heart Full of Flowers

*I will praise You, O LORD, with my whole heart; I will tell*
*of all Your marvelous works. I will be glad and rejoice in*
*You; I will sing praise to Your name, O Most High.*
PSALM 9:1–2 NKJV

Look outside the window during class or at home and see the many beautiful things about spring. The sun seems to hug the earth and warm the frozen ground. The flowers put on their best blooms of pink, orange, red, and purple. Colors we haven't seen all winter long now greet us as we walk out the door. All of these wonders are God's, and He has placed them on this earth for us, as well as the wonder of His Son, Jesus Christ. When you see a flower, think, "God made that for me. God loves me."

Sometimes being thankful is extremely hard, especially when your hair wants to look like a bird's nest, your clothes don't fit well, or you didn't get the part in the play or make a spot on the team. We don't know why God withholds certain things from us. But we can be certain that He only gives us what is good for us. It is hard to give thanks when things don't go our way, but when we do give thanks, our hearts are happier. Without giving thanks, our hearts become like a flower that isn't watered. What would happen if there was no rain this spring? All the flowers would wither and wilt; they wouldn't wear their beautiful blooms. When we give thanks, our hearts can grow and bloom.

*Lord, help me be more thankful. I feel closer to You when I am*
*thankful. Being thankful is prettier than being fashionable. My heart*
*is Yours, Lord, and I want to thank You for things that You have*
*blessed me with to help me remember all Your wonderful gifts.*

## Day 93

# Crayons in a Box

*And David said to his son Solomon, "Be strong and of good courage,
and do it; do not fear nor be dismayed, for the LORD God—my God—
will be with you. He will not leave you nor forsake you, until you
have finished all the work for the service of the house of the LORD."*
1 CHRONICLES 28:20 NKJV

Have you ever been in a large crowd? Either at a fair or at a mall where thousands of people seem to be squished together like crayons in a box and you are the only one traveling against the crowd? Did some people give you funny or mean looks when you squeezed your way past them? It's much easier to walk in their direction rather than your own. But there are many times the Lord calls us to walk against the crowd for Him. The amazing thing is, He walks with us! He is right beside us moving the crowd, making a path for you and picking you up when you fall. How wonderful that He doesn't run away or abandon us when we feel most scared!

God created the whole world, and did you know He created this world with you in mind? This time of year, flowers pop their heads out of the earth as if to say, "Cheer up, it's spring!" The trees dress themselves in small buds of green, tired of the brown, frayed coat they've worn all winter. All creation seems to burst forth and sing to the Lord. He has never abandoned the trees, flowers, or birds. Don't you know how much more He loves you than the earth?

*Lord, help me trust that You are with me. You will never
leave me; You will never laugh at me or call me hurtful
names. You make me strong and courageous.*

## Day 94
# God Doesn't Want Texts

*I called on Your name, O LORD, from the lowest pit. You have heard my voice: "Do not hide Your ear from my sighing, from my cry for help." You drew near on the day I called on You, and said, "Do not fear!"*
LAMENTATIONS 3:55–57 NKJV

How great is our God that He would hear our cry! In the midst of all the hustle and bustle, He hears us and answers us. God does not see some people as more important or interesting than others. To Him, you are just as important, special, and loved as Selena Gomez or Kate Middleton. Notice in the verse above that we must call on God's name; we cannot just sit around silently hoping for an answer to an unasked question. God delights in hearing your voice and thoughts.

If a friend suddenly stopped talking to you, what would you think? You would be confused, hurt, and sad. The relationship would not feel like a friendship. See, you cannot have a relationship without communication, and that is exactly why you need to talk to God. The more you talk to Him about good and hard things, the stronger your relationship will be with Him. He does not want a text-message relationship with you; He wants to sit down and hear all that is going on in your heart.

*Lord, I am sorry that I have not talked to You as much as I should. Help me listen and speak to You more often. Thank You for hearing me and giving me so many things to celebrate.*

## Day 95

# As Sure as the Dawn

*Let us know, let us pursue the knowledge of the LORD.*
*His going forth is established as the morning; He will come*
*to us like the rain, like the latter and former rain to the earth.*

HOSEA 6:3 NKJV

What are some things that make you want to stop trying? Is it a difficult math question or that you can't seem to get the ball in the basket or goal? Maybe your best friend has stopped talking to you and you have no clue why. It is easy to give up and "throw in the towel," but what good would stopping do? If you did not work to score the goal, understand the math, or reach out to your friends, you would rightly earn the title of "lazy," "uncaring," or "dud." If you think you have learned everything there is to know about God, you are wrong.

God is greater, mightier, cooler, smarter, funnier, and lovelier than any Hollywood star or person in your life. Knowing Him, reading His Word, and talking to Him through prayer is the greatest adventure you will ever have! God has never stopped loving you; He has never stopped chasing after your heart. God is not "lazy," "uncaring," or a "dud." God reminds us with every sunrise that He is coming back for us, that He has not forgotten us. Don't stop searching for God. Never let Satan or anyone in your life make you think He is boring. Who do you think created laughter? God did! Everything that you enjoy this spring (puddles to splash in, flowers in bloom, rainbows that have no end) was created by God.

*God, thank You for all the beauty this spring.*
*Thank You for the ups and downs in my day, because*
*they fashion me into a young woman who seeks You.*

# Boasting in Christ

*But God forbid that I should boast except in the cross of our Lord Jesus Christ, by whom the world has been crucified to me, and I to the world.*

GALATIANS 6:14 NKJV

You know when someone is proud. They tend to always talk about their skills or talents, possibly even show them off. It is annoying to be around a show-off who wants all of the attention. The apostle Paul in writing a letter to the church in Galatia (which is located near modern-day Turkey), said that the only thing he will boast in is Jesus Christ.

Now imagine one of your classmates saying, "I take pride in the fact that I am a sinner and don't deserve forgiveness, but Jesus Christ saved me! I am proud of Jesus' grace and mercy." Kind of a strange thing to boast about, but what are some things you take pride in? Maybe you have good grades or an excellent singing voice. Do you have a certain outfit that is super stylish? In comparison to Jesus Christ, these things are worthless.

Some day you will not be in school anymore and grades will not matter, and one day your outfit will go out of style, but Jesus never changes. God's love, grace, and power that He showed through Jesus Christ's death and resurrection will never fade away; they are as true today as they were two thousand years ago! We take pride in the gospel and Jesus' death and resurrection because we have no hope outside of Jesus Christ.

*Lord, forgive me for taking pride in my own abilities; all my gifts are from You. Thank You for the blessings in my life, and help me never grow tired or bored of being thankful.*

# God Isn't Scared

*"Blessed be the name of God forever and ever, for wisdom and might
are His. And He changes the times and the seasons; He removes kings
and raises up kings; He gives wisdom to the wise and knowledge to
those who have understanding. He reveals deep and secret things;
He knows what is in the darkness, and light dwells with Him."*

DANIEL 2:20–22 NKJV

I am sure there are kids in your class that you listen to and think, "Wow!
They are smart." Have you ever had a teacher that you did not like or
one that you absolutely adored? Things like knowledge, wisdom, and
authority are all blessings from God. Nothing is outside of God, and by
that I mean everything you interact with on a daily basis (iPads, siblings,
weather, parents, your crazy hair. . .) all comes from God! Whoa! So
does He control everything? Does He know everything? Yes! He knows
everything about you.

"He knows what is in the darkness, and light dwells with Him." I
love this line because it shows that God knows the scary stuff, the things
or secrets we don't want to know, and He is not scared by them. In fact,
He is in control of them. The "light" in this verse can mean knowledge,
healing, or peace, and it lives with God. Light was created by God. Isn't
it wonderful to know that when you are scared, you have a God who
will bring light and peace into the darkest places? In those frightening
times, call out to Him, ask Him to calm you, and rely on Him to save
you, because He has defeated the darkness.

*Lord, I am so glad You control everything! Help me trust You in
the darkest times, knowing that You control the darkness.*

## Day 98

# Out of Style

*"The grass withers, the flower fades,
but the word of our God stands forever."*
Isaiah 40:8 nkjv

How much change occurs throughout your day? Most likely a whole bunch! You are not the same person each day—you grow a little taller, your opinions about movies or clothes change, and your hair never falls in quite the same way as the day before. The Bible, God's Word, has never changed! The same verses you read in the Old Testament are the same words the Israelites read. God is as constant as the waves on the seashore. His Word does not change, nor does He change His mind. Here in Isaiah, we see that God's Word is untouched by time.

Have you ever dealt with a person who can't make up their mind, or have you ever had a hard time deciding on the best outfit for school or a church function? It can be pretty frustrating. Now imagine serving and worshipping a god who changes his mind all the time. Talk about a headache and nightmare! We would always be frustrated. There is such peace and comfort knowing that His love for you and me, His power and majesty, are untouched by time. God will never go out of style.

*Lord, I am so happy that You do not change. Thank You for being
a solid rock that I can cling to when frustrating times come.*

## Day 99

# The First Shepherd

*Behold, the Lord God shall come with a strong hand, and*
*His arm shall rule for Him; behold, His reward is with Him,*
*and His work before Him. He will feed His flock like a shepherd;*
*He will gather the lambs with His arm, and carry them in*
*His bosom, and gently lead those who are with young.*
ISAIAH 40:10–11 NKJV

Have you ever held a baby animal, such as a lamb or a rabbit? If so, did you feel their heartbeat pulsing faster as they tried to scramble from your hold, and then slowly, as you pet their fur, they calmed down and possibly even fell asleep in the warmth of your arms? This is one picture of how God quiets our worried hearts, but He can't calm your heart unless you give it to Him.

There are many times that we don't believe God will answer or hear our prayers, and His silence makes us nervous. Should I say yes or no? Do I tell the teacher I saw my classmate cheat on the test? Should I try out for the team or play? All these questions buzz in our heads like bees around spring flowers, but they never seem to settle. Isaiah gives a beautiful picture of how God handles our buzzing minds and hearts. He draws us near, gathers us into His arms, hugging us as He carries us. We serve an amazing God who brings justice to the wicked and also cares tenderly for you and me. God knows your heart, and He delights to hear your prayers, no matter how silly they may sound. Give your heart and questions to God and know that He will answer you.

. . . . . . . . . . . . . . . . . . . . . . . . . . . . . . . . . . . . . . . . . . . . . . . . . . .

*Father, please take my worried heart. Help me feel Your*
*hugging presence and know that You are in control.*

## *Day 100*

# God Literally Said This!

*And the LORD smelled a soothing aroma. Then the LORD said in*
*His heart, "I will never again curse the ground for man's sake,*
*although the imagination of man's heart is evil from his youth;*
*nor will I again destroy every living thing as I have done.*
*While the earth remains, seedtime and harvest, cold and heat,*
*winter and summer, and day and night shall not cease."*

GENESIS 8:21–22 NKJV

I'm sure you've heard the story of Noah. The verses above come right after God brought Noah and all the animals safely out of the ark and after Noah built an altar for the Lord out of praise and thanksgiving. God promises that He will never bring about another flood that will cover the whole earth. God also says that so long as the earth remains, He will not disrupt "seedtime and harvest, cold and heat, winter and summer, and day and night." In all of history, have we ever gone a whole year without spring? No, which means God has been faithful to His promise. Each day is a promise kept by God. He has not changed His mind, nor will He deceive us. We can fully trust God, and if you ever doubt that He keeps His promises, just look at the changing seasons, sunrises and sunsets, because He made them all for you.

*Lord God, thank You for the changing seasons and thank You for the*
*beauty of spring! Thank You that You do not leave me all to myself.*
*Thank You that You are constantly watching and caring for me.*

## Day 101

# Persevere

*Let us hold fast the confession of our hope without wavering,
for He who promised is faithful. And let us consider one another in
order to stir up love and good works, not forsaking the assembling
of ourselves together, as is the manner of some, but exhorting one
another, and so much the more as you see the Day approaching.*

HEBREWS 10:23–25 NKJV

"Holding fast" is the same as holding strong, like grasping a life preserver in rough waves. What do you hold fast to? Is it the knowledge that school will be out for the summer, and you are holding on to the hope and promise of a break? Summer will come to an end, and you will return to school and studies, but God will never quit on you. But the best news is that the one who holds the other end of the lifeline is God, and He is faithful. He will never let go of you.

There are definitely times when God seems distant, but those are times when He is growing your perseverance and trust in Him. If you have ever watched the Olympics or any professional sporting event, then you know those athletes trained for most of their lives and gave all of their time to get in shape and become professionals. God trains you so that in hard and sad times, you can trust Him and know that He hears your prayers.

*Lord, it is great to know that You train me. Help me realize the
work You are doing in my life and the lives of my friends and family.
When things get tough, help me persevere and hope in Your promises.*

## *Day 102*
# He Spins Time

*I know that whatever God does, it shall be forever. Nothing can be added to it, and nothing taken from it. God does it, that men should fear before Him. That which is has already been, and what is to be has already been; and God requires an account of what is past.*

ECCLESIASTES 3:14–15 NKJV

How many times a day do you look at the clock? We always want time to speed up when we're in school and slow down on the weekends. Did you know that God doesn't rely on time? God doesn't check His watch or look at a clock. Time relies on God because He created it. God's Word and everything He does, from creation to the death and resurrection of His Son, Jesus, will last forever! His plan is perfect because He is perfect. In the verse above we read that "nothing can be added to it, and nothing taken from it." So when God says He loves you, He cannot love you more, nor can He love you less. He has mapped out your life, and He knows every desire of your heart. God does these wondrous works in your life so that you can know Him more and build a deeper relationship with Him. God is not wishy-washy like TV stars or testy teachers. He is eternal.

*Father God, it is crazy to think that nothing about You or Your plan changes. I change my mind almost every minute, but I can always rely on You. Thank You for being an infinite and all-knowing God.*

## Day 103

# God Fights for You

*Strengthen the weak hands, and make firm the feeble knees.*
*Say to those who are fearful-hearted, "Be strong, do not*
*fear! Behold, your God will come with vengeance, with*
*the recompense of God; He will come and save you."*

ISAIAH 35:3–4 NKJV

Have you ever talked in front of a large group of people or had to perform on stage? Was there ever a time you were afraid to ride a roller coaster or go to a new school? It seems that every day there is something new to be afraid of. Most of the time we are nervous or scared of embarrassment, and it seems to paralyze us like porcelain dolls.

Now think of all those scary times and imagine that you had a friend who knew all the answers to the test, spoke perfectly in front of others, sat in the front seat of the ride, and made friends with the whole class on the first day of school. Would you feel more confident with a person like that by your side, who encouraged, loved, and guided you? Of course!

God is that friend. He is strong, mighty, all-knowing, and nothing is outside of His power. He knows all of your fears, even the ones you have not faced, and He walks right beside you in the darkest of times. "Be strong, do not fear!" God fights for you and is your Savior. He will rescue you and your heart from the most frightening times.

*Father, there are times where there is seemingly no hope, and right now I'm terrified. Calm my heart, Lord. Help me see Your rescuing hand in this time, and thank You that You have not left me alone.*

## Day 104
# Royalty

*The royal daughter is all glorious within the palace; her clothing is woven with gold. She shall be brought to the King in robes of many colors.*
PSALM 45:13–14 NKJV

Do you want to know a secret? You are a daughter of the King. When God calls you to be His child, you are adopted into His royal family! How often do you feel like a princess or treated like royalty? How often do you wish you looked like the girls in magazines or TV shows? There are many times we don't like what we see in the mirror, but do you ever stop to think that God loves you and created you for a great purpose? Go back and read the first verse of the passage above, and pay attention to the words the psalmist uses. Did you catch it? "The royal daughter [that's you!] is all glorious within." He is talking about your heart—your compassion, kindness, humor, creativity, imagination, and joy. It is more delightful and fun to hang out with a kind and warmhearted person than a rude person, no matter how popular, rich, or pretty they may seem.

God, the King, delights in your heart once you have given it to Him. He loves your company, and He enjoys speaking to you and hearing what is on your mind. He makes us laugh, and He is a God who enjoys joy. How great is our King, and we are His daughters!

*Lord, thank You for making me a part of Your family, and thank You that You are the great and mighty King who I can call Father.*

# Who Holds Your Arms Up?

*And so it was, when Moses held up his hand, that Israel
prevailed; and when he let down his hand, Amalek prevailed.
But Moses' hands became heavy; so they took a stone and put
it under him, and he sat on it. And Aaron and Hur supported
his hands, one on one side, and the other on the other side; and
his hands were steady until the going down of the sun.*

EXODUS 17:11–12 NKJV

One of the many ways God does not leave us alone is through friends and family. I am sure there have been plenty of times that you were not feeling well—maybe you were sick or someone had made a mean comment about you. God sends a friend, sibling, or parent to come encourage you.

Moses was in a difficult state. He was physically exhausted, and God provided Aaron and Hur to support him for hours and hours. God uses the people in your life to help you along in the hard times and good times. Sometimes encouragement and discipline seem unfair and harsh, but God uses everything to make you stronger and more secure in Him. God is always looking out for your good. The family and friends in your life are not mistakes. God put you exactly where you need to be, even though at times it may not feel like a perfect or fair life.

*Lord, thank You for the people in my life. I have been blessed to have
friends, teachers, coaches, and family that love and support me.*

## Day 106

# Waiting Room

*My soul waits for the Lord more than those who watch*
*for the morning—yes, more than those who watch for the*
*morning. O Israel, hope in the LORD; for with the LORD*
*there is mercy, and with Him is abundant redemption.*

PSALM 130:6–7 NKJV

What is the longest you have ever waited for someone or some
thing? Was it a vacation to the beach or Disney World? Maybe you were
going to see your best friend or grandparents. Whatever you waited for,
the time seemed to pass *so* slowly! In the psalm above, David was being
pursued by men who wanted to kill him, and David was waiting on the
Lord to rescue him. Talk about a nail-biter! You would definitely want
the Lord to answer your cries—and fast! But David anchored his hope
in the one person he knew could save him; he anchored his hope in God.
God is loving-kindness, mercy, and the only true peace on this earth.
Nothing is outside of God's plan, and nothing that happens ever startles
or surprises God. With such power and might, it is no wonder David
waited expectantly for God to rescue him. And at the right time, God
did rescue David from his enemies. Our only redemption, safety, and love
in this world is the Lord.

*Father, may I hope in You at all times. Thank You that You*
*have not left me to be captured by my enemies, but that You*
*hear me and answer my cry because You love me.*

## Day 107

# You—He Called You

*But now, thus says the LORD, who created you, O Jacob, and He who formed you, O Israel: "Fear not, for I have redeemed you; I have called you by your name; You are Mine. When you pass through the waters, I will be with you; and through the rivers, they shall not overflow you. When you walk through the fire, you shall not be burned, nor shall the flame scorch you. For I am the LORD your God, the Holy One of Israel, your Savior; I gave Egypt for your ransom, Ethiopia and Seba in your place. Since you were precious in My sight, You have been honored, and I have loved you."*

ISAIAH 43:1–4 NKJV

When the Lord speaks to Israel, He is speaking to His children. Go back through the passage, and wherever you see "O Jacob" and "O Israel," I want you to insert your name. Now reread the passage with your name in those spots. God is talking to you. You are His child. He "formed" you, "redeemed" you, and "called" you by name; even before your parents knew your name, God saw you and called you. God promises that you are His, and He will not sell you for gold; He will not give up on you. When you walk through dark and confusing times, He will be with you. He is your Lord and protector. He is the ultimate Father who will lead, comfort, discipline, grow, and fight for you!

*I love You, Lord. In fire and darkness, in scary, sad, and happy times, You are always by my side, sometimes carrying me when I can't walk. Thank You.*

## Day 108

# Wrapped Up Like a Blanket

*But it is good for me to draw near to God; I have put my trust
in the Lord GOD, that I may declare all Your works.*
PSALM 73:28 NKJV

Have you ever been extremely cold and all you can think of is getting close to a warm fire or snuggling up in a cozy blanket? And once you do, there is instant relief and you feel safe, as the warmth starts to melt your icy fingers and nose. It is a great feeling because we know and our body knows that it is good to be warm when it is cold outside. Do you know that it is just as good to be near to God and to put your trust in Him? The nearness of God is like having the best soccer player on your soccer team—you can't be beat! God never fails. The nearness of God is knowing that the thunder and lightning may crash and boom, but you are safe and snug in your bed. Being near God means having the ruler of the universe on your side and watching over you. Have you ever felt God's comfort and security, as though He is sitting right next to you?

We can draw close to God through His Word, praise, and prayer. Anything you do for His glory will draw you closer into His wonderful presence. Think of your favorite spot in the world, a spot that makes you feel calm and happy. Those places and joyful moments are given to you by God. He made them just for you!

*Father God, thank You for the peace and rest You give me.
Help me draw near to You through scripture and prayer.
Help me worship You in the hard times and happy times.*

## Day 109

# Every Last Penny

*So He called His disciples to Himself and said to them, "Assuredly, I say to you that this poor widow has put in more than all those who have given to the treasury; for they all put in out of their abundance, but she out of her poverty put in all that she had, her whole livelihood."*

MARK 12:43–44 NKJV

Have you ever gotten a gift, either for Christmas or your birthday, that you really wanted? Were you thankful and super excited? It is easy to give thanks and be appreciative when you have that thing (money, the newest game, a cool phone or hair style). But what if your haircut looks awful and the gift your grandma gave was the ugliest color in the world? That is when gratitude and a thankful heart are really hard to show.

In the passage above, Jesus points out that a poor widow gave her last penny. Without money, how could she buy food or pay rent? She never hesitated to give to the Lord, and she was blessed tenfold because of her sacrifice.

Jesus wants every last penny you have, and He's not speaking about just money. Jesus wants your time, thoughts, actions, worship, conversation, and heart. Sometimes He asks us to give up our pride, maybe ask forgiveness or be kind to a person who has been mean to us. Each time Jesus takes something from us, we may feel hollow and sad, but He is refining us like gold and getting rid of anything that is not precious! There is great beauty in the breaking apart of yourself; the more you break away from selfish actions, the more free and more blessed you will be.

. . . . . . . . . . . . . . . . . . . . . . . . . . . . . . . . . . . . . . . . . . . . . . . . . . . .

*God, sometimes I don't want to do the things You tell me, but help me obey. I give You every last penny of myself.*

# Hope in a Shepherd

*Now faith is the substance of things hoped for,*
*the evidence of things not seen.*
HEBREWS 11:1 NKJV

Even though we can't see the wind, we can feel its power and presence when we step outside. How can you believe in something you cannot see? Faith is much more than believing without seeing. You know the sun will rise in the morning, and you know that you will turn a year older each year, but faith is hoping in what God will bring each day and in the future. We tend to place our hope and faith in things that do not always succeed. Have you ever been let down by a friend or parent? It hurts when what we expected didn't come true.

There is only one person who will never fail us. God will always provide; He will always come through in the brightest and darkest of times. God is more constant than the seasons, and He will never be late to pick you up or watch your game. God will always provide what is best for you. Though you may not exactly like His plan, He will never harm you. Jesus is called the Good Shepherd, and a good shepherd does not hurt or handle His sheep roughly. Jesus gently speaks to us in our pain and hurt. He is the Savior and friend we hope in.

*Father, I am so blessed to have You as my God.*
*Thank You that You will never harm me or yell at me.*
*You speak so kindly to me. Thank You for loving me.*

# Hurricane Heartache

*God is in the midst of her, she shall not be moved;*
*God shall help her, just at the break of dawn.*
PSALM 46:5 NKJV

Have you ever seen pictures of towns after a tornado or hurricane has run through them? Everything—houses and trees—has been flattened, and the result is a mess. There are times when our hearts and lives feel wrecked and broken, as though an emotional hurricane erupted in our heart. What can we do when a loved one or beloved pet has passed away, or when all the things in our lives seem to be going wrong? We turn to God.

The verse above gives us a very important truth about living and surviving the rough and tragic times. With God as the center and focus of our lives and souls, no emotional pain will conquer us because Jesus protects our hearts. Did you see the sun rise this morning? Did the birds chirp a springtime song or the rain dance a jig on the roof? All of these little ordinary moments—the bird's song, the rain's refreshment, and the bright sun—are promises that God protects you. He cannot be your protector unless you choose to make Him the center and focus of your life. But once you do, He will never leave you.

. . . . . . . . . . . . . . . . . . . . . . . . . . . . . . . . . . . . . . . . . . . . . . . . . . . . . . . .

*Lord, I can't make things right. I don't have the power or energy to*
*fix everything, though there is so much that is broken. With You, nothing*
*is impossible. Please be the center of my life. Help me focus on You.*
*I love You. I know You will come as sure as the springtime to save me.*

# Annoying Siblings

*"These things I have spoken to you, that in Me you
may have peace. In the world you will have tribulation;
but be of good cheer, I have overcome the world."*

JOHN 16:33 NKJV

Does it ever feel like nothing will change—as though your brother or sister will never stop pestering you, your outfits will never be in style, and the cute boy in second period will never smile at you or take notice? Did you know that Jesus faced every possible temptation and struggle that we do today? His younger siblings teased him, other kids at school or in the town bullied Him, and He wasn't a rich child, so His clothes were probably ordinary.

In the verse above, Jesus is talking to His disciples, and His message is troubling but also hopeful. Jesus knows that we will face trials and "tribulation"—that the road we walk will be rocky and hilly, sometimes dark and sinister, but because of His sacrifice on the cross, because He was tempted and overcame sin, He is the victor of death and sin. He overcame the evil and sin in this world so that we can find peace in Him! He is telling us to cheer up; all the troubles will end; He will get us through these hard and frustrating times.

. . . . . . . . . . . . . . . . . . . . . . . . . . . . . . . . . . . . . . . . . . . . .

*Jesus, thank You for taking notice of my troubles. Thank You for conquering
the evil in this world and knowing what I am going through.*

## Day 113

# What to Do?

*He has shown you, O man, what is good; and what does the Lord require of you but to do justly, to love mercy, and to walk humbly with your God?*
Micah 6:8 nkjv

Do you ever wonder, *What should I do?* or *What do I say?* Maybe a friend has asked you for the answer on a test and the teacher has said you can't swap answers, or you overheard others talking behind a person's back. These are tough times when we either say or do something or we walk away. So what do we do?

Whatever the circumstance, God has given us the answer. In the verse above He has told us to do justice, love mercy, and walk humbly with our God. By walking humbly with God, we take on a personal relationship with Him through praying and reading His Word. The Bible is a way to find out more about God's character and power, as well as His love and glory. He is the greatest teacher we'll ever have.

In the scene above, where your friend asks you for an answer, it is very tempting to help them out, but what would be "justice" and "mercy" in this situation? Justice would be not giving them the answer because that would make you both cheaters, and mercy would be encouraging them to ask the teacher for help. When God calls us to do the right thing and we obey, God blesses us beyond our imagination, and He is so proud of us!

*Father God, help me stand strong, obey, and act justly in hard times. Please forgive me for the times that I have disappointed You, and thank You for loving me.*

## Day 114

# Sing Like No One Is Around!

*Sing, O daughter of Zion! Shout, O Israel! Be glad and rejoice*
*with all your heart, O daughter of Jerusalem! The LORD has taken*
*away your judgments, He has cast out your enemy. The King of*
*Israel, the LORD, is in your midst; You shall see disaster no more.*
ZEPHANIAH 3:14–15 NKJV

Shout for joy! Jump up and down! Sing with the birds and buzzing bees!
All the colors of spring are yelling the glory of God! Why are they so
happy? Because they know their God has redeemed them and that the
Lord provides for them. The Lord has taken away all your debt and all
your sin so that you may be called His child. The Lord God has taken
your enemies down; no one can defeat our God.

We serve a King, and He is the King of kings and Lord of lords.
There is no one greater or stronger than Him. Satan cannot defeat Christ
because Christ came down and defeated all sin and death. Rejoice and
sing loudly as if no one is around you! Did you know you have been
purchased at a great cost? Did you know that Christ is the *only* one who
could save us from death? There is no plan B outside of Christ. He knows
you by name and protects you every time you take a breath.

Sing with creation; rejoice with all your heart that God reigns and
no one can take Him from His throne!

*O God! How You have loved me and protected me!*
*I don't need to fear a single thing because You are with me.*
*Thank You for Your Son and His defeating death!*

# Wilderness Training

*"Therefore, behold, I will allure her, will bring her
into the wilderness, and speak comfort to her."*

HOSEA 2:14 NKJV

What makes something scary? For me, it is unfamiliar places that are dark with loud noises. When we are scared, there seem to be a million different thoughts racing through our heads. This verse from Hosea shows that God is in control of the scary places. In fact, He brings us into those difficult times. Why would He take us into a terrifying place? Good question. God is always concerned about your good, and He will never give you a difficult teacher, class, or friend that you and He can't handle together. God uses those scary and hard times to make us stronger and trust Him. He brings us into the "wilderness" and speaks "comfort" to us. He never leaves us when we feel abandoned, nor will He ever leave us! All the times you've felt as though you've failed or made a huge mistake, God is right next to you speaking comfort. God's comfort comes in many shapes and sizes. He comforts us through song, the birds singing in the trees this spring. He gives us laughter and all the new baby animals being born. He shows us beauty through the budding flowers. God has wrapped us up in a blanket of creation for us to enjoy!

*God, thank You for giving me comfort. Thank You for being in
control and making me stronger. Help me rely on You in scary times
and call on Your name. Thank You for always being with me.*

## Day 116

# Flourish Like the Lilies

*"I will be like the dew to Israel; he shall grow like the lily, and lengthen his roots like Lebanon. His branches shall spread; his beauty shall be like an olive tree, and his fragrance like Lebanon. Those who dwell under his shadow shall return; they shall be revived like grain."*

Hosea 14:5–7 nkjv

Have you ever had an exhausting day, and when you finally crawled into your soft bed, it seemed like your whole body relaxed with relief? When your heart is troubled and someone gives you an encouraging word or you remember God's promise, does a sense of peace cover you like a warm blanket?

When we plant our hopes, dreams, and heart in the Lord, He will grow us "like the lily." Lilies are elegant, white, sweet-smelling flowers that are beautiful to see. What a glorious picture of how our hearts flourish in the Lord! No plant can grow without water and sunlight; they need both to survive. Just like lilies and olive trees, we cannot grow and blossom unless we love and walk with the Lord.

God provides comfort in His shadow and shade, just like a big oak tree on a hot summer day. In the verse above, we glimpse God's refreshing character, like jumping in the pool or snuggling on a comfy couch. He is not only beautiful, but He smells wonderful! All the fragrance of springtime flowers and rain are part of His aroma, and what a wonderful scent it is. Relax in the Lord, go to His shade, and know that He will grow and strengthen you.

*Lord, thank You for rest and peace. Thank You for being my shade and quiet place. Help me think of Your Word and promises. I love You.*

# Six Kept Promises

*The LORD is near to all who call upon Him, to all who call upon Him in truth. He will fulfill the desire of those who fear Him; He also will hear their cry and save them. The LORD preserves all who love Him, but all the wicked He will destroy. My mouth shall speak the praise of the LORD, and all flesh shall bless His holy name forever and ever.*

PSALM 145:18–21 NKJV

Our God is an attentive God, meaning He knows everything that is going on in your heart and mind. You cannot hide anything from God: a lie, a secret crush, or the fact that you cannot stand vegetables. He knows you better than your parents, siblings, or closest friends do. His ability to be with you at all times, know your pain, and hear your cry for help is called omnipresence. Because God is so great and powerful, He can be everywhere at once. How? We don't know because He has not told us, but it is a promise that He will always be with us.

In the verse above, count how many promises God makes to us. Did you count six? The psalmist declares that the Lord will do the following: He is right next to all who call on Him in truth; He will fulfill the desire of those who love Him; He hears their cries; He saves His children; He protects all who love Him; and He destroys the wicked. How many times have you made six promises and kept them all? Probably not often, but God keeps His promises, and He keeps them for thousands of years and will continue to hold His promises until His return!

*Dear Lord, thank You for keeping Your promises and for always being close to me in happy and sad times.*

# Something Old for Something New

*"Remember the former things of old, for I am God, and there
is no other; I am God, and there is none like Me."*

ISAIAH 46:9 NKJV

Why do we study history? Why is it important to know how wars began, what people ate, and where the Great Wall was built? Because we can learn from these events and apply them to our lives today. Even in the modern world of iPhones, laptops, Google glasses, and electric cars, the lessons we learned from medieval knights and the pilgrims are very important.

Life will be overwhelming at times: you have a solo in the school performance, or you have three tests and two quizzes on the same day! Take a deep breath and remember past times when God answered your prayers and calmed your heart. Remember what God did for you in those crazy days—a certain worship song calmed your heart and made you glad, or a friend spoke kind and encouraging words.

Go outside and look at God's beautiful creation, knowing that if He feeds all the birds bobbing in the trees then He will definitely take care of your worries. Rely on God, and remember His good works. There is no other person like God. He is in His own league! He has protected us and bailed us out more times than we realize. Give thanks that He is unchanging and will never stop loving you. Take time this week to remember how God answered your prayers and the prayers of others around you. Thank Him for His goodness.

*Dear God, thank You for saving me!*

# Nicknames

*For unto us a Child is born, unto us a Son is given; and the government will be upon His shoulder. And His name will be called Wonderful, Counselor, Mighty God, Everlasting Father, Prince of Peace.*
ISAIAH 9:6 NKJV

How many names do you have? Well you have a first, middle, and last, and maybe a few nicknames. Each of your names means something different about you. God is so great, and His character is more infinite than the galaxy! There are so many names for God that are used throughout the Bible.

First, He is Wonderful. What do you consider wonderful? Maybe it is a magenta sunset or roaring waterfall. Something wonderful could be a diamond necklace or a hug from a best friend or loved one. Whatever you think is wonderful is part of Christ's beauty and the wonder of His sacrifice. The name Counselor gets a bad rep in today's world, but what if you had a counselor who knew exactly what was going on in your heart and mind and knew how to help you? Jesus knows the desires, fears, dreams, and sorrows of your heart, and He wants to hear what you have to say. Mighty God—there is nothing that God cannot do. Nothing is outside of His power and control. Everlasting Father—God will never leave you, and He will shepherd and guide you forever. He is the best Father you will ever have. Prince of Peace—Jesus is royal, and He owns and gives peace to all His children, which is why we ask Him for peace when worries come our way.

*Dear Jesus, You have so many wonderful names that all show different parts of Your character. Thank You for being an Everlasting Father!*

# Dripping with Honey

*The heart of the wise teaches his mouth, and adds
learning to his lips. Pleasant words are like a honeycomb,
sweetness to the soul and health to the bones.*

Proverbs 16:23–24 NKJV

How do you show your friend you care and love them? Do you give him or her little gifts or pass notes? Maybe you spend tons of time together outdoors or you share part of your lunch. There are numerous ways to show friends, family, and classmates love.

Speaking kindly and keeping others' feelings in mind when you talk is a great gift! Think of all the times a compliment about your clothes, talents, schoolwork, or character has made your day. The quickest way to make a friend is to give a compliment, and the easiest way to ruin someone's day is to say something rude or harsh. To give a compliment or encouraging word is better than giving chocolate!

What you believe in your heart will be obvious in how you speak. "The heart of the wise" thinks before speaking or making a comment. There are many times we say something that we wish we could take back; it's embarrassing and humiliating, and sometimes we are punished for the words we say. Learn from those mistakes and ask yourself, "Is this something I'd like said about me?" or "Would this be encouraging or mean?" I challenge you to compliment three different people each day. Give a compliment that you truly mean, don't lie, and see how much easier it becomes to speak kindly.

*Dear God, forgive me for speaking mean and hurtful things
about others. Help me find true compliments to give to others.*

## Day 121
# He Wins

*Then the women said to Naomi, "Blessed be the LORD,
who has not left you this day without a close relative;
and may his name be famous in Israel!"*
RUTH 4:14 NKJV

What are some of the first things that pop in your head every morning? Are they, "Ugh! School!" "What am I going to wear today?" or "I am so ready for this test"? We think about tons of things during the day, from gym class to shopping to what gross food the cafeteria is serving to how much you love the song on the radio. But how much thought do you put into God? Is He one of your thoughts besides when you pray before bed?

God, because He is always with us through the Holy Spirit, pays a lot of attention to our hearts and minds. As the verse above proclaims, He has not left us without a Redeemer, and His name is to be more remembered than all the Hollywood stars in history! God is the ultimate celebrity because He sent His Son to save us from death and sin.

Outside of Christ there is only darkness. Don't be fooled into thinking that there are other ways to find true peace; remember, Jesus is the Prince of Peace. Satan will distract you at all costs from thinking about God and thanking Him. Praise the Lord that He has won the battle! We know one thing about the future, and that is our Lord and Savior is coming back for us, and He wins.

*Dear Lord, I am so glad to know that You have won the
fight and You are the victor! Thank You for saving me,
and help me tell others about Your great love and sacrifice.*

*Day 122*

# Just. Two. Rules.

*One of [the Pharisees], an expert in religious law, tried to trap
him with this question: "Teacher, which is the most important
commandment in the law of Moses?" Jesus replied, "'You must love
the LORD your God with all your heart, all your soul, and all your
mind.' This is the first and greatest commandment. A second is equally
important: 'Love your neighbor as yourself.' The entire law and all the
demands of the prophets are based on these two commandments."*

MATTHEW 22:35–40 NLT

Don't you just love rules? Rules at school, rules in sports, rules at home.
Sure, we all have to live by the rules around us so that everything runs
smoothly, but it's a lot of rules, and it's easy to feel like we'll never measure
up or get them all right. But Jesus showed us how to simplify everything
with *just two rules.*

Instead of arguing with those who tried to trick Him, Jesus gave
them—and us!—a great answer and blessing. His simple reply is all the
guidance and direction we need.

Just two rules. Two things to remember. Two points to consider.
Only. Two. Only two rules to guide you in living a life that honors God.
When you have to decide something, just answer these questions: *How
will this choice love God? How will this choice love someone else?* Like Jesus
said, if we let everything we do follow these two rules, all the other rules
don't matter so much.

· · · · · · · · · · · · · · · · · · · · · · · · · · · · · · · · · · · · · · · · · · · · · · · · · · · · · · · · · · · · · · · ·

*Lord, thank You for Your two rules—
the only ones I need. You make my life simple.*

# Where It Started

*We love because God first loved us.*

1 JOHN 4:19 NCV

Every moment, God says, "I love you." If that's all you ever remembered about Him, that would be enough.

No matter what we're doing or where we are, God's love surrounds us. John wrote many words about God's love, the love that's part of God's unchanging nature. He first *loved* us—not judged us or taught us or trained us—but *loved* us. His "I love you" means "I cherish you and protect you, guide you and comfort you. I lead you and teach you, hold you and help you. I'm your biggest fan. I'm your Father, full of forgiveness and grace, wisdom and security. I'm everywhere, but My favorite place is your heart."

He first looked at you and said to Himself, "Wow, that young lady is Mine, *all Mine*, and I love her more than she'll ever know. I'll love her every moment, and in that love, I'll grow her and redeem her and challenge her to be all that I've prepared her to be in this amazing life in front of her!"

And in God's love we see how we can love those around us too. It's about hope and help and seeing the best yet to come. It's an enduring love modeled by God that we can share. It's a peaceful love that comforts others the way God comforts us. It's a growing love that never stops because God's love never stops.

He loves us, we love Him, and away we go!

*Father, help me remember—and let others see—all I mean to You.*

## Day 124
# Never Ever Give Up

*Keep your eyes open, hold tight to your convictions,*
*give it all you've got, be resolute, and love without stopping.*
1 CORINTHIANS 16:13–14 MSG

✦

Do you ever wonder if you're following Jesus right? Do you run into things you don't understand and situations you can't control? Life is more tangled up than the insides of a broken cell phone, and that's why Jesus simplifies and clarifies things for us. He never says give up. He never says you can't make it. He never stops following you or unfriends you. Paul's pointers to the church members at Corinth guide us too.

Keep your eyes open—look for Jesus in all you do and claim His strength in every situation.

Hold tight to your convictions—don't let anybody make you doubt your faith or God's ability and grace.

Give it all you've got—Jesus needs bold and brave disciples today just as He did when He walked the earth, and He has special work just for you.

Be resolute—finish that work! Keep your focus on the goals Jesus has given you. You'll complete some quickly, some take time, and some are ongoing. Keep at it.

Love without stopping—that's what Jesus does. He loves you through every good moment and every tough moment. Love Him back and pass that love on to others.

No matter what's happening, these guidelines will work you through it. Jesus' love straightens it all out.

• • • • • • • • • • • • • • • • • • • • • • • • • • • • • • • • • • • • • • • • • • • • • • • • •

*Thank You, Lord, for always teaching me and guiding me. You know*
*how I can get lost sometimes, and I know Your directions never fail.*

# Receiving Grace, Reflecting God

*"Therefore, I tell you, her many sins have been forgiven—as her great love has shown. But whoever has been forgiven little loves little."*
LUKE 7:47 NIV

The woman in Jesus' story is an example to us today of great love and devotion from her *and* Jesus. The woman led with her heart, despite her mistakes in the past and perhaps her fear of Jesus because she'd done some wrong things. We never have to be afraid of Jesus or His reaction to us—it will always be one of love and forgiveness.

Every day is full of choices and options. We make the wrong decision sometimes. Others do too. But the story shows us that Jesus is waiting for us to come to Him with the mess, to just love Him and leave everything else at His feet and let Him choose how to handle it. Here's a hint—He'll always choose love! He'll use it all to teach us and make us stronger so we'll know what it means to feel His great love and then be able to share it.

No matter how much we love Him, He loves us more, and with that example of love and mercy, we can pass it all on to others. We can be generous and kind and forgiving because our love will never be misplaced when it's given as Jesus gives it to us.

We receive God's grace and reflect Him to others. It's a simple and simply wonderful plan.

. . . . . . . . . . . . . . . . . . . . . . . . . . . . . . . . . . . . . . . . . . . . . . . . . . . . .

*Lord, thank You for Your love and Your mercy.*
*Please know my gratitude, and make me merciful too.*

## Day 126

# One Prayer, Every Day

*His mother said to the servants, "Do whatever he tells you."*
JOHN 2:5 NIV

Sometimes our minds can feel like a computer that's lost its operating system. Sure, we've got plenty of computing that needs doing, but our poor processor has no idea how to process, what to do, where to start.

The confusion comes from everywhere, but the solution comes from one place—one strong, easy-to-find, never-out-of-range place. Prayer!

Early in Jesus' ministry, He and His friends attended a wedding in Cana in Galilee. The custom at the time was for the host to share wine with all the guests, but the host ran out. Jesus' mother gave the problem to Him and then told the servants to obey His directions, whatever they were. They did, and water from the well became wine for everyone.

Mary's wise words gave them—and us—comfort and direction. All our confusion can be tossed away like an old password when we *do whatever He tells us.*

So when your computer freezes up—in your mind, your heart, your thoughts—find the Jesus-answer key and the instructions you need. Keep your prayers and your follow-through simple.

. . . . . . . . . . . . . . . . . . . . . . . . . . . . . . . . . . . . . . . . . . . . . . . . . . .

*Jesus, please help me remember that You respond to all my prayers with comfort and direction. Please help me do whatever You tell me in every moment. Thank You for Your guidance and care.*

# Help Wanted: ME!

*"O Sovereign Lord," I said, "I can't speak for you! I'm too young!"*
JEREMIAH 1:6 NLT

Some jobs for God can feel easy—being kind, being grateful, even telling others about Him. Other jobs are tougher, and we don't always feel ready. Jeremiah was young and scared when God called him to a big job. He said no. But God isn't in the habit of taking no for an answer, because when He asks us to do something, He's already planned it and prepared us to accomplish it.

We don't have God's long-range vision, but we can simply trust Him to know what He's doing. He loves us so much that He would never set us up to fail. People might do that—ask you to do something you know you're too young or inexperienced to do or lead you to the wrong place—but not God. The jobs He gives you fit you perfectly, and you're never too young to say yes.

Maybe you'll start slow; maybe you'll master a few things and grow your confidence in yourself so that you don't feel so afraid. Good. Remember that your courage comes from your faith in God to give you whatever you need. God comforted and reassured Jeremiah so that he could carry out the big job ahead. He'll do the same for you.

Go ahead and answer, "Yes, Lord, I'm young, but I'm Yours. Let's go!"

*Here I am, Lord. Please help me along on the big jobs You've created for me. Thank You for trusting me, and help me trust You more every day.*

# He Calls Your Name

*Jesus said to her, "Mary." She turned toward him and cried out in Aramaic, "Rabboni!" (which means "Teacher").*

John 20:16 niv

Learn what Jesus' voice sounds like. It's never mean, never unloving, never wrong.

Mary Magdalene went to be near Jesus in the tomb after He was crucified, but He was gone. She recognized His voice when He called her name.

If a friend turns against you or if someone tells lies about you, those voices are hurtful and mean. If you fail at something, your own voice can be damaging and unkind. If your family members sometimes don't understand you or you have an argument with one of them, their voices can be cruel and frightening. All of those other voices, including your own, are part of the noise of the world, but they're a mumble compared to the voice of Jesus.

Listen for Jesus' voice in every situation. Is He prompting you to make an apology? Is He guiding you through the next step of a difficult process? Is He reminding you of your worth and value to Him?

Know Jesus' voice by knowing *Him*. Spend time learning about His life and ministry and understand how He leads those who love Him. Listen. His words will be simple, but they will explain everything you need to know.

* * * * * * * * * * * * * * * * * * * * * * * * * * * * * * * * * * * * * * * * * * * * * * * * * * * * * *

*Please help me hear You, understand You, and follow Your loving words, Jesus. Help me silence all other voices and respond to Yours in love and trust.*

# Mother's Courage

*When she saw that he was a fine child, she hid him for three months.*
*But when she could hide him no longer, she got a papyrus basket*
*for him and coated it with tar and pitch. Then she placed the child*
*in it and put it among the reeds along the bank of the Nile.*
*His sister stood at a distance to see what would happen to him.*

Exodus 2:2–4 NIV

You might not even remember the name of Moses' mother (Jochebed), but it doesn't matter. "Mother" is the name that says it all.

The king of Egypt was afraid of the Israelites becoming powerful, so he wanted every baby boy killed. You can imagine how horrified the parents were! Moses' mother made a risky and brave decision to save her baby son, putting her trust in God—and it worked. The pharaoh's daughter rescued Moses, and his mom even got to raise him for a little while.

When Moses was just a toddler, his mom was separated from him again, but when she held him, sang to him, told him stories, and spoke words of God's love, she formed something in him that helped make him the leader of his people and the follower of God that he was.

Look at your mom, grandmothers, aunts, teachers—they each have their "Moses" story of bravery and trust to tell. Learn it. Repeat it.

* * * * * * * * * * * * * * * * * * * * * * * * * * * * * * * * * * * * * * * * * * * * * * * * *

*Father, please help me honor my mom and all the strong and courageous*
*women in my life who've shown me how to make good choices that*
*benefit others. Help me be thankful for them today and every day.*

# The Faith to Follow Through

*Ruth said, "If you say so, I'll do it, just as you've told me."*
RUTH 3:5 MSG

We read Ruth's Old Testament book and wonder how it can apply to us, but it's a tremendous story of her faith in God and those He provided to help her. And now she's part of everything we do today. Because of her strength and courage, she became the great-grandmother of David, ancestor to Jesus.

Ruth was married to Naomi's son. Times were very different then, and when he died, Naomi and Ruth were unable to care for themselves, so Naomi decided to go home to Israel. Ruth wasn't from there, and going to a new place was a lot harder then, but Ruth's loyalties and faith led her there. She told Naomi, "Where you go I will go, and where you stay I will stay. Your people will be my people and your God my God" (Ruth 1:16 NIV).

Still, it had to be scary, but Ruth knew God, and she put her faith in Naomi's leadership and direction. Even though they were alone when they got to Israel, Ruth followed Naomi's advice and carried herself with dignity and grace.

She kept her faith in her mother-in-law and the God she chose to serve. She married Boaz, and they became parents to their son Obed, father of Jesse, father of David. Ruth's simple, deep faith made it so.

*Father, help me keep my faith in You and those You
provide to help me. Please guide me in new places and
lead me on to the great things in my future.*

## Day 131

# It's Your Boat

*When they had rowed about three or four miles, they saw*
*Jesus approaching the boat, walking on the water; and they were*
*frightened. But he said to them, "It is I; don't be afraid."*
*Then they were willing to take him into the boat, and immediately*
*the boat reached the shore where they were heading.*

JOHN 6:19–21 NIV

Jesus sees everything. He sees all the good and the bad around you. He'll "walk on water" in whatever form that means to get to you. So the question isn't whether Jesus is holding the doorknob of your life—it's whether you'll unlock it and let Him in.

The disciples had that same choice. They were scared until they knew that it was Jesus "standing at the door," and then they invited Him in. He didn't jump in the boat uninvited, and He won't come crashing into your life. He's not pushy, but He is sticky—once in, He's in for good. He wants you to do the same as the disciples—have faith in Him and *willingly* ask Him near you. That's because *it's your boat.* You decide who's in and if you want Jesus' help in guiding it. His flawless guidance is all the GPS you'll ever need.

Just like it's your choice to accept or reject a phone call or to post or delete a photo, it's your choice to invite Jesus in or leave Him out. It's the simplest choice with the most personal and powerful results *ever.*

*Thank You, Jesus, for the power of choice.*
*I choose You in my life, everywhere, always.*

## Day 132
# Onward!

*Jesus was quick to comfort them. "Courage, it's me. Don't be afraid."*
*Peter, suddenly bold, said, "Master, if it's really you, call me to come to*
*you on the water." He said, "Come ahead." Jumping out of the boat,*
*Peter walked on the water to Jesus. But when he looked down at the*
*waves churning beneath his feet, he lost his nerve and started to sink.*
*He cried, "Master, save me!" Jesus didn't hesitate. He reached down and*
*grabbed his hand. Then he said, "Faint-heart, what got into you?"*
MATTHEW 14:27–31 MSG

When you're scared, it's hard to keep your focus where it should be. Peter learned that on high, shifting waves when he lost his footing and his focus on Jesus.

Even when we're doing something good, something we know Jesus approves of and will help us with, we can still be like Peter, upended by the elements around us. Fear is strong, and we have to fight it with everything we have, no matter how it shows up and tries to knock us under. Fear that threatens you like a crashing wave can be anything: others who don't believe in what you're doing, others who are too afraid to have faith themselves, even your own mind feeding itself with doubt instead of Jesus' words.

All that's just crashing waves that mean nothing because Jesus will never let you go under the scary water. He'll grab your hand and remind you He's *always* there.

*Thank You, Jesus, for walking with me and having faith in me.*
*Help my faith grow as we go onward everywhere together. Let's go!*

## Day 133

# Wake Me When It's Time

*Then the time came for Herod to bring him out for the kill. That night, even though shackled to two soldiers, one on either side, Peter slept like a baby. And there were guards at the door keeping their eyes on the place. Herod was taking no chances!*

ACTS 12:6 MSG

Faith means believing in our God to do His job while we do ours. It means carrying on in hard experiences and being an example to those around us. Do you ever find yourself worrying about a test you've already prepared for? Do you spend too much time thinking about what someone else said or did instead of focusing on what you can do? Do you ever wonder if God's paying attention to what's bothering you?

When Peter was in jail, waiting to be tried and possibly killed for teaching about Jesus, do you know what he was doing? He was *sleeping*, of all things. He wasn't screaming or plotting or pouting. He had prayed and turned everything over to God. He had demonstrated his devotion and faith to those around him. And then, because he'd done that part of his job and probably needed rest to carry on, he closed his eyes and simply slept.

Can you do that the next time you're worrying about something you can't change? Can you pray, do whatever's required of you, and then rest in faith, sleeping "like a baby"? Yes, you can!

*Lord, please help me have Peter's faith when I'm scared, and help me rest in Your promises. Just wake me when it's time for more work!*

*Day 134*

# Joy at the Door

*Still shaking his head, amazed, he went to Mary's house, the Mary who was John Mark's mother. The house was packed with praying friends. When he knocked on the door to the courtyard, a young woman named Rhoda came to see who it was. But when she recognized his voice— Peter's voice!—she was so excited and eager to tell everyone Peter was there that she forgot to open the door and left him standing in the street.*

Acts 12:12–14 MSG

Remember Peter, who was in prison, all full of faith and sleep? Once free, he went to his friends. Now let's meet Rhoda, a young girl who spent her time in service to others, including answering the door. She was with those praying for Peter and didn't know of his miraculous escape. When she recognized his voice outside, she was so overjoyed that she ran to tell the others, leaving Peter at the door.

Rhoda may have been embarrassed, but that's okay. Her faith in God joined with her joy at Peter's release, and she couldn't contain it. God probably smiled and thought, *What a wonderful daughter of Mine, unafraid to rejoice in My work. I like that.*

When we react out of love and pure joy for God's grace, He says the same thing about us. Look for miracles, have faith in God to accomplish them, and then tell everyone in the house what new miracle is standing at the door of *your* life.

*Thank You, Lord, for answering prayers and bringing miracles to my life every day. Help me celebrate You with those I love.*

## Day 135

# Say It; Make It Count

*Run away from childish indulgence. Run after mature righteousness—*
*faith, love, peace—joining those who are in honest and serious*
*prayer before God. Refuse to get involved in inane discussions; they*
*always end up in fights. God's servant must not be argumentative,*
*but a gentle listener and a teacher who keeps cool, working firmly*
*but patiently with those who refuse to obey. You never know how*
*or when God might sober them up with a change of heart and*
*a turning to the truth, enabling them to escape the Devil's trap,*
*where they are caught and held captive, forced to run his errands.*

2 Timothy 2:22–26 msg

Have you ever heard the saying that God gave us two ears and one mouth for a reason? It's a silly little way of saying we should talk less and listen more. Yet we know people (sometimes it's even us) who have to have the last word, who can't stand to be corrected, who spend a ton of time jabbering about stuff that doesn't even matter.

God says there's a better way. When the arguing and complaining start, spit out your own unhelpful ideas like you would spoiled food because that's what bad thoughts and words do: make you sick.

Listen twice as much as you talk. Use words that tell the wonderful truth about God and why your faith is in Him. Then at least from *you*, everyone will hear love, hope, compassion, and direction.

*Lord, please help me be a good leader in every situation,*
*representing You and telling others about You.*

## Day 136
## "Directions, Please?"

*"They pile heavy burdens on people's shoulders and won't lift a finger
to help. Everything they do is just to show off in front of others.
They even make a big show of wearing Scripture verses on their
foreheads and arms, and they wear big tassels for everyone to see."*
MATTHEW 23:4–5 CEV

✦

Did you know that in Jesus' time some of the Jewish leaders who wanted to look impressive wore a box on their heads with a Bible verse or two inside (called *phylacteries*)? Maybe you know the type.

They act like they're friends with others and then spread rumors behind their backs. They look like good students but cheat on tests. The truth is that no matter what others appear to be or how they portray themselves to others, God knows their hearts.

He knows if your faith is real or if it's paraded around for some selfish reason. The claim to be God's follower only matters when you live it. He asks for His words to be written not on your head but on your *heart* where they can never be removed. Jesus called the Jewish leaders "blind guides" (v. 24 NIV), but we know exactly where we're going.

No matter what comes up, with God's love and directions imprinted from the inside out, there's no need to unstrap a box from your head and check for instructions. Simply read your heart and you'll know how to practice what Jesus preaches.

. . . . . . . . . . . . . . . . . . . . . . . . . . . . . . . . . . . . . . . . . . . . . . . . . . . . . . . . . . . .

*Lord, I know every day is a chance to be a guide for others.
Please make my words and my actions wise as I follow You.*

## Day 137

# Knowledge Is Power

*All wisdom comes from the LORD, and so do
common sense and understanding.*

PROVERBS 2:6 CEV

You'll hear this statement all your life, and it's true: *knowledge IS power,* because what you know is something no one can ever take away from you. No one can steal it or hide it. It's yours forever. It's valuable and powerful, so be sure your knowledge comes from the right place.

Some people will tell you what *they* want you to know, maybe try to convince you to do whatever they're doing or make a risky decision. It happens all the time, but your response is simple. To decide if they're leading you the right way or the wrong way, stand their wisdom up alongside God's Word and see if it agrees with it or argues with it.

And do you know how you'll know? When *YOU* know God's Word. The knowledge and understanding and wisdom that He gives is the knowledge and understanding and wisdom you need. It's *that* knowledge that's power, and it gives you a plan. When someone comes to you with an idea, take a minute and take a measurement, seeing if it matches what you know from God.

The more you study God's Word, listen to Him, and see Him work in your life, the quicker you'll be able to make those decisions, making your life much simpler. *That's* where you put your trust—in what God tells you and teaches you.

Knowledge is power—God's power.

. . . . . . . . . . . . . . . . . . . . . . . . . . . . . . . . . . . . . . . . . . . . . . . . . . . . . . . . .

*Please help me learn and follow Your wisdom,
Lord, and claim it for my own.*

## Day 138

# He's Here, Now, Always, Real

*"Starting from scratch, he made the entire human race and made the earth hospitable, with plenty of time and space for living so we could seek after God, and not just grope around in the dark but actually find him. He doesn't play hide-and-seek with us. He's not remote; he's near. We live and move in him, can't get away from him! One of your poets said it well: 'We're the God-created.' Well, if we are the God-created, it doesn't make a lot of sense to think we could hire a sculptor to chisel a god out of stone for us, does it?"*

ACTS 17:26–29 MSG

Some call it "blind faith" or "misplaced trust" in a God they can't see or touch. We just say no worries!

Our God needs nothing to survive. He isn't dependent on air, water, or food the way we are. He spends all His time caring about us fragile little things that can't even see Him. He wants our trust yet doesn't demand it. He waits for it.

He's made of love and wisdom and mercy and gives it all to us. He doesn't post pictures of Himself or create clever hashtags, but He helps us quicker than the rest between heartbeats. When we reach for Him, He's already here. If we ask to be part of His work, He simply shows us the list of stuff we can do, and we succeed when we trust what we can't see or feel to make everything real.

*Thank You, Lord, for being all I need, right beside me, bigger than anything else—real!*

## Day 139

# The Place to Start

*In fact, we felt sure we were going to die. But this made us stop trusting*
*in ourselves and start trusting God, who raises the dead to life.*
2 Corinthians 1:9 cev

Paul traveled through some hostile territory to tell the story of Jesus, and he was often in real danger. He told the church in Corinth about being fearful for his life in Asia. He could've kept relying on his own ability, but he found a better source of strength and courage. His fear didn't win. He changed it into faith and trusted God to be with him. God responded, Paul learned, and so can we.

Lesson #1: When you're scared out of your mind, trust God.

Lesson #2: Don't wait until you're scared out of your mind to trust God.

This story doesn't mean we shouldn't be competent and skillful. It's about learning everything you can and doing your best to be a faithful disciple, all while you're trusting God to take care of whatever you can't. When hard, scary things are happening, that's when relying on our trust in God should come *first*. That's when we want to remember God's promises are for us, when we want to remember all the times before that He's helped us and know He's still not scared of anything. He's still the same strong and powerful God who has us in the palm of His hand.

We can't save ourselves, and what's wonderful about that is we don't have to.

*Lord, please help me remember You never tune me out.*
*My trust is the call You wait for.*

## Day 140
# Yes or No?

*When Jesus saw him lying there and learned that he had been in this*
*condition for a long time, he asked him, "Do you want to get well?"*
*"Sir," the invalid replied, "I have no one to help me into the pool when*
*the water is stirred. While I am trying to get in, someone else goes down*
*ahead of me." Then Jesus said to him, "Get up! Pick up your mat and*
*walk." At once the man was cured; he picked up his mat and walked.*

JOHN 5:6–9 NIV

✦

It's easy to complain and find excuses. The people believed that the pool
of Bethesda would heal them if they stepped in the water at the right
time, but the man Jesus met couldn't walk. Jesus, in all His love and
compassion, didn't pick him up or call for others to do it—He asked the
man if he really wanted a better life. "Do you want to get well?" might
be a question He asks us sometimes, and we can answer like the man
in the story.

Do we really want to overcome a fear, break a bad habit, stop following
poor role models? *Do we really want to get well?* The man walked because
Jesus said he could. He trusted Jesus and began a greater life. What will
*you* do when you hear Jesus say you can?

It's a simple question. Let's be ready when He asks, "Do you want
to get well?"

. . . . . . . . . . . . . . . . . . . . . . . . . . . . . . . . . . . . . . . . . . . . . . . . . . . . . . .

*Jesus, my answer is yes! I want to be well in You, growing stronger*
*and wiser every day, doing everything You say I can do.*

## Day 141

# Building High, Building Wide

*"'Yes, get to work! For I am with you.' The GOD-of-the-Angel-Armies is speaking! 'Put into action the word I covenanted with you when you left Egypt. I'm living and breathing among you right now. Don't be timid. Don't hold back.'"*

HAGGAI 2:5 MSG

The Israelites were trying to rebuild the temple of God after being captives far from home for seventy years. Imagine how afraid and unprepared they felt, and then they met up with a whole town of bullies who didn't want them there. They were tempted to give up, to say the job was just too hard and scary. God had other plans.

He sent them there, and He wasn't going to forget about them or ignore their fear. Haggai the prophet delivered God's message they needed to keep building. It's a timeless message that comforts and inspires us today. It's so simple, so profound, so *God*: "Do not fear, I am with you."

"Remember who I am?" God's saying. "Do you think these problems and people are bigger than I am? Do you think we should just let them have their way and forget about My plans? That would be a no."

Following God's lead doesn't mean never running into trouble, but it does mean He's there right in the middle of it with us—and He's a whole lot bigger. And just like the Israelites, we'll build temples of our own that He designs, no matter what gets in the way.

........................................................

*Thank You, Lord, for being with me all the time, just like You promise. Help me avoid being afraid while we build everything You have planned.*

## Day 142

# Gut-Check Time

*The king wanted [Queen Vashti] to wear her crown and
let his people and his officials see how beautiful she was.
The king's servants told Queen Vashti what he had said, but
she refused to go to him, and this made him terribly angry.*

ESTHER 1:11–12 CEV

Have you ever felt pressured in a situation, with little room to refuse whatever was asked of you? It takes courage to stand up for yourself, especially if you have a lot to lose by saying no. The book of Esther tells about two courageous women who did just that. We learn about Esther, but we also learn about Vashti, the queen before Esther, who lost everything but decided that was a risk she was willing to take.

Her husband, King Xerxes, wanted to show her off in front of his guests. She refused, and that's what made the way for Esther to become queen. Who knows what might've happened if Queen Vashti had been less courageous? But she trusted herself enough to make the tough choice. Maybe God was speaking to her somehow, even though we have no indication she even knew God. Still, through her, He made a way for Esther.

The right choice is one of courage and trust in what God's taught us. We can ask ourselves: *Would God want me to do that?* The answer might feel like "trusting your gut" because that's God speaking to you. And when we listen, we'll find the same courage, conviction, and decisiveness Vashti and Esther had.

* * * * * * * * * * * * * * * * * * * * * * * * * * * * * * * * * * * * * * * * * *

*Thank You, Lord, for leading me the right
way. Help me trust You every time.*

## Day 143

# "Good Morning, God!"

*Listen, GOD! Please, pay attention! Can you make sense of*
*these ramblings, my groans and cries? King-God, I need your help.*
*Every morning you'll hear me at it again. Every morning I lay out*
*the pieces of my life on your altar and watch for fire to descend.*

PSALM 5:1–3 MSG

What's the first thing you think of in the morning? Is it school, family, what you're going to wear? Is it a decision you have to make *today?* The best way to attack all of it is with God as your first thought.

David says that he gave everything to God first thing, and it doesn't say then he worried or gave up on getting an answer. Verse three in the NIV translation says, "I lay my requests before you and wait expectantly." There. Done. He's trusting God to handle it all, and he's expecting God's grace to guide him through the next steps, whatever they are.

God's up all night, waiting for you to wake up and talk to Him. He's ready with the grace you need for the day, like raindrops on a warm afternoon or a tidal wave you can ride to safety.

Those first thoughts of your morning can guide your entire day. Let them be to God and of God, your expectation and His response. Trust Him to hear you and respond. Trust Him to surround you with His grace that makes you able to make every day better than the last.

*Some days are more of a challenge than others, Lord.*
*I love knowing You're here every moment, no matter what.*

# Friends Matter

*Don't fool yourselves. Bad friends will destroy you.*
1 CORINTHIANS 15:33 CEV

During the time Paul was preaching and teaching about Jesus, he was talking and writing to people who were influenced by many things, and not all of them were good. Many groups denied Jesus, and they wanted others to turn against Him too. You may have people around you every day who try to influence you the wrong way or convince you to go against what you know to be true. Those are friends you don't need.

God knows that running away from bad friends can be hard though, and that's why His grace surrounds you and gives you courage and direction, because your choice of friends is so important. For better or worse, we tend to become like those around us. It's part of being human, which can work out for the good because we can choose to be around godly, kind, and humble people. Just as bad company can take us away from what we know is right and true, good company can help us hold on to it more and become an even better example to those around us.

God helps you find people who'll help you grow, and He also puts people in your life that you can help. Trust Him to continue building your character every day, making you a stronger and wiser friend.

Good influences come from God—be one of them.

* * * * * * * * * * * * * * * * * * * * * * * * * * * * * * * * * * * * * * * * * *

*Jesus, You said You are my friend. I believe You. I trust You. Let me be a good friend to others and find more good friends to grow with.*

## Day 145
# Perfect for Your Part

*"Here's what I want you to do: Find a quiet, secluded place so you won't be tempted to role-play before God. Just be there as simply and honestly as you can manage. The focus will shift from you to God, and you will begin to sense his grace."*
MATTHEW 6:6 MSG

During school time, you bend to the teacher's demands and class rules. During sport time, you put on the team jersey and do your part. During home time, you're the daughter with responsibilities to your parents. If you have brothers or sisters, that's another role, and if you have a job or volunteer, you're hitting your marks there too. You are one committed girl!

And that's all wonderful, just as it should be. But to do your best in all those slices of your life-pie that's getting bigger by the day, you need help. You need God's guiding grace, and you know what? You don't have to be *anything* when you come to Him. You don't have to prepare to talk to Him—He prepares *you* for everything you have to do. You don't have to impress Him—receive from Him. Give Him your love and attention and devotion, and He will give you all the energy and wisdom and ability you need.

Thank Him for His daily grace. Ask for what you need. Receive all that and more. It's never an audition, just dancing high on the stage of God's plans.

*Father, here I am, and more importantly, here You are.*
*Thank You for loving me as I am. I love You too.*

## Day 146

# Right Words, Wrong Words

*But you will not really be the one speaking.*
*The Spirit from your Father will tell you what to say.*
MATTHEW 10:20 CEV

We learn quickly that words matter. What others say to us and about us matters a lot and can have a good or bad impact on how we feel and what we do. Maybe it shouldn't, but it does. And sometimes we're wordless as a tree, unable to respond to hurtful things people say or know what to say ourselves when a friend needs comfort. But we can learn what to say every time with God's help because He *always* has the right words.

Jesus prepared His disciples for the less-than-friendly treatment they might run into as they traveled to preach His teachings and tell others about Him, knowing that others weren't always going to open their doors with hospitality and kindness. "Don't worry," He told His followers. "Open your heart and then open your mouth—let God speak." That simple plan of trust still works today for us, no matter what anyone says about us or to us. Our Father's words never fail.

You might meet people who make fun of your faith or condemn you for something or don't see your value to God. Often not responding is the best choice, and hitting DELETE works amazingly well; but when you have to reply, trust God to give you the words. Everyone is listening.

*Thank You, Lord, for helping me find the right words and not say the wrong ones. Remind me to hear from You before others hear from me.*

## Day 147

# More Than Enough

*Peter asked [Sapphira], "Tell me, did you sell the property
for this amount?" "Yes," she answered, "that's the amount."
Then Peter said, "Why did the two of you agree to test the Lord's
Spirit? The men who buried Ananias are by the door, and they
will carry you out!" At once she fell at Peter's feet and died.*
ACTS 5:8–10 CEV

Sapphira and her husband, Ananias, both died because of their greed and mistrust. Who knows what examples they might've been for us if they'd simply been witnesses of God's grace instead of trying to secretly work deals for themselves?

You're learning more and more every day about managing your own money and being responsible for some of your own needs, but that's the point—to be managers of what God's given us, not captors. Everything we have is God's. It's our job to use it well and trust Him to continue to provide for us and sustain us every day. God doesn't do anything "barely" or "not quite." He always supplies more than enough when we're following Him in trust and doing our best to carry out His plans.

It's no glory to Him if we go around whining, "Well, God's just not big enough for this project" or "God didn't make me smart enough to do that" because whatever God's planned for, He's prepared for. And His abundant grace, coupled with our trust and unselfishness, makes it all possible.

*Lord, please help me conquer my greed and worry and focus on
Your generosity and wisdom. Your supply is overflowing!*

## Day 148

# Growing Gifts

*God's various gifts are handed out everywhere; but they all
originate in God's Spirit. God's various ministries are carried out
everywhere; but they all originate in God's Spirit. God's various
expressions of power are in action everywhere; but God himself
is behind it all. Each person is given something to do that shows
who God is: Everyone gets in on it, everyone benefits. All kinds of
things are handed out by the Spirit, and to all kinds of people!*

1 CORINTHIANS 12:4-7 MSG

What are your gifts? Do you wonder that sometimes? Do you wish God
would just send you a text and tell you what gifts you have and how to
use them? Well, He sort of does. More immediate than a text is the
evidence of gifts all around you and a special one for you to participate
in all the time.

Every day you can practice the gift of *encouragement*. It doesn't cost
a thing, and it helps others focus on God's help and kindness coming
through you. Also, when others share their gifts with you, learn from
them, thank them, and thank God for putting them in your life.

Keep it simple. See your good qualities and natural abilities as buds,
little beginnings to grow. Think about the tiny acorn that grows into the
gigantic oak tree and see your God-given gifts as a basket full of acorns.
God's grace grows those acorns into your own forest of gifts to share.
Start with a little encouragement for yourself.

*Thank You, Lord, for all my gifts! Please help me learn
from and encourage those around me. We all grow!*

# Start Anywhere, Finish Strong

*For there is no difference between Jew and Gentile—the same*
*Lord is Lord of all and richly blesses all who call on him.*
ROMANS 10:12 NIV

Jesus was born a Jew, but that didn't mean all Jews would follow Him. Many persecuted Him and His disciples. Others who weren't Jewish and were typically the enemies of the Jews trusted and believed Jesus and became His disciples all over the world. We can't change what nationality we are. We can't change when or where we were born or who our parents are or how tall we grow. And none of that matters.

Paul told the Romans and all of us that God doesn't care about any of that stuff—because it's all out of our control. He won't blame us for something we can't create or change. But we can control ourselves and grow and become all He sees for us, and that's what He cares about, not where we start.

So you can't become French if you're born Chinese, but you can become a surgeon because your education is something you can change. You can't grow yourself younger, but you can take care of your body and grow stronger every day. You can't erase mistakes and become sinless like Jesus, but you can correct your wrongs and work every day to make better choices.

The grace Paul was talking about covered the fighting Jews and Gentiles, and the same grace covers you now. God always answers your call.

*Lord, help me see the way You do, and let nothing stand*
*between me and Your blessings as I grow.*

## *Day 150*
# **Powerful Grace**

*For we are God's masterpiece. He has created us anew in Christ Jesus, so we can do the good things he planned for us long ago.*
EPHESIANS 2:10 NLT

You can't work your way into God's heart. You can't impress Him enough with your good grades or trendiest outfit or newest gadget. He's focused on you—His already-masterpiece—and He cares about how you receive His grace, not because He needs the recognition, but because He wants to give you more. The more we use, the more He gives!

When you think you can't learn something or achieve something or overcome something, that's doubt in your heart and mind trying to keep God's grace out—because when grace comes in and you use it, the doubt gets rubbed out like a fading ghost in a cartoon. And then more grace comes in, and you use that too. Then more and more. So just tell that doubt that God's already worked out the plan and He's preparing you and equipping you to achieve it. You're His daughter, the only one who can do the jobs He's prepared for you. Get to work!

That special something that makes you *you* and makes you able to do all you do is God's powerful grace. It's His once-and-forever grace that's saved us from a lifetime lost and abandoned, and it's His every-moment grace that meets us where we need it.

*Lord, how much grace do You have to give me? I know—I'll never use it up! You keep giving it to me so we can do great things. I like this plan.*

## Day 151

# God Doesn't Forget

*But the king's personal servant completely forgot about Joseph.*
GENESIS 40:23 CEV

Bad things happen—people forget, but God never does.

Joseph knew a few things about sibling rivalry. His brothers even sold him to slave traders thinking they'd be free of him, but Potiphar, an Egyptian captain of the guard for Pharaoh, bought him. Because of Joseph's intelligence and respect, Potiphar put him in charge of running things, but he eventually wound up in prison, accused of something he didn't do.

Even there, Joseph kept trusting God, made friends, and even helped a worker get his job back. Joseph asked the worker to just mention him to Pharaoh when he was released, but like people often do, he forgot. For two more long years, Joseph stayed in prison, forgotten by people, lovingly remembered by God. Once finally released from prison, Joseph went on to save his brothers and many others from starvation because of his wisdom and obedience to God.

For far too long, others have sacrificed so that we are saved today from all kinds of evil, that we're free to worship God in peace. For the many brave men and women who've died protecting us, let us never forget.

. . . . . . . . . . . . . . . . . . . . . . . . . . . . . . . . . . . . . . . . . . . . . . . . . . . . . . . . .

*Thank You, Lord, for those who live out their wisdom and*
*obedience to You every day so that we may live in joy and peace.*
*Let us always remember the heavy price paid for our freedoms*
*and help us honor the memory of those who paid it.*

# That's a Lot of Love!

*But now, GOD's Message, the God who made you in the first place, Jacob,*
*the One who got you started, Israel: "Don't be afraid, I've redeemed you.*
*I've called your name. You're mine. When you're in over your head, I'll*
*be there with you. When you're in rough waters, you will not go down.*
*When you're between a rock and a hard place, it won't be a dead end. . . .*
*That's how much you mean to me! That's how much I love you! I'd sell*
*off the whole world to get you back, trade the creation just for you."*
ISAIAH 43:1–2, 4MSG

God doesn't see you and look for the little trash can at the bottom of the screen. He doesn't lose you and your messages to Him, no matter how many others are filling up His inbox. He knows YOU. He loves YOU. Just as you are, this moment.

He knows your name—no matter who else doesn't, no matter where you go, no matter what changes about you—because He's claimed you for His own, forever and ever. He said so, right there. And what God claims, He blesses, He guides, He protects, He loves.

His love is what caused Him to make you and what keeps Him near you. It's His precious, everlasting, unfailing, never-let-you-go, greater-than-you-can-imagine blessing that matters more than anything because it's what makes all other things possible.

Keep it simple—believe Him, trust Him, love Him. If we just loved God back one one-hundredth as much as He loves us, we'd probably explode. But let's try.

*I love You, Lord. You love me. Help the meaning*
*of these truths fully sink in today.*

# First Love

*"I know your persistence, your courage in my cause, that you never wear out. But you walked away from your first love—why?"*

REVELATION 2:3–4 MSG

During wedding season, you may find yourself witnessing the wonder of a groom in awe of his bride as she makes her way down the aisle. He beams as she approaches in all her radiance. A smile stretches clear across his face, and there's a good chance for tears of joy. This love. This is just a glimpse of the way God loves *you*! In fact, God loves you infinitely more, with overwhelming depth and completeness.

It's impossible not to wonder whom you may one day marry and what that day might be like. Yet God Himself is first trying to win you over to an important first love. He longs for you to fall for Him. He encourages us over and over in scripture to focus on His love, the greatest love we'll ever know. He has to remind us because we have a tendency to wander. Our hearts easily stray away, and too often it takes heartbreak for us to see how much we need Him.

Thankfully, no matter how much we get bumped off course, there is always grace from God. He loved us first (see 1 John 4:19), and He is constantly trying to show us just how much.

*God, help me make You my first love so that I'll grow into the woman You created me to be.*

# At the Heart

*"Do not consider his appearance or his height, for I have rejected him. The LORD does not look at the things people look at. People look at the outward appearance, but the LORD looks at the heart."*

1 SAMUEL 16:7 NIV

The fan pages on social media. Movies on the big screen. They reflect plenty of beauty, that's for sure. Magazines and Snapchats send a lot of pretty pictures your way. If you're not careful, you can get to thinking that you are supposed to look a certain way to be valuable. But that is so far from the truth! God said so.

Looks, finances, family status—none of these matter in God's eyes. He sees you as a standout beauty no matter what kind of hair day you're having. If your home is a wreck with peeling paint, He doesn't care. If your family vehicle is a ten-year-old minivan, that's quite all right. It's your heart that matters. *You* are what God wants. You matter. And right where you are, God has beautiful plans for you.

*Dear God, help me see that the way You made me is beautiful, inside and out. Give me the strength to do the heart work that I need in order to grow into the strong woman of God You are preparing me to be.*

## *Day 155*
# **Balancing Life**

*Do not conform to the pattern of this world, but be transformed*
*by the renewing of your mind. Then you will be able to test and*
*approve what God's will is—his good, pleasing and perfect will.*
ROMANS 12:2 NIV

Olivia spends several hours a day online, and judging by her posts, she seems truly miserable. Claire wants to read all the time. When her friends text her or want to hang out, it seems like she has no time for them. Leah is crazy involved at her church, and it's all she ever talks about. She doesn't take time to really get to know people and hear their hearts.

There are so many activities we can choose to spend our daily life on. Social media, good books, great friends, time with God, family time, going to practices, and church activities. In between all the things you get to choose are things you simply should do, like chores and homework.

If you're not careful with your choices, life can get overwhelming and start to feel really out of balance. Making a habit of spending time with God, just reading the Bible, and quieting your heart will help you see and hear what God wants to show you.

*Lord, I quiet my heart before You. Help me make decisions today that*
*give me a balanced life, shining Your love in me and through me.*

# Navigation Plans

*The LORD directs the steps of the godly. He delights in*
*every detail of their lives. Though they stumble, they will*
*never fall, for the LORD holds them by the hand.*
PSALM 37:23–24 NLT

People often ask Zoe what she wants to do when she grows up. She likes it when they leave off the "when you grow up" part. She's in the process of growing up, being more like an adult, and they're noticing. But when she contemplates what job she wants when she's older, she can't help but think about all the adults she knows who still don't know what they want to be! She sees that she has time and that it's a process too.

A mentor is helping Zoe to see that God is always working on helping her recognize the gifts He's given her and the many opportunities where she can use them. The best thing, her mentor says, is that when you step out in faith to use your gifts, God helps you grow stronger in them.

Right now Zoe has her hands full navigating these teenage years. She has volleyball games and practices over the summer, 4-H, and youth group too. Each day she is trying to spend time with God. As she reads the Bible and asks God for understanding in applying what He says to life, she's starting to sort out what is important for her growth and what isn't really a good use of her time.

*Dear God, give me eyes to see what is best for my walk*
*today, that I would grow in strength and wisdom.*

# You Are Good Enough

*There has never been the slightest doubt in my mind that the God
who started this great work in you would keep at it and bring it
to a flourishing finish on the very day Christ Jesus appears.*

PHILIPPIANS 1:6 MSG

Sara feels like nothing she does is ever quite good enough for her parents,
for her coach, for her grades. Life can be so demanding. She tries so hard
to do things well, but she feels like she is always coming up short. Or
maybe she is putting herself up against the wrong standard.

God says she is good enough, after all. He made her with unique
giftings, a great style all her own, and abilities that little by little she is
getting better at.

God has great plans for the work He began in Sara, and He doesn't
quit something He started. He is going to do great things with her life
experiences. What she's learning is that those things often don't look like
she thought they would! Sometimes she can't see what God's doing at all,
and sometimes He shows her much later. So she's learning to trust that
God is at work, and that means she is always good enough.

*God, thank You that You made me good enough for everything I
face. Help me go through my day with confidence in what You are
doing in and around me, even though I can't see a lot of it.*

## Day 158

# Me, a Leader?

*God doesn't want us to be shy with his gifts,*
*but bold and loving and sensible.*

2 TIMOTHY 1:7 MSG

People often tell Chloe to "be a leader." They intend this to be encouraging of course, but they don't realize that she has a lot of introvert in her. To her, being a leader doesn't sound like her thing at all. She gets really nervous when she has to say something in front of the class or is chosen to be a group spokesperson in science.

What God has helped her see, though, is that leading isn't always in front of a group or even spoken. Oftentimes it is just doing the right thing, and if one person sees it and makes a better decision, then she is a leader.

Like at lunch, when Chloe was nice to this one girl who other kids were mean to. Soon after she did that, one of her other friends asked a new kid to come sit with them. That was really cool.

She's learning to be brave and grow in the strengths God has put in her. It makes her feel really good about her life!

*God, show me today how You want me to lead, whether it's with words or not. Give me the strength to choose the right actions today.*

## Day 159

# Struggling Friends

*You already know these things, dear friends. So be on
guard; then you will not be carried away by the errors of
these wicked people and lose your own secure footing.*

2 PETER 3:17 NLT

One of Hunter's friends has been making some really bad decisions lately. It makes Hunter not want to spend too much time with her so she's not pulled in the wrong direction too. If Hunter's mom knew the whole story, she wouldn't let Hunter near this friend. Yet Hunter can't help but think of how Jesus loves every single one of us, no matter what we've done or what we struggle with. Hunter knows that her friend needs encouragement and grace.

Hunter started praying about this and for her friend. She decided to talk to her mom and told her how her friend is struggling, how she needs truth given to her in love, but she also needs grace. Hunter felt that she was supposed to be a friend who offered those things to her, that maybe she could be like Jesus in these ways. She asked her mom to support her with this. Hunter's mom was so surprised by her maturity and was happy to help. They began praying together for Hunter's friend and talking through what a healthy balance of time with her would look like. Her mom had some great ideas for encouraging healthy decisions for Hunter's friend.

Hunter is so glad she asked God what to do and thankful for a mom who would pray with her and help.

*God, guide me today in friendship decisions.
Give me wisdom so that I can grow stronger in my faith.*

## Day 160
# The Roaring

*Be alert and of sober mind. Your enemy the devil prowls around like a roaring lion looking for someone to devour.*
1 PETER 5:8 NIV

You can feel like you're on the right track. That you're growing just how you should in your faith, your friendships, and your decisions. Then—without you even noticing, you are distracted by something that seemed harmless, and just that fast—you're off track.

The noise of the world around us makes it incredibly difficult to focus on what God has for us. There are unhealthy messages being thrown out at you all the time. There are people who will lead you astray because they're lost themselves. There are false teachers (see 2 Peter 2:1), and you never know where they'll turn up. Sometimes certain friends are bad for us, and we have to stop hanging out with them.

The roar of the world around us reminds us that the enemy is lurking and waiting for a chance to bring us down. Thank God that He is with us always wherever we go. Walking with Him is the only way we can make our way through safely.

*God, help me hear Your still, small voice amid the deafening noise of the world around me, that I would walk in strength with You.*

*Day 161*

# Your Radiant Beauty

*Your beauty should not come from outward adornment, such as
elaborate hairstyles and the wearing of gold jewelry or fine clothes.
Rather, it should be that of your inner self, the unfading beauty of
a gentle and quiet spirit, which is of great worth in God's sight.*

1 PETER 3:3–4 NIV

When Sam was thirteen, she wanted Alan to notice her. He seemed like
a nice boy (and she really liked his hair). He noticed her in the way that
he didn't run her over in the hallway. Clearly she wasn't standing out to
him though. What she really wanted was for him to think, *Wow! She's
really something!* Well, she *was* really something. What she didn't realize
then was that she was expecting someone to notice who she really was
by the way she looked.

What Sam learned was that she just needed to concentrate on growing
in her knowledge, strengths, and faith. When she relaxed and did that,
people noticed the most valuable things about her. These are the people
who ended up being her good friends, because strong character and faith
mattered to them too. *That* is beautiful.

. . . . . . . . . . . . . . . . . . . . . . . . . . . . . . . . . . . . . . . . . . . . . . . . . . . .

*God, help me look to You today as I grow, that I would shine for You
and attract friends based on who I am rather than how I look.*

## Day 162

# Reflect Purity

*Don't let anyone look down on you because you are
young, but set an example for the believers in speech,
in conduct, in love, in faith and in purity.*

1 TIMOTHY 4:12 NIV

Summer's Dad became very upset when he saw the bathing suit she
wanted to wear to hang out with her friends by the pool. "No one should
see her like that," she heard him telling her mother. Summer knew he
was trying to protect his little girl, but it seemed so overboard.

She later came to understand the impact of how she dresses, how it
affects others and potentially her faith walk too.

No one is perfect, not one. Yet we are asked to strive to do our best.
For Summer, that meant thinking about how she dresses and acts so that
her decisions wouldn't cause others to make poor decisions. Whether
we're young and figuring these things out or a little older and wiser, at
every age we want to aim to reflect the purity of Christ.

*Dear God, help me listen to You and the wisdom of those who
know more than I do so that I will grow stronger in You.*

# Minding My Messages

*The weapons we fight with are not the weapons of the world. On the contrary, they have divine power to demolish strongholds. We demolish arguments and every pretension that sets itself up against the knowledge of God, and we take captive every thought to make it obedient to Christ.*

2 CORINTHIANS 10:4–5 NIV

Zoe really liked this one popular song. A lot. She added it to her playlist, looked up the lyrics, and read about the band too. It was such a cool song that she sang it a lot for a good week or more. Her brother pointed out that some of the words were a little shady, and he explained it a little in detail. Now her mom was paying attention to what he was saying, and Zoe was upset. "I just liked the song," Zoe said. How bad could it be?

She didn't want to talk to them about it; she was just mad. She spent some time in her room alone thinking and eventually praying. She realized that the parts of the song her brother pointed out were not good messages to hold on to. She started writing down in a journal the good messages in songs she liked, the ones that she should hold on to and think about applying in her life. It became a lot clearer that there were a lot of negative messages, and Zoe decided to be more careful with the things she let herself think about.

*God, help me guard the door of my mind so that I am thinking on things that help me grow strong and faithful.*

*Day 164*

# Face-to-Face Friends

*"Therefore, if you are offering your gift at the altar and there remember
that your brother or sister has something against you, leave your gift
there in front of the altar. First go and be reconciled to them."*
MATTHEW 5:23–24 NIV

Emma found herself in a heated texting conversation with one of her
best friends, Jade. It was all a misunderstanding, which Emma was
trying to explain, but it wasn't getting across apparently. The messages
that kept going back and forth were based on faulty information, and it
compounded with each reply. Emma became so upset and found herself
angry with her friend. She started wondering if BFF would no longer be
an interchangeable name for Jade, and that made her really sad.

That night at youth group, Emma's mentor noticed how down she
was, and Emma was eager to share her situation. Her mentor encouraged
her to talk with her friend in person and go back to the original misunderstanding. She shared with her that whether it's our fault or not, or
whether it's just a misunderstanding, God asks us to be the initiators of
mending broken relationships (see Matthew 18:15).

Emma asked her mom that night if she could walk over to Jade's
house. Her honest conversation with Jade taught her valuable things. She
began taking greater responsibility for her words in texting and realized
that face-to-face friendship is always the best.

*Dear God, help me be the kind of friend that You instruct
me to be in Your Word, genuine and true.*

## Day 165

# Understanding the Parents

*"As the heavens are higher than the earth, so are my ways higher
than your ways and my thoughts than your thoughts."*
ISAIAH 55:9 NIV

It seems absolutely impossible sometimes trying to figure out how your parents think and why they make some of the decisions they do.

They aren't God, but understanding their way of thinking can be *likened* to God in the way that they understand many things that are just way beyond you at this point in your life. As crazy as it sounds (majorly crazy), they know a lot more than you, for no other reason except that they've lived through things you haven't yet.

Add to this the fact that the human brain is not fully developed until you're in your twenties—and some studies believe this to be as late as twenty-eight years of age. (What?!)

Even at full brain development, remember that your parents are still just human. They have hurts in their lives and hearts too. They're not perfect, but they love you more than you can imagine.

Even if your parents don't have it together or make some decisions you question, they are usually trying to protect you and do what's best for you (even when it seems ridiculous).

*Dear God, help me in my relationship with my parents,
whom You've placed in my life to care for me and lead me.
Give me understanding and patience as I put my trust in You.*

## Day 166
# Freedom

*And the Spirit and the bride say, "Come!" And let him
who hears say, "Come!" And let him who thirsts come.
Whoever desires, let him take the water of life freely.*
REVELATION 22:17 NKJV

A missionary couple spoke at Sara's church. They couldn't tell everyone where they serve because it could put their lives in danger as well as those they minister to. It's pretty crazy to think about this when in our American culture most of us take our religious freedom completely for granted. We can have church services and openly talk about our faith. It's amazing when you compare this to places where people are dying every day for their faith in Christ.

The great freedoms of our nation exemplify the freedom God gives us to choose Him. American soldiers have given their lives and their service to provide and protect the many freedoms we experience every day. In a far greater way, Christ gave His life to give us a way to choose a life of freedom in Him.

No matter which nation we live in though, living free in Christ begins with choosing Him, and then it beautifully unfolds in a lifelong living and learning process.

. . . . . . . . . . . . . . . . . . . . . . . . . . . . . . . . . . . . . . . . . . . . . . . . . . . . . . .

*God, help me be mindful of the freedom You give me,
in this nation and, most importantly, in You.*

## Day 167
# God's Love

*But because of his great love for us, God, who is rich in
mercy, made us alive with Christ even when we were dead
in transgressions—it is by grace you have been saved.*
EPHESIANS 2:4–5 NIV

Claire's new friend Brie, who started coming to youth group, thinks
the things she's done make it impossible for God to love her. She told
Claire some of the things she is ashamed of, and some of them were
things she couldn't control because people treated her horribly. Other
things she chose to do.

Their pastor shared one night at youth group that there isn't anything we can do that God finds unforgivable. He said there's nothing
that keeps God from loving us. Claire and Brie talked about this later
when everyone was playing ping-pong. "It's just so hard to believe," Brie
said, "because I feel too bad to ever be loved by someone good." Yet she
wanted what was good. She wanted forgiveness.

They had some great conversations over the next few weeks and asked
their pastor some questions too. It took time, but Brie finally accepted
God's love and forgiveness. She seems so much happier. It makes Claire
pretty happy too!

*God, thank You for Your love—so great I can't comprehend it.
Help me reflect Your love and grace to those around
me, that they would be drawn to You.*

## Day 168
# Hurt

*When you pass through the waters, I will be with you; and when you pass through the rivers, they will not sweep over you. When you walk through the fire, you will not be burned; the flames will not set you ablaze. For I am the LORD your God.*
ISAIAH 43:2–3 NIV

✦

Lainey's uncle was divorcing her favorite aunt. Her mother cried a lot lately. The whole family was upset about it. Lainey wondered if she would still get to see her aunt. Would this happen to her parents too? The week before that, the sweet elderly man who lived next door died. Lainey had helped him with his garden. She was already sad about losing him, and now her favorite aunt might be out of her life too. How could things fall apart so fast at any time? As quickly as she could wonder about that, she found out that her youth pastor was moving to another church out of state.

Weeping into her pillow that night, Lainey cried out to God. *What is solid and certain in life?*

She really hoped for an audible voice. Instead what she felt with all her being was God's strong presence with her.

*Dear God, thank You for being the constant, certain, solid thing in my life. Help me trust in You during the scary and uncertain times.*

# A Mentor

*These older women must train the younger women to love their husbands and their children, to live wisely and be pure.*
TITUS 2:4–5 NLT

Sammie's dad was working most of the time, and her mom just wasn't there for her very much. It wasn't that her mom didn't care, but she seemed to be struggling and distracted by her own issues. It was really hard for Sammie to learn how to work through a lot of things and grow in her faith. Her pastor referred to his mentor many times, so Sammie decided to find a mentor too. If her pastor had one, why shouldn't she? There was a woman at church, Linda, who spoke at youth group before and often asked Sammie how she was doing. Sammie asked Linda if they could start meeting.

Linda was clearly busy—a working woman balancing motherhood—but she cheerfully said yes. Sammie's mom was happy that she was seeking the friendship of a trustworthy woman of faith. It was such a great experience for Sammie to talk through the things she was uncertain about. Linda recommended some great books and Bible studies that Sammie loved. Even Sammie's mom started reading some of them, and they began talking more about the things that were on both of their hearts.

*God, give me wisdom to choose faithful people to model after, that I would grow strong and be a mentor someday myself.*

## Day 170
# Kindness Anyway

*Be completely humble and gentle; be patient, bearing with one another in love. Make every effort to keep the unity of the Spirit through the bond of peace.*
EPHESIANS 4:2–3 NIV

Maddie's younger brother, Henry, frustrated her. Over the weekend she had a birthday sleepover with some girlfriends, and he would not stop running through the living room yelling while they were watching a movie together. He ate up half the snacks that Mom bought for the night, and it seemed impossible to just enjoy talking to her friends.

Her older brother, Jake, is a little better, but his friends are so awkward and irritating to have around. These boys are ridiculous! Her mom told her that they're just not sure how to act around her, and they're just trying to navigate these growing years too. "It's an uncomfortable time in life for everyone," her mom said.

Maddie thought about that and how many uncertain things she faced too. She decided to try following Paul's words she'd read in Ephesians and work on being more patient and kind. The boys are still super silly (that's the nicest word she could think of), but she's noticing improvement, and she knows she's doing what she's supposed to.

*God, give me a heart to treat the annoying people in my life with kindness. I need Your help to be more like You.*

# Greatest Father Love

*"Look at the birds of the air; they do not sow or reap or*
*store away in barns, and yet your heavenly Father feeds*
*them. Are you not much more valuable than they?"*

MATTHEW 6:26 NIV

Skylar's dad has been gone a little over a year now. It has gotten easier since the shocking day that an aneurysm took him from them in a moment's time, but Father's Day is a poignant reminder of how much she misses him. Thankfully he left her a great example of fatherly love. His great big heart of love for her has made it easier to see that her heavenly Father loves her. Her dad used to tell her, "He loves you way more than I do. I can't understand that because I love you so much!"

There are a lot of friends in Skylar's life who aren't as blessed as she was. Some of their fathers aren't in their lives at all. Others have been treated badly by their dads. What Skylar realizes is that no matter who our father figures are, we can always count on our heavenly Father. Looking to Him helps point her friends in that direction too, and His love can't be matched.

. . . . . . . . . . . . . . . . . . . . . . . . . . . . . . . . . . . . . . . . . . . . . . . . . . . . .

*God, thank You for the father you have placed in my life, and thank You*
*for being the perfect Father who loves and protects me exactly as I need.*

# Filled

*"When I discovered your words, I devoured them. They are my joy and my
heart's delight, for I bear your name, O LORD God of Heaven's Armies."*
JEREMIAH 15:16 NLT

Sometimes there's a hunger to know something and understand. Other
times there's a void in you, like an empty spot that you can't seem to fill.

Sasha was feeling all of this and more when someone she thought
was a good friend betrayed her. The girl said awful, untrue things about
her that a lot of people believed. The damage and hurt were something
Sasha had not experienced before. Uncertain how to respond, Sasha
reached out to trusted friends and family. Her mom began praying for
and with Sasha. She also pointed her to Psalms where King David cried
out to God about more struggles and emotions than we could list.

Sasha gave reading Psalms a try and found herself immersed in
sections of David's raw outpouring to God. There was so much encouragement there as she realized that God welcomed her crying out. Not
only that, but He could and He would fill the hurting, empty places in
her. It was the first time Sasha truly understood that the words in the
Bible were food for her heart and soul.

*Dear God, show me today in Your Word what I need.
Fill the gaps in my understanding, or simply help me
trust You in what are still mysteries to me.*

## Day 173

# Finding God's Voice

*"Then you will call on me and come and pray to me, and I will listen to you. You will seek me and find me when you seek me with all your heart."*
JEREMIAH 29:12–13 NIV

Do you ever wonder how to hear God's voice, or *if* you're hearing His voice? How can you tell the difference between your own thoughts and temptations versus God's actual voice?

Thankfully God gives us some clear answers to this question in His Word. First of all, we are invited to come boldly before God (see Hebrews 10:19) and inquire of Him. Before Christ's sacrifice on the cross, it was only priests who had this privilege, and even then there were tight limits—they could be struck dead if they didn't do things right! Now we have access to God at any time. This is way more prestigious than you being able to, say, walk right in to the president's Oval Office at any time.

God so wants a two-way conversation with us that He never leaves, much like with Adam and Eve in the garden. He is always right here. So you can be sure He wants you to hear Him.

One thing you can count on is that He will never communicate something that doesn't line up with His Word. If we are one of His children (meaning we have invited Him into our lives), we are given the ability to hear His voice (see John 10:27).

So go!

*Dear God, help me discern Your voice in the midst of the loudness of this world. I need You today.*

# Good Boundaries

*A person without self-control is like a city with broken-down walls.*
PROVERBS 25:28 NLT

We all know them, the girls who fell into just a little loss of self-control. They don't know how they got so far off course, and before they knew it, they ended up with a permanently altered plan so early in life.

So many things that we know we shouldn't do are enticing, that's for sure. Thankfully, avoiding a damaging invasion on your life is not a mystery. Self-control starts with putting yourself in safe places with healthy boundaries rather than tempting places with broken boundaries. Listen to God's leading, and ask Him to be your strength and wisdom.

You'll be thankful if you're one of the girls who keeps up boundaries of control. Someday it will be a blessing if pregnancy is something you get to experience with full joy when you're married to a great guy. Later in life, these same boundaries can keep you from unhealthy friendships and even affairs that could damage you, your marriage, and your family.

*Dear God, help me make strong decisions and strengthen me so that my choices will be a blessing that pave the way to good things in my life.*

## Day 175
# The Chase

*Yet when I surveyed all that my hands had done and what I had toiled to achieve, everything was meaningless, a chasing after the wind; nothing was gained under the sun. . . . I saw that wisdom is better than folly, just as light is better than darkness.*

ECCLESIASTES 2:11, 13 NIV

King Solomon was one of the richest men who ever lived, and the Bible tells us he was also the wisest man who ever lived. He had everything a person could dream of having. He planned his own majestic dream house and had it built exactly as he desired. It sat next to the temple of God Himself, and God granted Solomon wisdom at his disposal.

Yet Solomon, with all of his possessions, boundless resources and ability, and beautiful surroundings, came to the conclusion that all of his efforts on earth amounted to nothing. Wisdom was his greatest gift.

It seems clear that no one will be given wisdom to match that of Solomon's any time soon, but God does give us the access to grow wiser. Not only access, though, He offers to generously give us wisdom if we will only ask (see James 1:5).

*Dear God, I need wisdom in the decisions I make each day. Give me what I need so that I would make sound choices and grow strong in You.*

## Day 176
# Confusing Emotions

*And now, dear brothers and sisters, one final thing. Fix your thoughts on what is true, and honorable, and right, and pure, and lovely, and admirable. Think about things that are excellent and worthy of praise. Keep putting into practice all you learned and received from me—everything you heard from me and saw me doing. Then the God of peace will be with you.*

<small>PHILIPPIANS 4:8–9 NLT</small>

Reeling from a terrible day with friends in her neighborhood, Tess couldn't tell if she was more angry or sad about how they were treating one another. When she got home from her friend's house, she had hoped to catch the one show she liked that was on in forty-five minutes. She'd also heard about a conversation that referenced her on Instagram that she should check out, and now her mom was all over her to get an hour's worth of chores done, one of which was taking a dead fish out of the aquarium. Her favorite fish had died!

How many emotions can a person experience at one time? She was sure she would lose it!

But in what seemed a rare moment of maturity, Tess focused on what was good around her. She had a family who loved her, plenty to eat, and air-conditioning on a pretty warm day. She reminded herself of what was true, rather than what was frustrating and sad. It changed her entire outlook, and before she knew it, she felt much more at peace.

*God, in the mixture of emotions that come my way, thank You for being the one true God I can rely on to be constant.*

## Day 177

# Temptation

*The temptations in your life are no different from what
others experience. And God is faithful. He will not allow
the temptation to be more than you can stand. When you are
tempted, he will show you a way out so that you can endure.*

1 CORINTHIANS 10:13 NLT

Hannah walked down the block with her friend to the store where they
planned to buy a few snacks for the movie they would watch later. A
young family walking just ahead of them dropped a twenty-dollar bill
and didn't realize it. Hannah hesitated for a moment.

She thought how much more they could buy with that twenty and
considered just picking it up and not saying anything. But she felt too
bad about it, and besides, she didn't want to involve her friend too. She
picked it up and called ahead to the parents of the small children. They
were so thankful for her honesty that they let both Hannah and her
friend pick out some candy at the store. Hannah's heart was at peace. It
felt good to do the right thing.

*Dear God, thank You for providing a way out of temptations
that come my way. Help me want to choose You.*

## Day 178
### Pouting

*Therefore, as God's chosen people, holy and dearly loved, clothe yourselves with compassion, kindness, humility, gentleness and patience.*
COLOSSIANS 3:12 NIV

Lizzie's little cousin didn't get her way at the picnic and pouted all the way to the other side of the shelter house. She leaned her three-year-old self against a post looking as sad as she was cute. Lizzie walked over to her.

"What's wrong, Audree?" asked Lizzie.

"Mommy say no more pop," she managed with her lip sticking out like a ledge.

"I'm thirteen years old, and my mom says that too, because she wants me to be healthy," Lizzie encouraged. "My mom also likes to make sure I know that I can't always get what I want, which I don't usually like either!" she said, mocking a stern face.

Audree wasn't buying any of it, so Lizzie scooped her up in her arms and smiled. "What can we do with what you do have?" she asked and picked up the sand toys nearby. "Want to make a castle?" Audree started to smile, and Lizzie was picking up on the lesson even though she was the one giving it.

*Dear God, help me do all I can with what You have given me and be content while I work toward what I hope for. I need You, God.*

## Day 179
# Stuff

*"If you are faithful in little things, you will be faithful
in large ones. But if you are dishonest in little things,
you won't be honest with greater responsibilities."*

<small>LUKE 16:10 NLT</small>

Maggie's dad was always bugging her to put her stuff away. She didn't
see the point when she was going to turn around and use it all again. It
would be right there ready to go—so much easier her way. The house
seemed like it was always a mess anyway, with their new puppy playing
and running all over the place.

Arriving home one afternoon, Maggie dropped her bag on the floor
in the living room, her shoes fell off in front of the couch, and she set
her phone on the ottoman. She went into the kitchen to get some juice,
and by the time she got back, the puppy had chewed a hole clear through
her right shoe. She was so mad, and worse, she knew she would have to
answer to Dad! Her shoes were only two weeks old. She regretted that
this was how she learned the benefits of putting things away.

* * *

*Dear God, help me with even the little things in life so I can
better prepare for the bigger things that come along.*

## Day 180
# Fitting In

*"We are here for only a moment, visitors and strangers in the land as our ancestors were before us. Our days on earth are like a passing shadow, gone so soon without a trace."*

1 CHRONICLES 29:15 NLT

We're always trying to fit in. We want to look and feel like we belong, which isn't all bad. But when we let fitting in be a measurement for our self worth, we're on a slippery slope down to places we will not enjoy at all. What if we weren't made to "fit in"? What if we were meant to march to a set of orders unique to our life? And what if that looked very different from a lot of your friends? Would that be okay?

It would.

There are measures in which we need to fit in for good reason and purpose so that we can understand and communicate well with others (see 1 Corinthians 9:19–23). Compared to eternity, this earthly life is a very short time, no matter how long we live. So let's use it well!

*Dear God, use my life for Your greater purposes.
Help me have the faith I need to walk in Your ways.*

# Masterpiece Me

*Thank you for making me so wonderfully complex! Your
workmanship is marvelous—how well I know it. . . . You saw
me before I was born. Every day of my life was recorded in
your book. Every moment was laid out before a single day had
passed. How precious are your thoughts about me, O God.*
PSALM 139:14, 16–17 NLT

Who you are is a great discovery of the gifts and opportunities that God
has placed in and around you. He granted you specific desires and abilities with a beautiful purpose. Even before you were formed, He had an
intricate plan for your life. As you grow, you get to discover the person
God made and is making as you walk through each day in faith.

Every time you wonder why God allows some frustrating or heart-
breaking thing to happen, and each moment that you doubt how you
will get through a hard time, remember this: you are a masterpiece in
the making by the master artisan. It *will* all be beautiful!

*Creator God, thank You for how You made me. Guide me
as I discover and learn. I need Your hand in my life.*

## Day 182

# He Never Leaves

*God is our refuge and strength, an ever-present help in trouble.*
*Therefore we will not fear, though the earth give way and the*
*mountains fall into the heart of the sea, though its waters roar*
*and foam and the mountains quake with their surging.*

PSALM 46:1–3 NIV

Sarah excitedly told her babysitter how her new shoes would help keep Jesus in her heart. "Every time I look at my sparkly shoes, I remember to listen to Jesus, so He never leaves my heart."

"Oh Sarah, Jesus will always be with you, and no matter what you do, He will never stop loving you!" her babysitter told her. "It's good to have a reminder like your pretty shoes to encourage you to do what's right, but you couldn't convince God to leave you if you tried. He's with us all the time."

Sarah seemed relieved. Her babysitter was surprised to find herself thinking over her own words. She realized how often she needed to remind herself of this truth. God *refuses* to leave us. He may be silent or misunderstood, but He stays.

. . . . . . . . . . . . . . . . . . . . . . . . . . . . . . . . . . . . . . . . . . . . . . . . . . . . . .

*God, thank You for Your steadfast and unshakable love*
*for me every day, all the time, anywhere I go.*

# Made for Creativity

*So God created mankind in his own image, in the image of
God he created them; male and female he created them.*

GENESIS 1:27 NIV

When you think of God, what is the first thing that comes to mind? His majesty and power? His gentleness and mercy? His justice and holiness?

Humankind was created in God's image. This means that God, the Three-in-One, made us to be like Him. Sin keeps us from being perfect reflections of Him, but despite that, His beauty remains in us.

One important way you bear God's image is through creativity. The Master Creator made us to be "little creators" after Him—we don't speak things into existence, but He gave us the ability to think, make, and speak. Adam first used the creative gift of language to name all the animals in the garden (see Genesis 2:19–20). He was also the first poet, speaking beautiful words to mark the arrival of his wife, Eve (see Genesis 2:23).

Whether or not you make fine art (like painting or sculpting), you still shine with God's creativity. The creative impulse radiates out of an awesome cannonball into the pool, in the smile lighting up your face, in a silly joke told at dinner. Our whole lives can be works of art as we practice creativity! He is delighted through our thankful enjoyment of His gifts.

What gifts has He given you—physical gifts, spiritual gifts, or ways you enjoy His creation? Praise Him for being able to think, laugh, and create!

. . . . . . . . . . . . . . . . . . . . . . . . . . . . . . . . . . . . . . . . . . . . . . . . . . .

*Dear God, thank You for this great gift of creativity.
Help me praise You by using it every day!*

# Nurturing the Soil

*Then he told them many things in parables, saying: "A farmer*
*went out to sow his seed. As he was scattering the seed, some*
*fell along the path, and the birds came and ate it up. Some fell*
*on rocky places, where it did not have much soil. It sprang up*
*quickly, because the soil was shallow. But when the sun came up,*
*the plants were scorched, and they withered because they had no*
*root. Other seed fell among thorns, which grew up and choked*
*the plants. Still other seed fell on good soil, where it produced*
*a crop—a hundred, sixty or thirty times what was sown."*
MATTHEW 13:3–8 NIV

When we hear the parable of the sower, we all want to say that we're examples of "good soil"—always growing in God's Word, right?

Guess what? Your heart is never just one type of soil. At different times, our hearts might be eager to hear the Word (like good soil), but we might abandon it during tough times (rocky soil), or get distracted by more "important" things (thorny soil). Thankfully, God is the sower *and* the one who nurtures the soil. The Holy Spirit is constantly cultivating our hearts, digging the rocks out, fertilizing, and watering the soil to prepare us to hear God's Word.

If today you're feeling like rocky or weedy soil, ask the Holy Spirit to help you change. The fruit that grows out of His work will be worth all the effort!

*Father God, I confess that sometimes I really don't care about*
*Your Word. Please forgive me and keep cultivating my heart!*

# More Than a Story

*Finally, my friends, keep your minds on whatever is true,*
*pure, right, holy, friendly, and proper. Don't ever stop thinking*
*about what is truly worthwhile and worthy of praise.*
PHILIPPIANS 4:8 CEV

Whether it's a book, a TV show, or a movie, we're wired to connect deeply with stories. Paul encouraged his readers to think on what's "truly worthwhile and worthy of praise" because what we spend time thinking about changes us. Stories have amazing power to shift how we think about the world and ourselves.

This summer, take time to think about the stories you're reading and watching. In light of what you know from the Bible, look at the characters and their decisions. Would their actions please God? How? Is there a character that you wish you could be like? Why? You may find that the characters you admire reveal something you need in your own life, or you might decide what actions *not* to take based on their decisions.

Each story you encounter becomes an opportunity to learn more about how stories affect you and for you to grow wiser as you search for truth woven into the fabric of the stories. All truth belongs to God, wherever you find it—it can even be in a story that wasn't written by a Christian! No story is a waste of time when we contemplate it in light of God's Word. Let your reading and watching keep your mind on what is "worthwhile and worthy of praise"!

*Dear Jesus, thank You for books and movies.*
*Please help me stop and look for Your truth in everything.*

## Day 186
# Freedom!

*"I will say to the prisoners, 'Come out in freedom,' and to those in darkness, 'Come into the light.' They will be my sheep, grazing in green pastures and on hills that were previously bare."*

Isaiah 49:9 nlt

You feel it in the bliss of summer vacation—hot, long days spending time with friends at picnics, the pool, and the movies. But maybe the word *freedom* brings something more serious to mind, especially if your parents or friends of the family serve in the military. You know how much peace can cost in this uncertain world.

As followers of Jesus, freedom runs deeper than the joy of summer or bravely pushing back the danger of war. Jesus saw His people enslaved to sin, and He came to earth to live among us and make us free. He paid the ultimate cost for us so we would no longer be enemies of God; instead, we'd be a part of His family. All we had to do was believe in Him—and He rescued us from the crushing weight of our sin, from the fear of death, from the fear of not being good enough, and He brought us into a life of lasting peace with God. Not only are you free from sin, you're free to thrive—to enjoy the abundant life that the Good Shepherd has for you (see John 10:10).

Today, remember the eternal freedom that Jesus has given you!

*Jesus, thank You for Your freedom! Thank You for giving Your life so I could be a part of Your family.*

## Day 187
# Beautiful Rules?

*The Law of the LORD is perfect; it gives us new life.*
*His teachings last forever, and they give wisdom to ordinary*
*people. The LORD's instruction is right; it makes our hearts glad.*
PSALM 19:7–8 CEV

Anywhere we go, we all have to obey rules that don't make sense to us.

"'Keep off grass'? Why?"

"Ugh! I hate that I'm not old enough for this movie!"

Have rules ever made us happy? Probably not, but God's rules should. His rules have always been meant for His people's protection, from the Garden of Eden's one rule to the Ten Commandments. God also gave His law to reveal His holy character to us and to help us live in a way that pleases Him. Our unhappy response to His rules is rooted in pride—we think we know better about what's good for us than God does.

Think about it. What sins are fun at first but never turn out well? Fighting with our friends, disobeying our parents, lying. . .even if there aren't immediate consequences, these things never produce peace in our lives.

Our hearts naturally push against rules, but Jesus can change them. Through His love and His example, He can teach us how to love God's commands. Through His salvation (accomplished by His perfect obedience), we can love God with all our hearts, souls, and minds. . .and by obeying too. Open the Word and ask Jesus to show you the beauty of His commands—He will do it.

*Dear Jesus, it's hard for me to see, so please show me how Your*
*commands are perfect. Thank You that You never stop teaching me.*

# What Lasts Forever?

*I pray that you, being rooted and established in love,*
*may have power, together with all the Lord's holy people,*
*to grasp how wide and long and high and deep is the love of*
*Christ, and to know this love that surpasses knowledge—that*
*you may be filled to the measure of all the fullness of God.*

EPHESIANS 3:17–19 NIV

✦

If you traveled a million years into the future, what might still be around from your time? Diamonds, cockroaches, maybe even pieces of nonbiodegradable Styrofoam? There would be one thing for certain. You can't touch it, but it's more precious than diamonds and would be there waiting for you as you exited your time machine.

It's the love of Jesus. The Bible says that His love "surpasses knowledge" with how "wide and long and high and deep" it is. It can find you whether you go up to the heavens or settle in the depths of the sea (see Psalm 139:8). Even if you had a spaceship, His love could reach you and hold you close amid the stars in the farthest reaches of the universe.

His love is unchanging. No matter what you do, you can't stop Jesus from loving you (see 2 Timothy 2:13). His forgiveness frees you from worrying whether you've done enough good things to outweigh the bad. You're free to grow into a closer relationship with the almighty Creator without fear. If you trust in Jesus, this love that lasts forever is yours.

*Jesus, I can't begin to understand how precious Your love is.*
*Thank You for loving me! Thank You that Your love lasts forever.*

## Day 189
# Not Giving Up

*And I am certain that God, who began the good work
within you, will continue his work until it is finally
finished on the day when Christ Jesus returns.*

PHILIPPIANS 1:6 NLT

✦

"Why do you have to keep *doing* that?" Have your parents ever said that when they're upset with you? You're trying to obey them better, but it seems like however hard you try, you're stuck struggling with the same things. It feels like you're never going to stop bugging your brother or talking back to your dad. It just happens!

All Christians experience the same thing, and thankfully, God doesn't expect perfection from us. That's why He sent Jesus to live a perfect life so that His righteousness covers us when we trust in Him for salvation (see Romans 3:21–24). God's work in us doesn't stop there. When we trust in Jesus, He gives us the Holy Spirit, and the Spirit works in you every day to teach you to be more like Him—helping you understand scripture (see 1 Corinthians 2:10–16), helping you pray (see Romans 8:26–27), and moving you to grow in the fruit—or character qualities—of the Spirit (see Galatians 5:22–23).

If you can't see any change in your life, go back and read Philippians 1:6 and think back to when you first started following Jesus. Believe it—you *have* been growing, and you'll keep on growing. God doesn't give up on His children.

. . . . . . . . . . . . . . . . . . . . . . . . . . . . . . . . . . . . . . . . . . . . . . . . . . . . . . . . . . . . . . . . . . .

*God, thank You that You're at work in my life even when it doesn't feel like it. Help me trust You and keep asking for Your help to grow and change.*

## Day 190
# Sacred Spaces

*Do you not know that your bodies are temples of the Holy
Spirit, who is in you, whom you have received from God?*
1 CORINTHIANS 6:19 NIV

Weird question: If you were a building, what would you look like? Do you imagine yourself as Solomon's temple from the Old Testament, covered in gold and beautiful carvings (see 1 Kings 6)? Or do you picture yourself as a regular house or even a camping tent? You receive so many messages about your body from movies, magazines, conversations with friends and family. Maybe you feel at home in your body, but there's probably something about it that you wish you could change.

By calling our bodies "temples," the Word declares that our bodies are sacred spaces inhabited by the third person of the Trinity. When you accepted Jesus, the Holy Spirit didn't look at you and say, "Well, that's not a temple I want to live in." Though you might have trouble liking your body, you were wonderfully made and are deeply loved just the way you are.

Remembering that the Spirit chose to make His home in you, treat your sacred space with kindness. Practice recognizing your God-given beauty, rejoice in all the things you can do, and lovingly care for yourself. This body won't last forever, but you can honor God by caring for His wonderful gift.

*Father, thank You for making me a temple for the
Holy Spirit. Thank You for loving every part of me,
even the parts I have trouble loving. Teach me how to
glorify You with how I treat and talk about my body.*

# So Annoying!

*If anyone acknowledges that Jesus is the Son of God, God lives in them
and they in God. And so we know and rely on the love God has for us.*

1 JOHN 4:15–16 NIV

Think of the most annoying person you know. Picture their face. Now,
remember what Jesus said: "Love the Lord your God with all your heart
and. . .your neighbor as yourself" (Mark 12:30–31 NIV). Yep, He even
calls you to love *that* person.

Whether it's a sibling or a youth group kid, the Bible has the solution
for how to love the annoying people in our lives. First John says that if we
don't love our brother whom we can see, how can we claim to love God
whom we haven't seen (see 1 John 4:20–21)? God's love reaches all people,
no matter what they're like, and He wants us to love like He does—He
lavished love on us before we ever loved Him back (see Romans 5:8).

Thankfully, God doesn't expect us to love in our own strength.
We "rely" on His love for us—when our love runs out, He fills us with
His love and teaches us how to be kind, how to be patient, and how
to serve others sincerely. We don't necessarily have to be close friends
with everyone, but we show that we belong to God by how we love
others. Also, chances are, you're on someone else's "annoying person"
list. Wouldn't you want them to treat you with God's love too?

*God, You know who the annoying people in my life are. Please help me
rely on Your love so that I can be patient and loving toward them.*

## Day 192
# No Matter What Happens

*Be cheerful no matter what; pray all the time; thank God no matter what happens. This is the way God wants you who belong to Christ Jesus to live.*
1 Thessalonians 5:16–18 MSG

Ella turned up her music to drown out the crying. Her mom and dad had already tried everything to calm little James down, but it was no use. *I hate car trips. We've been in the car for two days now!* Her brother seemed to agree, red-faced and wailing. *Yeah, James, we're all miserable; thanks a lot.*

Unexpectedly, the scripture passage from Sunday's lesson came to mind. "'Thank God no matter what happens,' huh?" Ella murmured. *Wouldn't hurt to try.* Looking out at the rolling hills of green cornstalks and the bright blue sky, Ella began to pray silently. *Jesus, thank You for the beautiful day. Thank You that my iPad still has a lot of battery left.* She looked over the seat at her baby brother, who was beating the air with angry fists. *Thank You for James. Can You help him feel better? I think only You can help him at this point. Amen.* James was still crying, but her mood felt lighter.

The corn swayed gently, and the van's tires rumbled along the highway. Later when Ella was switching to a different music album, James drifted off to sleep. Two big sighs of relief came from the front of the van, and Ella smiled. *Thank You, God.*

. . . . . . . . . . . . . . . . . . . . . . . . . . . . . . . . . . . . . . . . . . . . . . . . . . . . . . . . . . .

*God, it's hard to always be thankful and cheerful, but I want to practice. Help me keep on praying so I can see the blessings You send.*

## Day 193

# Treasure Hunt

*Don't store up treasures on earth! Moths and rust can destroy them, and thieves can break in and steal them. Instead, store up your treasures in heaven, where moths and rust cannot destroy them, and thieves cannot break in and steal them. Your heart will always be where your treasure is.*
MATTHEW 6:19–21 CEV

In light of these verses, it might feel silly to mourn one of your prized possessions that accidentally gets broken, whether it's a favorite necklace or the dog eats most of your favorite book. But the Bible doesn't tell us to "store up your treasures in heaven" because we're not supposed to enjoy anything here on earth. God made this beautiful world for delight—His and ours. Instead, we're given this warning so that we won't put all our happiness into things that don't last forever—in this imperfect world, that's setting ourselves up for heartbreak.

There is a treasure that will never break your heart—Jesus, the most precious one of all. He cares about all your heart's hurts, no matter how small (see 1 Peter 5:7). Trusting Him changes how you look at everything that happens in your life. He gives you strength to forgive the sibling who ripped your posters, and He's there to listen when you cry about your MP3 player that went through the wash. When you treasure your relationship with Him, it gets easier to hold on gently to earthly treasures because you realize you lack nothing when you love Jesus (see Psalm 23:1). What do you treasure most?

*Dear Jesus, help me keep my heart focused on You, my greatest treasure.*

# Fear of the Maybe

*"The LORD himself goes before you and will be with you; he will never leave you nor forsake you. Do not be afraid; do not be discouraged."*
DEUTERONOMY 31:8 NIV

"Maybe it's going to be too hard and I won't get good grades next year."

"Maybe I won't make the softball team."

"Maybe the older youth group kids will make fun of me."

Have you ever had an attack of the "maybes"? What are you afraid of, deep down? Are you afraid of making the wrong decision and messing everything up?

God has a lot to say about fear in His Word. Frequently, He reassures His people of His presence (see Isaiah 41:10 and Matthew 28:20). The possibilities of what could happen are scary, but God is the all-powerful King of the universe—nothing can happen outside of His plan (see Isaiah 46:9–10), and His love for you has no end (see Lamentations 3:22). Because His perfect love casts out fear (see 1 John 4:18), you can step out with courage, trusting that He will keep His promise to take care of you no matter what happens.

Sometimes it's hard to feel the reality of His care when the "maybes" close in. When anxiety hits, remind yourself of God's love with a memory verse. Pray in the moment. Seek help from older, wiser Christians. Fear doesn't have to keep you from moving forward—God will go with you every step of the way.

*Dear God, whenever I am afraid, I will trust in You.*
*Thank You that You're always with me!*

# If You Can't Say Anything Nice...

*Gossip is no good! It causes hard feelings and comes between friends.*
PROVERBS 16:28 CEV

The book of Proverbs has several verses about gossiping (see 11:13, 17:9, 18:8). Why is something that's so fun also so destructive? When we gossip, we share juicy tidbits about what's going wrong in other people's lives. Dragging out those details makes us feel better about the secret messes in our lives—we build ourselves up with the pieces we've torn off others.

Though gossip can make us feel indestructible, it reveals a shaky spot in our hearts—our self-worth. If we think that we have to tear down others in order to be cool or accepted, we have forgotten an important truth. We are enough in Jesus. We no longer have to try to prove ourselves to Him, and we don't have to prove ourselves to anyone else. When we are confident in His profound love, forgiveness, and acceptance of us, we no longer have to camouflage our imperfections in front of others.

Refusing to gossip is one beautiful way to love your neighbor. Praying for those who gossip about you or others is the kindest way you can repay their meanness. Gossip is no good! Make a practice of standing confident in Christ's love and leave gossip far, far behind.

*Jesus, help me stop gossiping completely! Let Your truth
about who I am in You fill me with confidence and bravery.
Teach me to share loving words instead of hurtful ones.*

# Starting the Conversation

*"Then you will call on me and come and pray to me, and I will listen to you. You will seek me and find me when you seek me with all your heart. I will be found by you," declares the LORD.*

JEREMIAH 29:12–14 NIV

Prayer is kind of weird. Maybe to you it feels more like writing a letter or email than a face-to-face conversation with God. If it feels funny to pray out loud, it definitely helps to write down your prayers, but if you're still not feeling confident in how to start praying, take a look at the person you're talking to.

We learn about God's character in the Bible. From Jesus, we learn that God is a loving Father who knows what we need before we ask (see Matthew 6:8). From Moses, we learn that God listens even when we come to Him with something too big for us to handle (see Exodus 32:30–32). From Gideon, we learn that God is gentle with His people when their faith is small (see Judges 6:36–40). From the blind man healed by Jesus, we learn that sometimes He lets things into our lives that don't make sense to us, but He will bring glory out of them (see John 9).

Starting can be the hardest part of praying. But as you get to know God better, it will get easier to share what's on your mind. And He's promised that if you seek Him, you will find Him.

*God, please show Yourself to me in Your Word. Thank You for always listening when I pray, and help me pray more often!*

## Day 197
# Joy!

*You will teach me how to live a holy life. Being with you will fill
me with joy; at your right hand I will find pleasure forever.*
PSALM 16:11 NCV

Contrary to popular belief, being joyful doesn't mean being happy all the time. When the Bible says to "count it all joy" (James 1:2), it doesn't mean we have to smile when our friends make fun of us or when we're having a really hard time with our parents. Instead, joy is a constant undercurrent of peace in our hearts—like an underground river that continues to flow even though the land above is dry from lack of rain.

Jesus, the Living Water, is the source of our joy. He has given so many promises—He is always with us to guide us and strengthen us (see 1 Peter 5:10), He has overcome the hard things we experience (see John 16:33), and He will bring peace and beauty out of those situations (see Isaiah 61:3). When we are connected to Him and believe His promises through faith, joy runs bubbling through our hearts, watering the places that are cracked and dry—our fears, our anxieties, our embarrassments.

This is what keeps our hearts from staying sunk on bad days. Is your joy a strong stream, or does it feel like a trickle? Spend some time with Jesus. His Word can quench any heart, no matter how parched.

*Jesus, I want to trust You more so my joy will grow.
Thank You for Your promises!*

## Day 198

# Attitude Check

*[Jesus] gave himself for us to redeem us from all wickedness and to purify*
*for himself a people that are his very own, eager to do what is good.*
TITUS 2:14 NIV

✦

The Bible tells us that when we received Jesus' salvation, God had already prepared good works for us to do (see Ephesians 2:10). He's also given each of us gifts we can use to serve others (see 1 Peter 4:10). Although He also promises to give us the strength we'll need to serve Him, we often don't feel like serving. . .and avoid it. Or we do it, but grumble and complain inside.

Unfortunately, our good deeds don't count for much when we have a bad attitude. The Pharisees of Jesus' day did many good works, but they did it so they would be praised by other people, not out of love for God (see Matthew 6:2). Jesus called them "whitewashed tombs"—they looked good on the outside but were dead on the inside (see Matthew 23:27). Paul reminds us that without love, good works are like meaningless noise (see 1 Corinthians 13:1).

When you don't feel like serving, pray. Tell God how you are feeling. Like the parable of the two sons working in a vineyard, God would rather you confess an unloving attitude and then do the work He's commanded, than the alternative (see Matthew 21:28–32). Ask Him to show you opportunities. (Being kind to your siblings is an everyday way to obey and please God.) And that should be the goal of all our service.

* * * * * * * * * * * * * * * * * * * * * * * * * * * * * * * * * * * * * * * * *

*God, please forgive me for when I've been selfish*
*instead of helpful. Help me be eager to serve!*

# The Bread and Wine

*There is now no condemnation for those who are in Christ Jesus.*
ROMANS 8:1 NIV

When your church serves communion, does a knot of dread form in your stomach? During the time of confession, you try to remember all your sins from the week, but the prayer time is never long enough. You nervously take the bread and cup, hoping you aren't eating them in "an unworthy manner" (see 1 Corinthians 11:27 NIV).

If communion is an anxious time for you, then you might be a little confused about the meal's meaning. Communion isn't about presenting a long list of your sins so that you are allowed to come to Jesus' table. You aren't able to make yourself worthy by your own effort—communion is a celebration of Jesus lifting the judgment for sin from us! The bread and wine remind us of Jesus' sacrifice on the cross and how by faith He forgives and cleanses us. While He is glad you want to live right, Jesus doesn't want you to worry that you haven't done well enough to eat at His table. He tells you, "I know you weren't good enough. That's why I gave Myself. So if you trust in Me for salvation, come and join Me!"

Next time you take communion, remember this: your sins are forgiven now and forever (see Psalm 103:12) because you've put your trust in the Savior's love, work, and forgiveness. Come and eat with joy!

*Jesus, at communion help me resist fear and believe*
*the truth that Your salvation has covered all my sins,*
*even the things I forgot to confess. Thank You!*

*Day 200*

# Internet Me

*The LORD's light penetrates the human spirit,*
*exposing every hidden motive.*
PROVERBS 20:27 NLT

You probably have Snapchat, Facebook, Twitter, Instagram, maybe a blog or two. You've likely been given advice on how to stay safe online and protect your personal info. But have you thought about who you are online?

We get to decide who we are every day. We act one way around our parents and another way around our friends—maybe sillier and more relaxed. While these different modes of self-expression are fine, new temptations arise when we realize what we can do online—especially if our identities are hidden behind a username. It's possible that no one would know it was you who left the mean comment on that video or that it's your blog that's peppered with gossip about kids in your class.

The internet itself isn't bad. It's a great tool for connection and self-expression. It's awesome to be creative and get to share your excitement for your favorite hobbies or movies with other fans around the world. But resist the temptation to leave behind your conscience when you're online. You may feel anonymous, but God still sees your actions and knows all the motives of your heart. Have you thought about how you can honor Him when you use the internet?

*Father God, the internet is such an awesome gift!*
*Please help me remember that You see all that I do online—*
*help me want to please You with these actions too.*

## Day 201

# Courage to Ask

*"So I say to you, ask, and it will be given to you; seek, and you will find;
knock, and it will be opened to you. For everyone who asks receives,
and he who seeks finds, and to him who knocks it will be opened."*

LUKE 11:9–10 NKJV

Bouncing her knee, Lauren scrolled idly through her phone, trying to be patient as her mom took the call from the hospital.

"Okay. So he's stabilized? Okay. Thank you for letting us know." Her mom ended the call and ran her hand through her rough red hair. "Sounds like Grandpa's doing a little better. The doctor said the fever hasn't come back since last night."

Lauren's eyes widened with recognition. Last night she had woken up and couldn't go back to sleep, her throat tight with worry for Grandpa. She'd tried reading for a while, but ended up hiding under the covers, praying hard against her fear. "Please let Grandpa's fever go down. God, I know You can heal him! Please heal him so he can come home." Finally, she'd been able to fall back asleep.

She gave her mom a hug. "Mom, God answered my prayer! I prayed for the fever to go away!"

Her mom held her close. "He always listens to our prayers, honey. We just need to be bold to believe that He does."

*And bold to ask for what we need*, thought Lauren. *Thank You, God.*

. . . . . . . . . . . . . . . . . . . . . . . . . . . . . . . . . . . . . . . . . . . . . . . . . . . . . . . . . .

***God, thank You that I can ask You for anything. Please give me courage to ask for the big things and not worry. You are strong enough to handle it all!***

# Summertime Blues

*Every good and perfect gift is from above, coming down from the Father
of the heavenly lights, who does not change like shifting shadows.*
JAMES 1:17 NIV

Sometimes the summertime blues hit hard. Maybe it's from looking at your friend's awesome vacation photos on Instagram or just feeling lonely and bored. But even when you're not sure why you're feeling down, your heavenly Father draws near to you, for He comes close to the brokenhearted (see Psalm 34:18). He knows your feelings before you tell Him anything, and He is ready and able to comfort you (see Matthew 6:8; 11:28).

Some ideas to beat the blues: Take your time. Give yourself permission to feel what you need to feel—pray, write out your thoughts, or make art out of them. Creativity can be a form of prayer. God also comforts us through His many good gifts. When we're feeling down, it's the perfect time to open ourselves to receive them. Spend a day enjoying His creation, something that lifts your spirits. Try visiting the zoo or the aquarium or picking wildflowers at the park. Maybe it's time for you to finally get that new haircut or try a new nail polish color. Maybe comfort means playing in the mud or getting friends together for volleyball or having a solo dance party in your room.

Hang in there and keep talking to God. The Maker of joy will be with you and comfort you on those unexplainably hard days.

*God, when I feel really down, help me keep my
eyes and heart open to receive Your gifts.*

## Day 203

# More Than Muscles

*The LORD gives me strength and a song. He has saved me.*
*Shouts of joy and victory come from the tents of those who*
*do right: "The LORD has done powerful things."*

PSALM 118:14–15 NCV

No doubt you've seen her: the "strong female character." Usually, this character is skilled at physical combat, hiding her emotions, and getting things done with sass. After the movie ends, you might feel a bit inadequate.

Despite what movies show us, strength isn't everything. Even if you're a martial arts/computer genius, God's strength is still greater. When you trust in Him, He lets you tap into His power and enables you to do great things, even if you aren't that strong.

Look at the women of the Bible. Though some were warriors—Deborah leading Israel's army and Jael and her tent peg—many of the women in the Bible were ordinary, but they accomplished mighty things through their faith in God. Esther risked her life to rescue her people; Abigail saved her foolish husband by offering hospitality to David; teenaged, unwed Mary carried the Savior in her womb; Anna the prophetess and Hannah, Samuel's mother, prayed earnestly until God answered them; Lydia is celebrated for her business savvy and love for God's people. If you're not that physically strong, don't worry. Strength takes on many forms—showing kindness, praying faithfully, being encouraging, speaking the truth. And you don't do it alone. Listen to God's voice, and trust Him to give you strength for the challenges that await.

*God, show me how true strength lies in trusting You.*

## Day 204
# Trust Me

*There are many who say, "You can trust me!" But can they be trusted?*
PROVERBS 20:6 CEV

How do we prove that we're trustworthy friends? One simple way is by faithfully doing things that show your care for your friends, like remembering birthdays or taking time to listen to them vent when they're having a bad day (instead of changing the subject to be about you), or doing something they like with them even if it's an activity you don't enjoy as much. In all our friendships, we should follow Jesus' command to "love your neighbor as yourself" (see Mark 12:31) and treat our friends how we want to be treated. Don't we want friends who will carry our burdens (see Galatians 6:2), speak honestly with us (see Ephesians 4:15), and forgive us when we hurt them (see 1 Peter 4:8)? Someone who will encourage us when we're down (see Ecclesiastes 4:9–10) and will tell us when we're doing stupid, sinful things (see Proverbs 27:5–6)?

Maybe you don't feel like you have any really trustworthy friends. It's a really tough spot to be in, but as you work on being the most trustworthy friend you can be, maybe God will move a friend to return the favor. Don't feel like you have to share any secrets until you feel like that person has earned your trust. Treat your friends as you would want to be treated, and make your trustworthiness undeniable—you'll be pleasing God in the process!

*Jesus, I want to be a trustworthy friend and have friends I can trust too. Teach me from Your Word how to be a better friend.*

# Feeling out of Place

*The whole body depends on Christ, and all the parts of the*
*body are joined and held together. Each part does its own work*
*to make the whole body grow and be strong with love.*
EPHESIANS 4:16 NCV

You've heard the biblical analogy of the Church (all Christians) being part of the body of Christ, with each individual part helping out the whole. When you're young, it's easy to feel like you're probably the tonsils or the appendix in the body—parts that could be taken out and no one would notice.

But God doesn't say that you're only useful to Him when you get older. The Bible says that *each* part helps the body grow and be strong in love. Paul had to remind Timothy, a new, young pastor, not to let older people look down on him because he was younger, but to set an example of faith and purity for all ages (see 1 Timothy 4:12).

You have God-given talents and skills to offer your fellow Christians and your community. Don't wait! The body has just as much it can learn from you as you can from them. Talk with your parents or someone in your church about ways you can get involved. It doesn't necessarily have to be at church—you can help in your community and do that work joyfully for Jesus too. If you are open and ready to receive it, God has good work for you!

* * * * * * * * * * * * * * * * * * * * * * * * * * * * * * * * * * * * * * * * * * * * *

*God, I want to feel like I'm part of the body.*
*Please guide me to how I can serve with love in Your Church.*

# Day 206
# Oh Yeah. . .

*Being confident of this, that he who began a good work in you*
*will carry it on to completion until the day of Christ Jesus.*
PHILIPPIANS 1:6 NIV

✦

Maybe you've just realized that you didn't read your Bible at all this past week. It was busy—full of lessons, hanging out with friends, and time with family. Or maybe it was the opposite—a week full of nothing that you spent watching TV, reading, or scrolling online.

*I'm a terrible Christian,* you think. *A real Christian would read the Bible all the time and always pray and not fight with her sisters and listen to Mom and Dad the first time. . .*

Good news: the only thing that makes a Christian "real" is that she trusts in Jesus to save her from her sin. Jesus justified you before God when He died on the cross—there is no more punishment for your sin, and His perfect life covers over your imperfect one. Instead of frantically trying to read the Bible and pray to avoid punishment, we do it because we want to know and love Jesus more. So before you start beating yourself up for forgetting again, talk to Jesus about it. Tell Him you want to love His Word, but you're having trouble. His Spirit will work in you, helping you read and learn from the time you spend in the Word. Don't give up! God has promised that He'll never give up on you.

. . . . . . . . . . . . . . . . . . . . . . . . . . . . . . . . . . . . . . . . . . . . . . . . . . . . . .

*Jesus, I want to follow You, but reading the Bible and praying is hard.*
*Remind me that spending time with You will help me see Your goodness.*

## Day 207
# Meant for Good

*Joseph said to them, "Don't be afraid. Am I in the place of God?*
*You intended to harm me, but God intended it for good to*
*accomplish what is now being done, the saving of many lives."*
GENESIS 50:19–20 NIV

Have you ever thought you were stuck in a hopeless situation? When those times come up, reread the story of Joseph in Genesis 37–50. Joseph, Jacob's favorite son, was so hated by his jealous brothers that they sold him into slavery. Joseph served faithfully but then was put in prison after being falsely accused of adultery. He spent years there until God gave him an opportunity to serve Pharaoh by interpreting his dreams about the coming years of plenty and famine and then serving as Pharaoh's second-in-command. Later, Joseph was reunited with his brothers. Incredibly, Joseph forgave them. He saw how God turned all the evil they meant him into good—because of Joseph, entire nations were saved from famine!

Whatever hard things we face, God works out everything for the good of those who love Him (see Romans 8:28). Nothing we go through is meaningless; often, hard times help us grow closer to God, and we learn how to comfort others better too (see 2 Corinthians 1:3–4).

Even if it feels like life's taking a wrong turn, God hasn't turned away from you (see Joshua 1:5). You can trust Him to guide you and work out the hard things for your good.

*God, I can't see how the hard things in my life are going to turn out okay, but I trust You. Help me see the good You'll bring out of them.*

# Tech Toys

*Teach us to use wisely all the time we have.*
PSALM 90:12 CEV

Isn't technology great? Whether you've got your own phone or you share with a sibling, or you have a laptop, gaming system, or iPad, you already know how to connect with other people online, play games, make art, and so much more.

So how much of your free time would you say you spend on your "tech toys"? They are among God's good gifts to us, but we easily use His gifts in unintentionally hurtful ways. For instance, staring at screens for hours can have long-term effects on your eyesight and upper spine. Also, when you and your family are investing more time in electronics than each other, relationships can suffer too.

Another gift God has given us is free will. We're allowed to choose how we use His gifts—our lives, our talents, our time, our money, our bodies. It makes sense that you might prefer to spend time talking or playing with friends online instead of spending time with family, but challenge yourself: try taking a Sabbath from your phone or computer. Maybe it'll only be once a month, but leave your screens off for the day and see what you end up doing. Maybe you'll explore a new hobby or drag your family along on an adventure. Enjoy that time—the tech toys will still be there when you get back.

*Jesus, thank You for all Your gifts—internet and computers too.*
*Help me value Your precious gift of time and use it wisely.*

## Day 209
# Crushed

*Just as Jerusalem is protected by mountains on every side, the LORD protects his people by holding them in his arms now and forever.*
PSALM 125:2 CEV

Crushes are tough. Whether you have a crush or if you're even interested in having a crush right now, you might feel that weird loneliness that comes from wanting someone to notice you—to see you and think you're amazing, fun, beautiful, and the best person to be around. Maybe those feelings seem stupid, but that longing for affection and attention is normal. Just like Adam, you weren't meant to be alone—God made you to be loved, by Him and also by the people surrounding you in your community.

This doesn't mean that He'll make your crush instantly like you back, but God can fill that longing in your heart. You need more than just romantic love to be a rounded person—you need the encouraging love from friends your age (and older). Their affection can help lift that strange loneliness, and they can boost your confidence with how they value you and appreciate what makes you who you are.

You also have the loving security of a relationship with your Creator. Know this—life will be okay whether or not your crush likes you back. God is the master of your days and the one who loves you best. Whatever you experience, He will hold you in His arms now and forever.

*God, please comfort me in the parts of my life where I feel lonely.*
*Thank You that You care about everything I go through.*

# Let Them Fly Away

*A curse you don't deserve will take wings and
fly away like a sparrow or a swallow.*
PROVERBS 26:2 CEV

Few things hurt worse than finding out a friend has been gossiping about you behind your back, and the bad things they're saying aren't even true. You want to stop the rumors right away, but they just keep spreading. . . .

If this happens, take heart. As hard as it is to resist defending yourself to everyone, you shouldn't have to if the rumor isn't true. Proverbs 26:2 says that if someone says false, unkind things about you, they won't stick—your character will speak for itself. Luke 6:44 says, "Each tree is recognized by its own fruit" (NIV). If your heart is good, you will bring good actions (fruit) out of it, and bad actions if your heart is holding on to evil (see Luke 6:45). You, your loyal friends, and God will be able to point to the evidence of good fruit coming from your heart even as others accuse you of bearing bad fruit.

It's tempting to spread gossip in return, but don't repay evil with evil (see 1 Peter 3:9). Forgive the rumor starter the best you can (for God has forgiven you), and pile kindness on them, even if that kindness is simply withholding the pounding you want to give them! Trust God to reveal the truth, and let those "sparrows" fly away and nest where they're deserved.

· · · · · · · · · · · · · · · · · · · · · · · · · · · · · · · · · · · · · · · · · · · · · · · · · · ·

*God, it really hurts to be gossiped about. Help me forgive and lean on Your truth. Help me obey You by being kind even when I'm really hurting.*

## Day 211
# Rushing and Lagging

*The Lord makes firm the steps of the one who delights in him; though he may stumble, he will not fall, for the Lord upholds him with his hand.*
PSALM 37:23–24 NIV

When it comes to making decisions, you might be a rusher or a lagger. The rushers are game for anything and jump right in. The laggers wait at the edge, watching the rushers, trying to figure out what's going on before deciding to join. . .or not—"Are you really going to lick peanut butter off his shoe? Gross!" "C'mon, it'll be awesome!"

Whatever your style, you'll find someone similar to you in the Bible. There are stories about rushers like Peter and Moses, as well as laggers like the disciple Thomas and Jonah. What do they all have in common? Though they all stumbled in one way or another, God worked out their stories for their good because they trusted in Him. Whether His children lag behind or jump ahead, whether they act wisely or make grand mistakes, God will not let them be snatched out of His hand, and He will not let them fall (see John 10:28; Psalm 37:24).

The important question is: Do you delight in your Creator? Do you make decisions with His beautiful, holy ways in mind? Even when you mess up (and you will), you can trust Him to keep you from falling.

*God, I know I'm going to mess up. Thank You that You keep me from falling when I make mistakes! Every day is a new day to try again.*

## *Day 212*
# Dream Hard

*Commit to the LORD whatever you do, and he will establish your plans.*
PROVERBS 16:3 NIV

What is your wildest dream? What if someone told you that a generous benefactor was willing to fund everything you needed to reach your dream? Not only that, but this person would believe in you 100 percent, even if you made lots of mistakes in the process. How quick would you go for it?

We Christians *have* that generous benefactor, our heavenly Father. He's certainly not a wish-granting genie, but the Bible tells us to bring all our petitions to God (see Philippians 4:6). He already knows what you're going to ask, and He gives good gifts to His children who pray in faith (see Matthew 6:8 and 7:11). Also, God is the one who plants dreams within us—dreams that are according to His plan—when we delight in Him (see Psalm 37:4).

Because you have access to the source of life and deep-down confidence, tell Him your dreams and wishes. Tell it all—worries, needs, anger, doubts—and commit to Him whatever you do. Give those dreams the best you've got, going forth in His strength and trusting Him to show you the way. God might shut some doors along the way, but keep going; He also opens doors to opportunities that we might not have expected to open. Your generous Father just wants you to ask and follow Him in faith. What's holding you back?

*God, help me believe that You care about my dreams. Help me seek You and commit these dreams to You and see what You have for me.*

## *Day 213*
# Speak Truth

*The LORD appeared to us in the past, saying: "I have loved you with
an everlasting love; I have drawn you with unfailing kindness."*
JEREMIAH 31:3 NIV

There is a truth you must tell yourself, one you need to hear every day.
You get pretty good at lying, telling yourself that you are unlovely and
unworthy. You have lots of reasons to explain why you're this way, but
those are lies.

The truth? You are loved. Even if you feel anything but lovable. Even
if your hair sticks up funny. Even if you've royally messed up.

You are loved. Even if it's hard to believe. Even if the guy you like
hasn't noticed you. Even if you feel the crush of loneliness more often
than not, you are loved.

You are loved. Carve it into the walls of your heart. Run your fingers
over the grooves of that truth whether the day is good or sour—find its
gleaming light and hang on to it. Know that your name is engraved on
God's hands—He will never forget you (see Isaiah 49:16).

You are loved. God formed you in secret, with delight (see Psalm
139). He calls you His dear one, the apple of His eye (see Zechariah 2:8).
The Creator of all things bestows His priceless love upon you without
stinginess, without waiting for you to love Him first (see 1 John 4:10).

Do not forget. But when you do, go back to the Word. Read and
speak the truth to yourself. *I am loved.*

*Father, thank You for loving me so much.
Help me always remember that You love me completely.*

## Day 214
# Who Am I?

*So God created human beings in his own image. In the image*
*of God he created them; male and female he created them.*
GENESIS 1:27 NLT

We're going to journey together through common questions girls your age ask. We might not have all the answers, but we do know the one who does, and we can seek His wisdom as we find advice from His Word.

Every girl gets to the point where she wants to know who she is and where she came from. We learn from birth who our relatives are, but then we figure out that life is more than just our families and friends. Ecclesiastes 3:11 tells us that God placed eternity right in each of our hearts from the very beginning. Psalm 139 shows us that God Himself created us inside our mother's womb and that He knows every word we say before we say it.

You are God's beloved creation, and He created you to know Him and know His love for you! No matter what kind of family situation you have grown up in or what you already believe about God, know this: God loves you more than you could ever imagine, and He is a good parent. Even if you have the best parents in the world, God is greater! If you have the worst family situation anyone could imagine, God is bigger than that and will reach down to show you His love if you let Him!

*God, I want to know who I really am and who*
*You are too. Please show me Your love.*

## Day 215
# Is God Real?

*The basic reality of God is plain enough. Open your eyes and there it is! By taking a long and thoughtful look at what God has created, people have always been able to see what their eyes as such can't see.*

Romans 1:19-20 MSG

Recently, a former atheist came to our church and shared his story. Lee Strobel was an investigative reporter for a large newspaper. After his wife committed her life to Christ, he wanted to prove that God was not real. Through years of research and studying eyewitness accounts of what happened while Jesus was alive, he came to the startling conclusion that it would take *more faith* to believe that Jesus wasn't who He said He was than to keep being an atheist! Did you catch that? He found that it would take more faith on his part to keep believing that there was no God than to accept the facts of history that Jesus was real, that He was God, and that He rose from the dead! Not only is the Bible the inspired Word of God. . .it is a reliable historical textbook. You can trust what it says about God!

You may have doubts about your faith sometimes, and that's okay. It's what we do with our doubt that matters! God understands our doubts and questions. He wants us to bring them straight to Him so that He can show us how faithful He is. Ask God to show you how real He is. You'll be amazed at the way that He shows up in your life!

*God, I want to believe You and trust You with my life.*
*Please help me see You in my world.*

## *Day 216*

# **What Is God Like?**

*But anyone who does not love does not know God, for God is love.*
1 JOHN 4:8 NLT

Some of us grow up with a weird view of God. We think He must be really old with a long white beard and sometimes a grumpy face. This is unbiblical and completely incorrect.

Jesus Himself tells us this: "No one has ever seen God, but the one and only Son, who is himself God and is in closest relationship with the Father, has made him known" (John 1:18 NIV). Since Jesus is the only one who has seen God, it's important that we get our ideas about God from Him. So what does Jesus tell us about God?

- "For God so loved the world that he gave his one and only Son, that whoever believes in him shall not perish but have eternal life." JOHN 3:16 NIV

- "For God is Spirit, so those who worship him must worship in spirit and in truth." JOHN 4:24 NLT

- "The Father and I are one." JOHN 10:30 NLT

The one true God of scripture exists as three persons: God the Father; God the Son, Jesus; and God the Holy Spirit. It doesn't have to be confusing, but it is a great mystery! Check out Colossians 1:15 and Isaiah 9:6 for more about who God is!

*God, please erase all of the wrong ideas I've had about You.
Help me know You as the one true loving and living God!*

# What's My Purpose?

*Jesus replied, "'You must love the LORD your God with
all your heart, all your soul, and all your mind.' This is
the first and greatest commandment. A second is equally
important: 'Love your neighbor as yourself.'"*

MATTHEW 22:37–39 NLT

What am I supposed to do with my life? Get good grades in school?
Go to college? Have a successful career? Start a family? That's what the
majority of people in this world consider their purpose, also known as
the American Dream! Those are all great goals. . .but is that really what
God wants from us?

Check out what 1 Corinthians 13:1–3 (NLT) tells us:

*If I could speak all the languages of earth and of angels, but didn't
love others, I would only be a noisy gong or a clanging cymbal. If I
had the gift of prophecy, and if I understood all of God's secret plans
and possessed all knowledge, and if I had such faith that I could move
mountains, but didn't love others, I would be nothing. If I gave
everything I have to the poor and even sacrificed my body, I could
boast about it; but if I didn't love others, I would have gained nothing.*

Basically, we could achieve the American dream and so much more,
but it would all count for nothing if we didn't do it out of love for God
and for others! God's purpose for us might not be easy, but it is simple:
love Him and love others.

. . . . . . . . . . . . . . . . . . . . . . . . . . . . . . . . . . . . . . . . . . . . . . . . . .

*God, please change my heart to match Your purpose for my life.
Help me work hard in all things out of my love for You!*

# If God Loves Me, Why Does Life Hurt Sometimes?

*Be merciful to me, LORD, for I am in distress; my eyes grow weak with sorrow, my soul and my body with grief.*
PSALM 31:9 NIV

King David was the author of many of the psalms. He experienced times of great blessing, but he also knew his share of deep pain. And still he trusted God no matter what. You can see his great faith in verses such as Psalm 37:25 where he says, "I was young and now I am old, yet I have never seen the righteous forsaken" (NIV).

David's pain came about because of the poor choices he made (adultery, murder, lying) and the choices of those close to him (King Saul hunted him; his own son betrayed him). He feared for his life on many occasions, causing him to cry out to God in sorrow and grief. Yet during that same psalm he was able to say: "Praise be to the LORD, for he showed me the wonders of his love" (31:21 NIV).

When life hurts, are you able to look to God and say: *I praise You for Your love for me. I'm hurting, but I trust You.*

Psalm 34:18 says, "The LORD is close to the brokenhearted and saves those who are crushed in spirit" (NIV). Jesus meets us in our pain. Sometimes you will never feel closer to God than you will when you are hurting. Reach out for Him. He is always reaching for You.

*God, thanks for being with me when I'm sad.
Please take away my hurt and fill me with Your love.*

## *Day* 219
# Who Am I in Christ?

*This means that anyone who belongs to Christ has become a
new person. The old life is gone; a new life has begun!*
2 CORINTHIANS 5:17 NLT

Once you've accepted Jesus Christ as your personal Lord and Savior,
His Spirit comes to live inside of you and changes everything for good.
God's Word tells us:

- I am free and clean in the blood of Christ
  (see 1 John 1:7; Galatians 5:1).

- He has rescued me from darkness and has brought
  me into His kingdom (see Colossians 1:13).

- I am a precious child of the Father (see
  Isaiah 43:7; John 1:12; Galatians 3:26).

- I am a friend of Christ (see John 15:15).

- Nothing can separate me from God's
  love (see Romans 8:38–39).

- God knows me intimately (see Psalm 139).

- God sees me as beautiful, and I am wonderfully
  made (see Psalm 139:14; Ecclesiastes 3:11).

- God is for me, not against me (see Romans 8:31).

Are you ready to step into a new life with all that God has in store
for you?

*Dear Jesus, I ask You to come into my heart and be in charge of my
life. I want to follow You and live for You all the days of my life.*

# What If I Feel Lonely?

*Yet I still belong to you; you hold my right hand.*
*You guide me with your counsel, leading me to a*
*glorious destiny. Whom have I in heaven but you?*
*I desire you more than anything on earth. My health*
*may fail, and my spirit may grow weak, but God*
*remains the strength of my heart; he is mine forever.*
PSALM 73:23–26 NLT

As you get older and change and grow, you'll notice many differences about you and your friends. Someone you used to be best friends with might suddenly like new things and new people. You'll find that you have new likes and dislikes too. It's all part of growing up, but it can feel really lonely at times.

When we give our lives to Jesus, the Spirit of God miraculously comes to live inside of us and we are no longer alone! Gods says: "Never will I leave you" (Hebrews 13:5 NIV), and even if you don't feel like God is with you, He is! That's a promise you can count on. When you are feeling sad and lonely, tell God about it. He promises to be close to you when you are feeling down and brokenhearted (see Psalm 34:18).

The next time you're feeling lonely, try writing a prayer to God. Ask God to fill your heart and help you know that He is near.

*God, You promise to be with me always. I'm feeling alone and sad,*
*and I need Your help. Please fill my heart with Your presence and love.*

## Day 221

# What If I Keep Messing Up?

*If we claim we have no sin, we are only fooling ourselves and not living in the truth. But if we confess our sins to him, he is faithful and just to forgive us our sins and to cleanse us from all wickedness.*
1 JOHN 1:8–9 NLT

When we're growing up, we make a lot of mistakes. We can either learn from our mistakes and make better choices next time. . .or we can keep making the same mistakes and hurting ourselves and others. If we love God, we want to make good decisions and follow His plan for our lives. But sometimes we still mess up. We get selfish. We want our own way. Our friends try to get us to do something we know is wrong, but we do it anyway. Sometimes life is just confusing and hard.

When we make mistakes, God wants us to come to Him and repent. To repent means to ask God to forgive our sins and help us change direction so that we turn away from sin. If you check out Romans 7:14–25, you can see that Paul felt this problem too. He asks God to rescue him from his mistakes and thanks God for His faithfulness to forgive us because of what Jesus did for us on the cross. Paul starts the very next chapter in Romans with this great truth: "There is now no condemnation for those who are in Christ Jesus" (Romans 8:1 NIV).

*God, I am so thankful and amazed that You took away my sin and mistakes on the cross. Please help me turn away from sin and seek You alone.*

## Day 222

# How Do I Find Help for My Problems?

*If you don't know what you're doing, pray to the Father. He loves to help. You'll get his help, and won't be condescended to when you ask for it. Ask boldly, believingly, without a second thought.*

JAMES 1:5-6 MSG

Lots of people head straight to the internet whenever they need help. They google everything, looking for answers to all their questions. James 3:17 says, "But the wisdom from above is first of all pure. It is also peace loving, gentle at all times, and willing to yield to others. It is full of mercy and the fruit of good deeds. It shows no favoritism and is always sincere" (NLT). The answers they find online, however, are rarely pure, peace loving, gentle, and unselfish. You might find the answer you're looking for, but it will be mixed with thousands of differing opinions and you have to sift through a bunch of junk to find some truth.

Pure wisdom is rarely found online unless you're looking up God's Word! When you need wisdom, the Bible tells us that we can ask God for it and He'll give it to us. Just because we asked Him (see James 1:5)! You never have to sift through any questionable content to find wisdom from God. Seek the Lord first before you google and before you ask for advice from others.

. . . . . . . . . . . . . . . . . . . . . . . . . . . . . . . . . . . . . . . . . . . . . . . . . . . . . . . . . .

*God, I definitely need lots of wisdom in this mixed-up world. Sometimes I get very confused about what is right and wrong. Please give me the desire to come to You for the answers to all my questions.*

# Is God Working in My Life?

*It was you who split open the sea by your power; you broke the heads
of the monster in the waters. It was you who crushed the heads of
Leviathan and gave it as food to the creatures of the desert.*

PSALM 74:13–14 NIV

Some days we need a good reminder that God is still working in our lives.
Maybe God seems far away and you need Him to show up again. In this
psalm, Asaph and his descendants needed help. They felt like God had
forgotten them. But instead of giving up on Him, they decided to make
a list of what God had already done. They reminded themselves of who
God was and how He had already worked on their behalf.

When you are tempted to doubt, speak truth into the moment:

- God will never leave nor forsake you (Hebrews 13:5).

- He is always working things out for your good
  (Romans 8:28).

- He is close to the brokenhearted (Psalm 34:18).

- He is not far from any of us (Acts 17:27)!

Make yourself an "It was You" list of all the times you know for
sure that God was there for you. Write down the blessings you have
experienced. Take note of hard times you endured and lessons that God
taught you. Then when you're tempted to doubt God's presence in your
life, go back and remember!

*God, thank You for always being with me even when I don't
feel You there. Thank You for working in my life!*

## Day 224

# How Can I Find Good Friends?

*One who has unreliable friends soon comes to ruin,*
*but there is a friend who sticks closer than a brother.*
PROVERBS 18:24 NIV

The Bible talks a lot about being wise in the friends you choose. The late Christian author and speaker Zig Ziglar said, "Life is too short to spend your precious time trying to convince a person who wants to live in gloom and doom otherwise. Give lifting that person your best shot, but don't hang around long enough for his or her bad attitude to pull you down. Instead, surround yourself with optimistic people."

It's so important to surround yourself with friends who love God and lift you up instead of drag you down. You want friends who are trustworthy and kind. A true friend sticks by your side closer than a sibling. This doesn't mean you should hide inside a "Christian bubble," because God wants us to share His love with all people. But do spend a lot of time with people who fill you up with the goodness of God. Then you have the strength and courage to go and fill others up with that same goodness. And you can serve and love unbelievers just like Jesus did!

*God, please surround me with people who love You.*
*Sometimes I have trouble making good friends. Will You*
*please bring the right people into my life? I trust You to meet*
*all of my needs. . .especially my need for good friends!*

# How Can I Be a Good Friend?

*Whoever would foster love covers over an offense,*
*but whoever repeats the matter separates close friends.*
PROVERBS 17:9 NIV

Imagine this conversation: A friend tells you she heard that another one of your friends hurt your feelings. You may be tempted to share the whole story so that the person listening will feel bad for you in the hopes that it might make you feel a little better. But the Bible says that a good and loving friend will cover that offense with love and not repeat it by gossiping. Instead, find a way to change the subject and let your friend know it's not something you feel comfortable sharing. Responding in such a way promotes love and protects friendships. You are covering the friend who hurt you with love and grace.

Proverbs 17:17 says: "A friend loves at all times, and a brother is born for a time of adversity" (NIV). True friends will promote love at all times. Even when they don't fully understand what their friend is going through. Be that kind of friend. Ask God to help you develop these kinds of friendships. Ask Him to help you respond to friends out of love and to treat friends—and conversations with friends—like you would want to be treated and in the way you would like to be spoken of when you're not around.

* * * * * * * * * * * * * * * * * * * * * * * * * * * * * * * * * * * * * * * * * * * * * *

*God, I really want to be a good friend. Help me not to*
*gossip and to be loving in my relationships.*

# Does God Like Me?

*"The LORD your God is with you, the Mighty Warrior who saves. He will take great delight in you; in his love he will no longer rebuke you, but will rejoice over you with singing."*
ZEPHANIAH 3:17 NIV

Hopefully, you have heard a lot about how much God loves you in your lifetime. But love and like are a little different, right? Do you ever wonder if God likes you? Pastor and author Dr. Charles Stanley says this: "Yes, God likes me. He approves of me. He likes spending time with me. He likes being with me. He likes hearing me when I pray to Him, and He also enjoys talking with me through His Word. I believe He loves me. He knows I make mistakes, but He sees my heart and my desire to know Him better each day." Think about that for a moment. Isn't that so amazing?

When you come to know Jesus as your Savior, God washes all your sins away and He sees you as the perfect girl you are. And you can say with confidence: "God likes me!" He rejoices over you, and the Bible says He even sings about you! You are liked. You are loved. You are His!

*Wow, God! This makes my heart smile. Thank You for loving me ...and for liking me just the way I am. Thank You for Jesus and seeing me as perfect. I love You. I like You a whole lot too.*

## Day 227

# How Can I Keep My Eyes on Christ?

*Then Peter got down out of the boat, walked on the water and came toward Jesus. But when he saw the wind, he was afraid and, beginning to sink, cried out, "Lord, save me!"*
MATTHEW 14:29–30 NIV

When our eyes are focused on Christ, He gives us the ability to rise above the storms of life. But just like Peter, when we get distracted and scared by the waves and problems all around us, we start to sink. Peter cried out to God for help when he realized how crazy and unbelievable it seemed to step out in faith. But the Bible says that "immediately Jesus reached out his hand and caught him" (Matthew 14:31 NIV).

Are you having trouble stepping out in faith and keeping your eyes on Christ? Do you keep looking at your problems instead of looking for God? Ask God to reach out His hand to you just like He did with Peter. Ask Him to forgive you for doubting and give you supernatural power to keep your eyes focused on Him. Trust Him to give you strength and peace in all situations.

*God, sometimes I'm scared to step out in faith and do the things You ask me to. I forget to keep my eyes on You, and I look at everyone and everything else instead. Please fill me with Your power to overcome so that I can keep my eyes focused on You!*

## Day 228

# Is the Bible True?

*The instructions of the LORD are perfect, reviving the soul. The decrees of the LORD are trustworthy, making wise the simple. The commandments of the LORD are right, bringing joy to the heart. The commands of the LORD are clear, giving insight for living.*

PSALM 19:7–8 NLT

+

Part of trusting God is trusting in the truth of His Word. As believers, we trust that the Bible is the inspired Word of God. Second Timothy 3:16 tells us that all scripture is God-breathed. What an amazing truth! God breathed the words of scripture through chosen believers in centuries past, and His Words still change lives today.

How can we know the Bible is true? Don't be afraid to search out the truth for yourself. Many an atheist has been converted by trying to prove the Bible wrong! AnswersInGenesis.org says this about the Bible: "It has been confirmed countless times by archaeology and other sciences. It possesses divine insight into the nature of the universe and has made correct predictions about distant future events with perfect accuracy."

God's instructions in the Bible are clear, and they give us wise advice for today. The Word of God can be trusted. If you want to know how to live your life for God. . .if you need wisdom for today and hope for tomorrow. . .if you want to hear God speak to you right now. . .get in God's Word. It will change your life!

*God, I want to believe in Your Word. Help me know and understand what You are telling me in scripture. Thank You that I can know for sure that Your Words are true!*

## Day 229

# How Do I Love God?

*If you keep my commands, you will remain in my love, just as I have kept my Father's commands and remain in his love.*

JOHN 15:10 NIV

In John 15, Jesus tells us how we can show our love for God: by obeying His commands. What are His commands? To love God and love others. Everything else depends on those two things (see Matthew 22:36–40).

To love God, you have to know and understand the truth about Him. John 10:27–30 says, "My sheep listen to my voice; I know them, and they follow me. I give them eternal life, and they shall never perish; no one will snatch them out of my hand. My Father, who has given them to me, is greater than all; no one can snatch them out of my Father's hand. I and the Father are one" (NIV).

In Bible times, a gentle shepherd would love and care for his sheep with compassion and kindness. The sheep would listen to the shepherd's voice. Jesus calls us His sheep. In the same way, Jesus wants us to love Him by learning to listen to His voice. Get to know His voice by reading His Word and talking to Him throughout your day. He loves to hear from you!

*God, please help me love You with all my heart and be faithful to obey Your words. I want to please You with my life.*

## Day 230

# How Do I See God?

*O nations of the world, recognize the LORD; recognize that the*
*LORD is glorious and strong. Give to the LORD the glory he deserves!*
*Bring your offering and come into his courts. Worship the LORD*
*in all his holy splendor. Let all the earth tremble before him.*

PSALM 96:7–9 NLT

Years ago at a famous newspaper, the religion editor received a letter demanding more evidence for God. They weren't convinced that there was a God. They wanted a sign. They wanted God to show up on the White House lawn and claim that He was real.

Looking outside at the phenomenal creation we live in, or gazing at any human being and recognizing the miracles of the human body, and then demanding further proof of the existence of God seems quite silly! God wants us to "see" His hand in everything with eyes of faith. This is part of worship: recognizing that God is the Creator and sustainer of our world and everything in it. And also thanking Him for it and taking care of all He has given us. Keep your eyes open and recognize the Lord in all things.

If you're not in the habit of recognizing and "seeing" God in everything, you can start changing that now.

*God, please help me see Your hand in all things. Thank You*
*for giving me life and watching over my family and friends.*
*Thank You for my home and my neighborhood. Thank You*
*for creating the stars and knowing me personally in the*
*midst of this great big world. Please open my eyes, Lord!*

# What If I Feel Ugly?

*Charm is deceptive, and beauty does not last;*
*but a woman who fears the LORD will be greatly praised.*

PROVERBS 31:30 NLT

Do you ever wish you looked just a little bit more like a movie star? Or maybe you have green eyes and you've always wanted blue? Or maybe your braces won't come off for one more year and you absolutely hate to smile?

Cheer up, friend. When God looks at you, He smiles! Braces, acne, long legs, bony knees. . .it's all part of growing up. God created you just the way you are with special traits and gifts that only you can use to serve Him! The Bible says that people look at outward appearances, but God looks at the heart (see 1 Samuel 16:7).

A truly beautiful person shines from the inside out. You've seen the movies! Actresses that are really beautiful but have a mean personality aren't loved for very long. And by the end of the movie, you can hardly stand them! Their bad attitude makes them look ugly even though they have beautiful features. So give everyone a great big smile—braces or not! Your beauty comes from the inside out. A great smile brightens everyone's day and warms the heart of God. And making God smile is all that really matters anyway.

*God, when I'm feeling ugly, remind me that I make You*
*smile. Help me remember that my beauty comes from inside,*
*and let my smile make someone else happy today too.*

## Day 232

# How Do I Know Which Direction to Take?

*Your word is a lamp for my feet, a light on my path. . . . The unfolding of your words gives light; it gives understanding to the simple.*
PSALM 119:105, 130 NIV

Imagine that you are hiking in a forest. As darkness approaches, you realize you had better start setting up camp. You hike a bit farther to find a spot that offers protection from the cold. It's getting darker and darker. You haven't found a safe place yet, so you keep going down the path, your flashlight guiding you so that you can see just enough to stay on the path. You finally find a safe spot and rest easy for the night.

In the morning, you look back and realize the path you were on was extremely dangerous. Any wandering to the left or right would have placed you in great danger. But you trusted your flashlight, and it provided enough light to get you to safety. If you had seen the condition of the path in the light of day, you would have been too scared to move on toward safety. You would have run the other direction, and that would not have gotten you to where you needed to be.

In the same way, God lights up our path just enough so that we can see how to obey Him—step by step and moment by moment. God's Word is a lamp for our feet. Reading and knowing God's Word provides us with light so our feet know the next steps to take.

. . . . . . . . . . . . . . . . . . . . . . . . . . . . . . . . . . . . . . . . . . . . . . . . . . .

*God, thank You for always having a plan for me. Help me get into Your Word so I know which direction to take.*

## Day 233

# How Do I Make Good Decisions?

*So letting your sinful nature control your mind leads to death.*
*But letting the Spirit control your mind leads to life and peace.*
ROMANS 8:6 NLT

You have a big choice to make today. Life and death are at stake. You can allow the Spirit to take over. . .or allow your sinful nature to do all the talking. Our sinful nature gets us into all kinds of trouble. When we allow our own nature to control us, we gossip, we do what we want without considering others, we hurt others, we sometimes lie and cheat, and worst of all—we forget about God's Spirit in our hearts.

But when we allow the Spirit of God to take over, we seek the things that God seeks: love, joy, peace, patience, kindness, goodness, faithfulness, gentleness, and self-control (see Galatians 5:22–23). Those things lead to life and peace and wisdom. We make good decisions by choosing to follow God's leading in our life. We ask ourselves what God would want us to do instead of just doing what everyone else is doing without even thinking about it. Every choice you make matters. Listen as God whispers truth from His Word into your heart each day.

*God, today I choose to lay down my own desires and let Your Spirit take control. It's so amazing to me that Your Spirit actually lives inside my heart! Help me never forget or ignore that! I want to make good decisions that honor You.*

*Day 234*

# How Do I Live for God?

*Surely the righteous will never be shaken; they will be
remembered forever. They will have no fear of bad news;
their hearts are steadfast, trusting in the LORD.*
PSALM 112:6–7 NIV

The dictionary defines *steadfast* as "unwavering, firmly established" and "firm in purpose." God's love is unwavering. He has firmly established His love for us by sending His Son, Jesus. His purpose for us is clear and steadfast too: love God, love others (see Luke 10:27).

Take a moment and pray that God will help you trust Him more. While you're at it, pray that God will make you strong, firm, and steadfast in your own faith. Jot down the following verse and pray it for your friends and family members too:

*And the God of all grace, who called you to his eternal glory in Christ,
after you have suffered a little while, will himself restore you and
make you strong, firm and steadfast. To him be the power for ever
and ever. Amen.*
1 PETER 5:10–11 NIV

Pastor and author Max Lucado says: "God became a man so we could trust Him, became a sacrifice so we could know Him, and defeated death so we could follow Him." Don't be afraid to follow Him wholeheartedly. His love is steadfast for you. You can trust Him!

. . . . . . . . . . . . . . . . . . . . . . . . . . . . . . . . . . . . . . . . . . . . . . . . . . . . . . . . . . . .

*God, please make me strong, firm, and steadfast in my purpose and my love
for You! Take my hand as I follow after You, and lead me closer to You.*

*Day* 235

# What If I Feel Discouraged?

*"This is my command—be strong and courageous! Do not be afraid or discouraged. For the LORD your God is with you wherever you go."*
JOSHUA 1:9 NLT

Discouragement is everywhere. Every step in the right direction is often criticized by others. Friends, family, and even well-meaning Christians can lose sight of faith and discourage you from following God's will to the fullest. It's so important to keep your eyes on Christ and concern yourself only with what He wants for you and not what others think. Find encouragement in the one who made you and has perfect plans for your life. Going against the norm takes courage! And God promises to be with you at all times. He is your constant encourager and comforter.

Philippians 4:6–7 says, "Do not be anxious about anything, but in every situation, by prayer and petition, with thanksgiving, present your requests to God. And the peace of God, which transcends all understanding, will guard your hearts and your minds in Christ Jesus" (NIV).

If you allow Him to be the center of your life and stop worrying, His peace will guard your heart and mind. Now *that's* encouraging!

*Jesus, You are my friend, my comfort, and my constant encourager.*
*Help me seek You always and not worry about what others*
*think. Your plan for my life is perfect and full of promise.*

## Day 236

# What Does a Relationship with God Look Like?

*Trust in the LORD and do good. Then you will live safely in the land and prosper. Take delight in the LORD, and he will give you your heart's desires. Commit everything you do to the LORD. Trust him, and he will help you.*
PSALM 37:3–5 NLT

It's easy to look at this verse and think, *Hey, if I just delight in the Lord, He'll give me everything I want!* But when we really start to delight in the Lord, God changes our hearts so completely that all we ever want is what *He* wants. When you commit everything you do to the Lord, you will begin to see how your desires line up with God's desires.

What does this look like in everyday life? Start your morning with thankfulness. Ask God to bless your day and for opportunities to be a blessing to those you encounter. Interact with God about each issue and problem you face. Thank Him for big and little blessings that come your way. Seek His will and guidance when you make plans. Pray for loved ones who don't know Christ and friends and neighbors who need God's help. Remember that He is with you in each and every moment.

* * *

*Lord, I commit my whole heart to You—and all of my plans and ideas. I want Your will in my life. Thank You for Your blessings and Your great love for me. Show me how to delight in You, Lord. I love You.*

## Day 237
# What If I'm Afraid?

*For I am the LORD your God who takes hold of your right
hand and says to you, Do not fear; I will help you.*
ISAIAH 41:13 NIV

✦

If there is a scripture you need to have handy in times of trouble, this is it! Post it on your mirror, write it on a sticky note to tack up in your locker or on your laptop, or commit it to memory so that the Spirit of God can bring it to mind when you need to hear it most.

Psalm 139 tells us that God created us and knows everything about us. He knows when we sit and when we get up, and He knows every word that's on our tongue before we speak it. It tells us that no matter where we go, His hand will guide us and hold us. God tells us not to fear literally more than a hundred times in the Bible! Why? Because He is already there making sure that everything is going to work out according to His will (see Romans 8:28).

Heading to the emergency room? Repeat Isaiah 41:13, and remember that God is holding your hand. Afraid of the future? Stop worrying and trust the God who loves you and has great plans for you. Facing a problem that you cannot possibly understand? Take hold of God's mighty hand and believe that He will help you.

* * * * * * * * * * * * * * * * * * * * * * * * * * * * * * * * * * * * * * * * * * * * * * *

*God, help me avoid fear. Take hold of my hand and
guide me. I put my faith and trust in You alone.*

# What If I'm Tempted to Do the Wrong Thing?

*The temptations in your life are no different from what others experience. And God is faithful. He will not allow the temptation to be more than you can stand. When you are tempted, he will show you a way out so that you can endure.*

1 CORINTHIANS 10:13 NLT

Is there a temptation in your life that is hard to get rid of? Temptation comes in all shapes and sizes, so what might be tempting to you isn't a problem for someone else. The opposite is also true.

It's so easy to get discouraged when we are tempted and then mess up. Especially when we're tempted by the same thing over and over again. Christopher Columbus said this: "I am a most noteworthy sinner, but I have cried out to the Lord for grace and mercy, and they have covered me completely. I have found the sweetest consolation since I made it my whole purpose to enjoy His marvelous Presence."

Here's the encouraging thing: whenever you face temptation, God promises to provide a way out. Look for it! In every moment that you are tempted, look for it! Pay attention to the interruptions that occur during temptation and grasp hold of them. They may just be "divine appointments" there to lead the way out!

*Dear God, help me find the way out in every temptation. Let me see Your faithfulness in these situations. Give me Your strength to resist and do the right thing.*

# Does God Understand Me?

*For this reason Jesus had to be made like his brothers and sisters
in every way so he could be their merciful and faithful high
priest in service to God. Then Jesus could die in their place
to take away their sins. And now he can help those who are
tempted, because he himself suffered and was tempted.*

Hebrews 2:17–18 ncv

God chose to come to earth in human form to be made like us. To understand what it's like to be human. To be able to fully take our place and remove our sins. Because He was fully human while being fully God, He can help. He can comfort. The Bible says that He "comforts us in all our troubles, so that we can comfort those in any trouble with the comfort we ourselves receive from God" (2 Corinthians 1:4 niv).

It's so encouraging that Jesus was just like us! Our God is not one who wants to remain as a distant High King, out of touch with the commoners. He wants a very personal relationship with each one of us. He lowered Himself to our level so that we could have personal and continual access to Him. His glory knows no bounds, yet He desires to be our friend. Take great comfort in that. He gets you!

*God, thank You for the great gift of Your friendship
and understanding. Allow me the opportunity to be a
friend and comfort to those around me in need.*

*Day 240*

# How Can I Be
# Like Jesus Online?

*And now, dear brothers and sisters, one final thing. Fix your thoughts*
*on what is true, and honorable, and right, and pure, and lovely, and*
*admirable. Think about things that are excellent and worthy of praise.*

<small>Philippians 4:8 nlt</small>

Negative and impure thoughts may cross our minds on a daily basis. Social media and TV don't help us out much in that area. Even Christian friends get sucked in and post thoughts and ideas online that make us cringe and hope our parents didn't see!

Instead of getting caught up in online gossip and looking at stuff you shouldn't, make it your goal to be a light in what can be a very dark, negative place. Encourage good and right thinking. Comment, post, and share God's love with your friends as much as possible.

For the next month, why not plan to post, text, or write at least one encouraging comment every day? Post encouraging scripture, text a friend a note to make her smile, tweet your favorite quote, or post a happy photo on Instagram.

Before you participate in something online that you know you shouldn't, stop and fix your thoughts on what is true, right, and pure.

*Father, help me see social media as a mission field. Help me be*
*an encouragement to everyone I communicate with online.*
*Keep my eyes away from bad things and help me be like You.*

# What If I'm Worried?

*"Come to me, all you who are weary and burdened, and I
will give you rest. Take my yoke upon you and learn from me,
for I am gentle and humble in heart, and you will find rest for
your souls. For my yoke is easy and my burden is light."*

MATTHEW 11:28–30 NIV

Jesus says, "Come to me." Just as He invited the little children to come to Him, Jesus calls us to bring all of our burdens and lay them at His feet. He wants to help. He wants to take away the heavy load we're carrying in our hearts.

A yoke is a harness placed over an animal or set of animals for the purpose of dragging something or carrying heavy equipment. Jesus liked to use visual imagery to get His meaning across. Can't you just picture all of the burdens you are carrying right now strapped to your back like an ox plowing a field? Now imagine yourself unloading each one onto Jesus' shoulders instead. Take a deep breath.

Jesus tells us many times throughout the Gospels not to worry. Worrying about something will never help you. Worry makes things worse and burdens seem larger. Worry clutters up your soul. Jesus wants us to find rest in Him. Hear His gentle words rush over you—"Come to me," and you'll find rest for your soul.

. . . . . . . . . . . . . . . . . . . . . . . . . . . . . . . . . . . . . . . . . . . . . . . . . . . . .

*Jesus, thank You for taking my burdens. I give them fully to You. Help me
never take them back! I want the rest and peace that You are offering.*

# What If I'm a Control Freak?

*"The LORD himself goes before you and will be with you; he will never
leave you nor forsake you. Do not be afraid; do not be discouraged."*
DEUTERONOMY 31:8 NIV

How comforting and freeing when we allow God to go before us! Stop
and think about that for a moment: you can relinquish control of your
life and circumstances to the Lord Himself. Relax! His shoulders are big
enough to carry all of your burdens. The Lord Himself goes before you.

The problem that has your stomach in knots right now? Ask the
Lord to go before you. The crisis that makes you wish you could hide
under the covers and sleep until it's all over? Trust that God will never
leave you and that He is working everything out.

Joshua 1:9 tells us to "be strong and courageous. Do not be afraid;
do not be discouraged, for the LORD your God will be with you wherever
you go" (NIV). Be encouraged! Even when it feels like it, you are never
truly alone.

If you've trusted Christ as your Savior, the Spirit of God Himself is
alive and well and working inside you at all times. What an astounding
miracle! The Creator of the universe dwells within you and is available
to help you make right choices on a moment-by-moment basis.

*Thank You, Lord, for the incredible gift of Your presence in each and every
situation I face. Allow me to remember this and to call upon Your name as
I go about each day. Forgive me for the times when I try to take control.*

*Day 243*

# How Can I Grow in My Faith?

*Two people are better than one, because they get more
done by working together. If one falls down, the other
can help him up. But it is bad for the person who is
alone and falls, because no one is there to help. . . .
A rope that is woven of three strings is hard to break.*
ECCLESIASTES 4:9–10, 12 NCV

One way you can grow in your faith is to find a mentor. God uses His people to encourage and strengthen one another. As iron sharpens iron, so a friend sharpens a friend (see Proverbs 27:17). We get more accomplished in life when we are open to the help and encouragement of others.

Ask the Lord to guide you in finding a "Three-String" mentor. Look for a Christian woman with a strong faith in the Lord who is willing to pray with you, encourage you in your faith, and be honest with you about your strengths and weaknesses. Make it a priority to meet together several times a month and allow your mentor to ask you some hard questions: Were you faithful to the Lord this week? Did you gossip? Is there anything you're struggling with right now? How can I pray for you?

With God, you, and a trusted Christian friend working together, you become a rope of three strings that is hard to break!

*Father, thank You for using Your people to encourage
and sharpen me. Guide me as I seek a mentor that will
help me grow in my relationship with You.*

## Day 244

# Does God Really Care about Me?

*I look behind me and you're there, then up ahead and you're there, too—your reassuring presence, coming and going. This is too much, too wonderful—I can't take it all in!*
PSALM 139:5–6 MSG

*How is it possible for God to care about my thoughts and feelings?* Is that how you feel sometimes? With billions of people to watch over, how can He possibly know you?

The truth is He *does* know you. He *does* care. He is the God of the impossible (see Luke 1:37), and He loves you beyond what your mind can fully understand. He just does. It's a faith thing. Ephesians 3:20 tells us that God is able to do exceedingly, abundantly more than what we could ever ask or even think!

Caring about us personally is one of those things.

Think about the heavens, the stars, the universe, the brilliant colors of the seasons, the miraculous way the human body works. God is behind *all* of that. And yet the Bible tells us that He even knows when a bird falls (see Matthew 10:29)! And He cares more about us than anything else in all creation. How is that even possible? What is impossible to us is possible with God (see Luke 18:27)!

* * *

*God, please open up my heart to You. I want to know You more every day. Give me eyes to see You and ears to hear You. Please make my faith strong and help me believe that You really do care about me more than anything else in all of creation.*

## Day 245

# An Eternal Perspective

*Then He said to them all, "If anyone desires to come after Me,*
*let him deny himself, and take up his cross daily, and follow Me."*
LUKE 9:23 NKJV

Evie walked slowly from the school bus drop down her long driveway. Heavy homework tucked into her backpack pulled hard on her left shoulder, and she adjusted it. As she entered the house, she pushed the front door closed with her foot. "Mom, I'm home," she announced.

"I'm in the kitchen," her mom, Yvette, called as she pulled the oven door open to put the roast in. Evie's downcast face appeared around the corner, and she slumped into the barstool across from her mom. "What is it, honey?"

"Over-the-top drama today, and it's so hard not to get sucked into it. Some people will do anything to be popular. I'm not cool because I was nice to a new kid today. Most of the girls aren't talking to me, including Christy, who I thought was my best friend."

"Evie—" her mom began, but Evie interrupted her.

"Don't worry, Mom, I'm okay. It's hurtful, but you have taught me to treat everyone with kindness and respect. I know it's more important to choose to please Christ over doing what my so-called friends want."

Her mother smiled as Evie continued, "Sure, I want to fit in and be liked. Who doesn't? But when it comes down to it, the choices I make today aren't just about today—they're eternal."

· · · · · · · · · · · · · · · · · · · · · · · · · · · · · · · · · · · · · · · · · · · · · · · · · · · · · · · · ·

*Heavenly Father, help me make choices that please You each*
*day. Remind me that my decisions can last an eternity.*

## Day 246
# Friendships Built to Last

*A perverse person stirs up conflict, and a gossip separates close friends.*
PROVERBS 16:28 NIV

A good and trustworthy friend is one of the greatest treasures you'll ever find. When you have someone in your life—whether you've known them forever or it just feels like they have been there that long—it's easy to be yourself. True friends share a give-and-take relationship, offering unconditional love and support. You know they won't misjudge or hurt you. You can laugh, cry, and safely share the deepest secrets of your heart with one another.

Building a friendship that lasts isn't easy. The rough times you journey through together tie the knot that keeps you strong. It's important to connect with the people He desires you to have in your life—those who will help you grow stronger in your relationship with Him. Have you given God the opportunity to give you the friends He wants you to have?

God is your friend too. He wants to mentor you and build a lasting friendship with you and those He puts in your life. Rely on His wisdom and let Him help your friendships become everything you need them to be for a successful, balanced life.

*God, help me to look at the friendships I have. Show me which relationships are positive and good—the ones You want me to have. Lead me and guide me to be the best friend I can be to others and help me choose the friends You have for me.*

# Dancing for Him

*This is what the LORD says: "Don't let the wise boast in their
wisdom, or the powerful boast in their power, or the rich boast
in their riches. But those who wish to boast should boast in this
alone: that they truly know me and understand that I am the
LORD who demonstrates unfailing love and who brings justice and
righteousness to the earth, and that I delight in these things."*

JEREMIAH 9:23–24 NLT

"Dance competition is fierce,"Tina commented to her friend Allyson, as
they walked back to the dressing rooms to prepare for their next round
of competition.

"I know," Allyson replied. "Sometimes I want to quit!"

Tina spun around to face her friend, stopping her abruptly in the
hall. "Why would you say that?" she asked.

"Well," she began, "I get tired of the drama from other girls and their
moms. They're always bragging on themselves and clucking around like
puffed-up chickens. I don't dance so people will look at me."

Tina looked down, feeling a little convicted. "I can get caught up in
that, and I know I shouldn't."

"When I dance, I try to remember my ability doesn't come from anything
I've done. The Lord gave me that gift. Instead of being one of those 'Hey!
Look at me!' kind of girls, I want others to see the Lord's blessing in me."

*Lord, You have created me with many gifts, some I haven't even
opened yet. When I'm tempted to become prideful in my own
ability, help me remember that I am here to point others to You.*

# Expect It to Happen

*Keep on being brave! It will bring you great rewards. Learn to be patient, so you will please God and be given what he has promised.*
HEBREWS 10:35–36 CEV

Grace was quiet. "What'cha thinking about?" her dad asked as he turned the car away from their neighborhood and toward her school.

Grace took a deep breath and then let it out with a huff. "I asked God to help me with something, and it's taking a long time."

"Is it something I can help with?" her dad prodded, knowing she liked to work things out on her own.

"Nope! It's a thing at school. People stuff, ya know!"

"Well then, hold on to your faith and believe. Don't give up on what you've asked God for just because it doesn't happen as fast as you want it to happen. Sometimes what we ask for takes time to move the situation around, much like moving a physical mountain into the sea. And when it concerns the heart of people, He often has to do a work in their heart first."

"I know, Dad. I'm just a little disappointed. You know it's hard for me to be patient." Grace finally smiled. "I'm not giving up though. I'll just keep believing."

. . . . . . . . . . . . . . . . . . . . . . . . . . . . . . . . . . . . . . . . . . . . . . . . . . . .

*God, it's hard to wait for You to work out the details after I pray. Help me keep believing. I know You're at work behind the scenes. The Bible says You will give me the desires of my heart when I pray according to Your purposes and plan. I won't let go but will receive what I've asked for in Your time.*

# Set Yourself Free

*"In a word, what I'm saying is, Grow up. You're kingdom subjects.*
*Now live like it. Live out your God-created identity. Live generously*
*and graciously toward others, the way God lives toward you."*
MATTHEW 5:48 MSG

✦

"Hey, Carrie," her brother, Pete, said as she walked through the den. No
answer. "When are you going to give that up? I told you I didn't break
your phone on purpose!"

"Still giving your brother the silent treatment?" her mother asked.

"Yes," she replied angrily. "I'm cut off from the rest of the world
now. Who knows when I'll be able to get another phone."

"You know, your brother isn't the only one you're hurting
by refusing to forgive him. Refusing to forgive can eventually con-
sume you and destroy your relationship with everyone you care about. I
don't want you to wake up from this and find all you have left is anger,
hurt, and tears."

"I'm going to take a shower," she replied to avoid the response she
knew her mother wanted to hear. As the water poured over her, she thought
about her relationship with her brother—and with God. She knew she
needed to let it go. "It's just a phone," she felt the Lord whisper. "I know,"
she said aloud. She got out, dressed, wrapped her hair in a towel, and went
to find her brother.

• • • • • • • • • • • • • • • • • • • • • • • • • • • • • • • • • • • • • • • • • • • • •

*Heavenly Father, it's easy to hold on to anger and hurt. I want to*
*think I'm punishing the one I don't want to forgive, but it really*
*hurts me more. Give me Your grace to let it go. Help me forgive.*

*Day 250*

# Thankfulness for Provision and Opportunity

*Indolence wants it all and gets nothing; the energetic
have something to show for their lives.*
PROVERBS 13:4 MSG

"Dad," Annie spoke up from the back seat of the car, "I don't get Labor Day. What's the point?" Her little brother, Jason, piped up, "We get out of school for it."

Dad glanced into the rearview mirror and caught Annie's gaze. "It's always the first Monday in September and was made into a holiday following the labor movement years ago. It was a time set aside for everyone to celebrate the social and economic achievements of American workers, especially the contributions workers made to the strength, success, and welfare of our country."

"So we're celebrating hard work and success as a country?" Annie asked.

"Yes," Dad continued, "and as Christ followers, we can also be thankful for the foundation God's Word provides to teach us the importance of hard work in the natural and in the spiritual. We thank God for providing everything we need, including the opportunity to earn a living and point others to God as we do it with honor and integrity."

*God, thank You for giving me opportunities to live a life for
You. Teach me the importance of giving my all in everything I do.
Help me grow and learn a good and godly work ethic in the natural
and the spiritual aspects of my life. May all my efforts honor You.*

# Your Heart's Mirror

*Therefore, whether you eat or drink, or whatever you do, do all to the glory of God.*
1 CORINTHIANS 10:31 NKJV

Elaine caught a glimpse of herself in the bathroom mirror. *Why do I have to be so ugly?* she thought. She leaned into the mirror, examining her freshly washed face. *Alyssa got the beautiful skin, the perfectly shaped lips, and I got this—freckles and dry skin.*

She jumped suddenly when her older sister, Alyssa, popped her head into the bathroom. "Sorry, didn't mean to scare you. Are you going to be much longer?" Alyssa inquired softly. "I'd like to get in here and get a shower."

"I jumped because I thought I might have said what I was thinking about you out loud."

"Oh yeah? And what were you thinking?" Alyssa said, teasingly.

"Just the same ol' thing. You're beautiful, and I'm not. I just feel awkward."

"I know you don't want to hear this," Alyssa began, "but you are beautiful. The heart of a person is really what matters. When people see you—the ones who really want to take a good look—see the character and nature of God in you. His light shines in all you do. That is more important than anything else."

⋯⋯⋯⋯⋯⋯⋯⋯⋯⋯⋯⋯⋯⋯⋯⋯⋯⋯⋯⋯⋯⋯⋯⋯⋯⋯⋯⋯⋯⋯

*Heavenly Father, I want to be a reflection of Your heart in all that I do. When I become discouraged and am tempted to see myself as the world sees me, remind me of what You see. You created me and made me who I am. I am beautiful in Your sight.*

# Go for It All

*But you are a chosen people, a royal priesthood, a holy nation,*
*God's special possession, that you may declare the praises of him*
*who called you out of darkness into his wonderful light. Once you*
*were not a people, but now you are the people of God; once you*
*had not received mercy, but now you have received mercy.*

1 PETER 2:9–10 NIV

Heidi closed her algebra book and tucked her completed assignment inside her folder before sticking both into her backpack. Her dad walked through the kitchen. "Honey, it's late. Why are you still up?"

"I just had to double-check my algebra assignment. This has been a really hard unit, and I need all the homework points I can get before the final."

Her dad tousled her hair. "I admire your persistence to pursue your goals. I believe God will honor you for all your hard work and help you remember all the things you've learned."

"Can you believe I started with a tutor?" Heidi smiled sleepily. "Now I am practicing good study habits that will ensure I can succeed now and into high school. Without the help of the Lord and encouragement from you and the rest of the family, I would not have gotten to this point. Now I actually understand what I'm doing—I'm doing math!"

*Lord, You have given me everything I need to succeed. I have the mind of*
*Christ and Your ability on my flesh to accomplish great things. Thank You*
*for wisdom and tenacity to set goals and achieve them with Your help.*

## Day 253

# Protect Your Reputation

*Those who are dominated by the sinful nature think about sinful things, but those who are controlled by the Holy Spirit think about things that please the Spirit. . . . Therefore, dear brothers and sisters, you have no obligation to do what your sinful nature urges you to do.*

ROMANS 8:5, 12 NLT

Perhaps you have heard the expression "His name is 'Mudd.'" Surprisingly, the origin doesn't have anything to do with someone's name or reputation being dragged through dirt, as you might suppose. Instead, the phrase comes from the circumstances surrounding a man involved in the life of John Wilkes Booth, the assassin of President Abraham Lincoln in 1865. Dr. Samuel A. Mudd went to prison for not reporting his patient's location after he set Booth's broken leg. The authorities felt Dr. Mudd misled them by not reporting Booth's location after treating his injuries. Although President Andrew Johnson pardoned Dr. Mudd in 1869, his reputation was lost to many.

Honesty, integrity, and trust are characteristics of a person with honor and a good reputation. Each decision you make is an opportunity to demonstrate the person God created you to be. Your choices reflect a picture of your true relationship with God. Within the quiet moments you share with God, you grow in your faith and discover His strength to do what is right when character is tested.

*God, instill in me a hunger to know You more. Help me grow in my faith. Let the decisions and choices I make each day speak loudly of who You desire me to become.*

## Day 254

# Competition Isn't Friendly

*Then I realized that we work and do wonderful things just because we
are jealous of others. This makes no more sense than chasing the wind. . . .
For example, some people don't have friends or family. But they are never
satisfied with what they own, and they never stop working to get more.
They should ask themselves, "Why am I always working to have more?
Who will get what I leave behind?" What a senseless and miserable life!*
Ecclesiastes 4:4, 8 cev

Jenny shut her locker door and turned to see her friend Meagan waving
at her with something in her hand. "Jenny! Look what I got," she called
as she half ran, half walked down the crowded hallway. *Oh great*, Jenny
thought as she tried to offer a smile for her excited friend. *Another gadget
she doesn't need.*

As Meagan chatted excitedly, Jenny's mind wandered. *Meagan is
always trying to impress people with the things money can buy.* Jenny didn't
resent Meagan for having things, but Meagan always had to one-up
everyone else. It drove Meagan nuts when someone had something better.

Jenny remembered a conversation she had with her grandmother
about King Solomon. "When someone is always trying to outdo someone else, it eventually leads to unfriendly competition," her grandma
had told her.

"I'm so happy for you, Meagan," Jenny said—and she really meant it.
She slid her arm through her friend's, and they walked together to class.

*Lord, help me avoid jealousy when others have something I want.
Help me be truly happy for them and remember it's not a competition.*

# Day 255

# Love—the Greatest Law of All

*Love never hurts a neighbor, so loving is obeying all the law.*
ROMANS 13:10 NCV

Gretchen's six-year-old little brother, Tyson, was full of questions about the Bible since his Sunday school class began a study on the Ten Commandments. "So why does God have so many rules, Gretchen?" he asked. "And how am I s'pose to remember them all?"

"You don't have to think about it like that," Gretchen said softly. "God promises to love us whether we do good or bad. What you do or don't do doesn't make Him love you any more or less."

"Then why all the rules?" Tyler asked.

"God wants us to know what makes Him really happy—like those things listed in the Ten Commandments. The most important thing to remember is God loves you no matter what—and He wants you to love others—no matter what."

"Even mean people?"

"Yes, even them. When you choose to love others, God will help you have love for them. God doesn't say to let them hurt you or put yourself in danger. Mom and Dad don't want that either. But maybe when you're nice to the mean people, it will help their hearts soften and maybe want to know God."

"What if I can't love them?" Tyler asked.

"Then you can pray and ask God to help you love them, and He will."

*Thank You, God, for loving me no matter what.*
*Thank You for pouring Your love into my heart and helping*
*me love others—even those who aren't so nice to me.*

# Take God at His Word

*God means what he says. What he says goes. His powerful Word is sharp as a surgeon's scalpel, cutting through everything, whether doubt or defense, laying us open to listen and obey. Nothing and no one can resist to God's Word. We can't get away from it—no matter what.*

HEBREWS 4:12-13 MSG

Deedra sat on the front steps of her house with her chin resting in her hands. *I won't cry this time*, she thought to herself, but as the minutes passed without her father in sight, she felt the lump in her throat rise higher. The tears came slowly and without sound.

Her friend Kylie sat down. "Waiting on your dad again?" she asked softly. Deedra nodded. "I'm sorry he didn't show," Kylie continued.

"You'd think I'd be used to it. It's the third time he promised he'd visit, and again, nothing!"

"You know what?" Kylie asked with a big smile on her face. "Now that you're God's child, you have a heavenly Father that always keeps His promises. In His book, the Bible, you can read all about His promises to love you and never leave you. He'll be with you and me both, always!"

"Yes, you are right," Deedra said. "I am learning about God and His promises for my life. He tells it like it is. He's always here for me."

*God, when others disappoint me for whatever reason, help me lean on You. Give me strength to forgive those who hurt me on purpose and unintentionally. Thank You for being the one who I can trust to keep all Your promises.*

# God's Definition of Beauty

*Do not let your adornment be merely outward—arranging
the hair, wearing gold, or putting on fine apparel—rather let it be
the hidden person of the heart, with the incorruptible beauty of a
gentle and quiet spirit, which is very precious in the sight of God.*
1 PETER 3:3–4 NKJV

The pages of the Bible tell the stories of beautiful people—those perceived as beautiful by God and those considered beautiful by their own culture. The prophet Samuel wanted to name Jesse's strongest, best-looking son as king, but he was not God's choice. Instead, the scrawny son that slept with the sheep was God's choice because he had a heart after God.

The apostle Peter, in the verse above, is not saying it is wrong to dress up, fix your hair, and wear nice things, but that is not where God looks for beauty. He sees you from the inside out. He knows what you're made of and the attitudes of your heart.

Inner beauty is about the actions someone takes to develop the qualities that God admires. Those with this inner beauty demonstrate acts of unconditional love for God and others, mercy, kindness, gentleness, and patience. They are peacemakers, quick to forgive and keep their hearts pure.

*God, You created me and made me lovely. I pray my heart is
filled with love and compassion, goodness, and all the things
You admire. Let me become the person who has a heart
like Yours. May I live my life from the inside out.*

*Day* 258

# Follow the Leader

*"The one who sent me is with me; he has not left me
alone, for I always do what pleases him."*

JOHN 8:29 NIV

"Do you always do what your parents want you to do?" Tara asked. "Just ask them to drop you at the mall, and then my sister will pick us up and take us to the party. They never have to know."

Lydia held her phone to her ear, listening and trying to decide what to do. Sensing her friend's hesitance, Tara pressed, "Everyone is going to be there. You have to go."

"It's time for dinner," Lydia's mother called from the dining room. "You kids wash up."

"I've got to eat dinner with my family," Lydia reported to Tara as she ended the call.

Lydia sat through dinner with a knot in her stomach. Even if her parents didn't find out, she knew the truth. She made a commitment years ago to follow Jesus. The knot in her stomach would only go away if she followed Him.

After dinner, she texted Tara: I CAN'T LIE TO MY PARENTS. I WON'T BREAK THE TRUST THEY HAVE IN ME. After a few texts in reply from a disappointed Tara, she went into the kitchen to help her mom with the dishes.

. . . . . . . . . . . . . . . . . . . . . . . . . . . . . . . . . . . . . . . . . . . . . . . . . . . . .

*Jesus, thank You for setting the right example for me to follow.
Help me always choose truth, even when it means rejection from
others. I value my relationship with You above anything else.*

# Letting Go of Resentment

*"But when you are praying, first forgive anyone you are holding a grudge against, so that your Father in heaven will forgive your sins, too."*

MARK 11:25 NLT

Hannah slid into the back seat of her mother's car. Normally a chatterbox downloading the events of the day, she was quiet.

"Tough day at school?" her mom asked as she made eye contact with her in the rearview mirror. She could see tears forming in her daughter's eyes. "Oh honey, I'm sorry," she said as she pulled out of the school parking lot.

"It was awful," Hannah choked out. "I don't want to talk about it."

"That's understandable," her mother said. "You're hurt and probably resent the person or persons who caused you pain. The important thing is to pray about it, give it to God, and let it go. Holding on to the hurt or carrying a grudge doesn't hurt them, but poisons you. Eventually you're going to have to talk to the Lord about it."

"I know," Hannah said softly. "I have to let go of the anger and the desire to get back at them first. It's going to take some work on my part to let go. The Lord will help me when I'm ready."

. . . . . . . . . . . . . . . . . . . . . . . . . . . . . . . . . . . . . . . . . . . . . . . . . . . . . . . . . . . . . .

*Lord, it's only natural to want others to pay for the pain they caused. That's not Your way. Help me let go of the anger and hurt. I choose to give it to You now. Give me the mercy I need to let it go so that I can be free from the poisonous residue of resentment.*

# When You Don't Feel Favored

*But if you treat one person as being more important than another,
you are sinning. You are guilty of breaking God's law.*
JAMES 2:9 NCV

Shelby saw the package on the front porch as they pulled into the driveway. "My gift from Aunt Sue!" she shouted. She pulled her backpack from the car and rushed to pick up the big box. She knew what was inside—her painting—the gift Aunt Sue made for each great-niece or great-nephew on their thirteenth birthday.

Aunt Sue, an exceptional artist, had created a beautiful piece of art for Shelby's older sister, Pamela, three years ago on her thirteenth birthday and for their cousin Max on his as well. It was a tradition she'd started with the two oldest that she said she would continue with the rest.

She lifted the box that held the precious canvas, carried it into the house, and placed it on the kitchen table. She very carefully opened the box after cutting away the thick tape. Her eyes fell on the canvas, and her heart sank. Max's and Pamela's paintings were tailored to their personalities and favorite colors, but Shelby's gift was generic and in no way compared to the gifts her sister and cousin received.

Mom put her arm around Shelby. "I'm sorry you're disappointed. It is a beautiful gift—just less than what you expected."

*God, thank You for loving me unconditionally and favoring me. Help me
love others unconditionally and forgive when others show favoritism.*

## Day 261

# Standing Tall

*Be brave and strong! Don't be afraid of the nations on the
other side of the Jordan. The LORD your God will always
be at your side, and he will never abandon you.*
DEUTERONOMY 31:6 CEV

Janna noticed Veronica picking on Cassandra. It wasn't obvious to anyone else, but Janna had been the recipient of Veronica's bullying last year. A group began to form around Cassandra's locker, blocking her way of escape. Janna could hear Veronica's taunts. By the time Janna stepped into the semicircle, Veronica had pushed Cassandra, and her books fell to the floor.

Janna took a deep breath and said in a voice as loud as she could, "I think that's enough, Veronica!" She slipped in between the two girls and tried to appear taller than she was.

Veronica frowned. "Are you sure you want to get involved? This has nothing to do with you."

"Consider me involved," Janna said. "I'm not afraid of you anymore, and I won't let you treat other people like you treated me before."

The bell rang. Veronica made a face and stormed off as the rest of the crowd disappeared. "Thank you," Cassandra whispered as she and Janna picked up her books together.

Janna smiled. "It makes standing up to a bully easier when you don't have to go it alone."

*God, thank You for being on my side. No matter what I face in
life, You are with me. Give me courage to stand tall in the face of
adversity and respond with Your wisdom in each situation I face.*

# Asking for Help

*"And if you ask for anything in my name, I will do it for you
so that the Father's glory will be shown through the Son.
If you ask me for anything in my name, I will do it."*

JOHN 14:13–14 NCV

✦

It was getting late, and dinner was not even close to ready. Shara wanted to cook a meal on her own. She had browned the roast in the skillet like she'd watched her mother do many times and then put it into the slow cooker, but she'd gotten a late start on the vegetables. She had the carrots cut up, but the potatoes were taking too long to peel.

Shara's mom stuck her head into the kitchen. "Are you doing okay?" she asked.

Shara stopped for a minute. She wanted to tell her mom that she had everything under control, but that would be a lie. "I wanted so badly to do this on my own, but I didn't realize how long the vegetables would take. So yes, I do need some help!"

"People like to help—they're just waiting to be asked." Her mother smiled and winked.

. . . . . . . . . . . . . . . . . . . . . . . . . . . . . . . . . . . . . . . . . . . . . . . . .

*Lord, I don't like to ask for help. I want to be independent,
but I need to learn to rely on others—and on You too. There are
things I just can't do by myself. Show me who I should ask for help.
Also help me appreciate their assistance and not take it for granted.*

# Prayer—the Open Door

*Make this your common practice: Confess your sins to each other and pray
for each other so that you can live together whole and healed. The prayer of
a person living right with God is something powerful to be reckoned with.*

JAMES 5:16 MSG

She'd hit the snooze too many times. Madalyn rushed to get ready for
school. Suddenly her grandmother's words flooded her mind. "God
wants you to share your life with Him. Time in prayer is the open door
to relationship with Him. Don't forget to invite Him in!"

*Oh, I miss Grandma so much*, she thought as she pulled on her clothes
and laced her shoes. Many mornings she woke up to find her grandmother
kneeling at the side of her freshly made bed, speaking to God about the
things she was thankful for and the things that concerned her. Grandma
taught her how to really talk to God simply by her own example.

Madalyn found her own conversations with God to have the power
to transform her heart, once filled with anger and resentment, and to
make lasting changes in her life. As she invited the Holy Spirit to make
God's Word real to her, she began to know Him in a tangible way.

She grabbed a breakfast bar and a banana and headed out to the
bus stop a little earlier. She wanted to make sure she had several minutes
alone with God since she'd started the day late.

*Heavenly Father, thank You for always having time for me.
Today I invite You to share in my life. May I never be too busy for You.*

## Day 264

# Extended Family

*And let us consider one another in order to stir up love
and good works, not forsaking the assembling of ourselves
together, as is the manner of some, but exhorting one another,
and so much the more as you see the Day approaching.*

Hebrews 10:24–25 nkjv

"Sometimes church gives me a charge. It's like plugging my spirit into a charger and powering up for the week," Rylie commented to her younger sister, Emma, as she sat down at the kitchen table to help do her homework.

Dad rinsed out his coffee cup in the sink and chimed into the conversation. "I try to go to church expecting God to respond to our faith. It's about the family of God living, learning, and growing together. I also experience strength from a faith shared with others. As believers come together, they grow in every area of their life."

"They are like our second family—our church family," Emma said.

"Yes," Rylie agreed. "Just like we help each other in our natural family. Our faith family encourages us to learn, live, and grow in our faith."

Dad continued, "Jesus said, 'Again I say to you, if two of you agree on earth about anything they ask, it will be done for them by my Father in heaven.' When you have a group of people trusting God for something specific, there can be miraculous results" (Matthew 18:19 esv).

. . . . . . . . . . . . . . . . . . . . . . . . . . . . . . . . . . . . . . .

*Lord, thank You for my church family. Help me develop positive
relationships with people who love You and love me. Give me
wisdom in how I can encourage others as I grow in my faith.*

## *Day* 265
# **Guard Your Gates**

*Don't you know that you yourselves are God's temple and*
*that God's Spirit dwells in your midst? If anyone destroys*
*God's temple, God will destroy that person; for God's*
*temple is sacred, and you together are that temple.*

1 CORINTHIANS 3:16–17 NIV

Halfway into their conversation, Hope realized her friend Bailey wasn't listening. "Hey, you're not listening to me. What's up?" she asked.

"I'm sorry," Bailey replied. "I've been distracted since I watched that horror movie the other night. I shouldn't have watched it, but I did it anyway."

"Oh," Hope said, "I did that once. It is awful to have those images stuck in your head."

"I convinced myself it wouldn't bother me, but I was so wrong. What did you do to get rid of the images?" Bailey asked.

"I asked God to forgive me for not guarding my heart. We choose what passes through our eyes and ears and what comes out of our mouths. These are the 'gates' to our thoughts, which impacts the condition of our heart. Then I asked God to help me remove those thoughts and images. I replaced them with positive ones through prayer and reading the Bible, and I even saw another movie that built hope instead of fear into my thoughts."

"That's good advice," Bailey said as the bell signaled the end of study hall. "Thank you!"

. . . . . . . . . . . . . . . . . . . . . . . . . . . . . . . . . . . . . . . . . . . . . . . . .

*Lord, thank You for reminding me that my spirit and mind*
*respond to what I choose to put into them. Help me choose wisely*
*what I allow to pass through the gates that protect my heart.*

## Day 266
# Are You Listening?

*"'For this people's heart has become calloused; they hardly hear with their ears, and they have closed their eyes. Otherwise they might see with their eyes, hear with their ears, understand with their hearts and turn, and I would heal them.' But blessed are your eyes because they see, and your ears because they hear."*

MATTHEW 13:15–16 NIV

Leann sat down in the swing on Grandma's front porch. She enjoyed the moments she had alone with her grandmother and the quietness of their ranch home that sat back away from the country road. Grandma sat next to her. She took a sip of her hot tea, closed her eyes, and breathed in the fresh midmorning air. "Are you listening?" she asked her granddaughter.

Leann tilted her head back and squinted her eyes to catch a glimpse of the sun as it slid behind the clouds. The birds were singing. She heard the chatter of two little squirrels chasing one another up and down the tree next to the house.

"Listening is a discipline," Grandma encouraged. "It requires self-control and a desire to hear instead of to be heard. The art of listening helps you interpret your world, understand others, and have a powerful relationship with God."

"Yes, Grandma, I'm learning. The question you asked me comes back to my mind often: 'How can we expect to hear God, who we can't see, when we can't even hear the people in our lives we can see?'"

*God, I want to hear You. I take time today to give You my undivided attention. Teach me to listen to You and to others today.*

# When You're Sinking

*Peter replied, "Lord, if it really is you, tell me to come to you on
the water." "Come on!" Jesus said. Peter then got out of the boat
and started walking on the water toward him. But when Peter
saw how strong the wind was, he was afraid and started sinking.
"Save me, Lord!" he shouted. At once, Jesus reached out his hand.*

MATTHEW 14:28–31 CEV

Fitting in at a new school really mattered to Melissa. She desperately
wanted to make friends. When a few of the "cool" kids invited her to
have lunch at their table, she hoped it was a good sign.

Melissa excitedly answered their questions about herself and listened
intently to their conversation. A red flag went up in her heart as the conversation shifted to what had happened the previous weekend at Jason's
house while his parents were out of town. "It was a sweet party, Melissa,"
Jason bragged. "Maybe you can come to the next one."

She smiled shyly and nodded, but her heart raced. *This is not the type
of cool kids my parents would approve of me spending time with. I don't want
to lie to my parents about my whereabouts in order to go to parties.*

As she exited the lunchroom and stopped by her locker to grab her
notebook before her next class, she felt herself sinking. "Lord, save me,"
she prayed.

*Lord, You are faithful to pull me from the raging storm and
bring me back to safety. When I'm tempted to compromise
Your truth, reach in and rescue me. I trust You!*

## Day 268

# Time for Goodbye

*Then David tore his clothes to show his sorrow,
and all the men with him did also.*

2 Samuel 1:11 NCV

Margo walked slowly across the parking lot toward her brother's car. She didn't want to go home. She was numb. She didn't want to face the grief in her own heart or on the faces of her family members. The words *Grandpa is gone* played over and over in her head, growing louder and louder with each step.

She felt a hand on her shoulder. "Hey! I've tried to catch up with you all day. What is going on?" Rachel stopped short when she saw the tears sliding quietly down Margo's face.

"Grandpa's dead," she said. *There, I said it*, she thought.

"Oh Margo! I'm so sorry. I have no words. I'll just wait with you for your brother to get out of class."

Margo nodded, and Rachel took it as a yes. Then Margo began to talk about her grandpa through her choking sobs and tears. "It's not any easier to accept just because we knew he was really sick. We knew it was going to happen, but I am not ready. Knowing he's in heaven and I'll someday see him again doesn't make the pain of not having him here go away."

. . . . . . . . . . . . . . . . . . . . . . . . . . . . . . . . . . . . . . . . . . . . . . . .

*Lord, when I experience loss, help me process my emotions and process the grief. Help me let go of the pain and embrace Your comfort and strength. Remind me I don't have to grieve alone.*

## Day 269
# God First

*But many believed in Jesus, even many of the leaders.*
*But because of the Pharisees, they did not say they believed*
*in him for fear they would be put out of the synagogue.*
*They loved praise from people more than praise from God.*
John 12:42–43 NCV

"Everyone wants to be liked," Natalie quipped as she followed her friend Dave to a spot on the bleachers to watch the volleyball game. "We want to feel loved, valued, and accepted by others. So what if we do things sometimes to get people to like us."

"But why should we have to 'do' stuff to make them like us? Shouldn't they just like us for who we are?" David argued. "I don't want to trade my relationship with God for friends and popularity."

"So you'd rather just be unpopular?" Natalie smirked.

"I hope I would choose to be unpopular rather than go against what I say I believe. It's like I have to pretend to be someone I'm not in order to fit into the popular crowd. I don't want to compromise. I want to believe that those who are truly my friends will accept me and my desire to do things God's way."

*God, I want to have lots of friends. I want to fit in and be a*
*part of the popular group. Help me always choose to please*
*You over pleasing others. Help me choose good friends who*
*share my faith and understand my choices for You.*

# Talking It Out

*A wicked messenger falls into trouble,*
*but a faithful ambassador brings health.*
PROVERBS 13:17 NKJV

✦

"It's so complicated," Lydia said in exasperation. "At first I thought living in a blended family would be terrible, but I don't think they are better or worse than any other families—just different."

"How so?" Olivia asked.

"There are just so many people involved. When my mom and stepdad make a decision, they try to consider how it will impact each person. How it will make them feel and if there are things they should talk to anyone about in order to avoid hurt feelings."

"So I imagine it's a real challenge to keep everyone straight. And what about having two houses—your mom's and your dad's?"

"Yes, that can get sticky too. Mom and Dad have different expectations and different rules. I can do some things at Dad's that I can't do at Mom's and vice versa," Lydia explained. "My mom and dad have worked really hard to hear me and my brother out. They listen when we have problems—but that wasn't the way it was at first. We had to learn to talk it out. It took a lot of effort on our part to hear what our parents were saying and for them to really listen to us. In the beginning I did a lot of crying and praying."

· · · · · · · · · · · · · · · · · · · · · · · · · · · · · · · · · · · · · · · · · · · · · · · · · · · · · · · · · ·

*Lord, help me understand the dynamics of a blended*
*family. Teach me how to express my feelings in a positive*
*way that helps me and my family grow in You.*

## Day 211

# Talk the Truth

*"A good man brings good things out of the good stored up in his heart, and an evil man brings evil things out of the evil stored up in his heart. For the mouth speaks what the heart is full of."*

LUKE 6:45 NIV

Jessica caught a glimpse of her older brother, Cole, standing in front of the mirror talking to himself. "Are you practicing for a speech?" she asked.

"Nope." Cole smiled. "I'm telling myself the truth. I'm talking to myself about who God says I am."

Jessica shot him a curious look. "How do you do that?"

"I find Bible verses that say who I am in Christ and then say them to myself."

"Okay. Let's see." Jessica stepped back and watched as her brother began to say Bible verses.

"In Christ, I am more than a conqueror," Cole began (see Romans 8:37). "I can do all things through Christ who strengthens me" (Philippians 4:13 NKJV). Cole paused between each statement as if he was letting the truth of God's Word sink into his heart and mind.

Jessica glanced at the piece of paper and saw that with each statement there was a Bible verse referenced. During the weeks that followed, she began to see some little changes in her brother's words and actions. "Hey," she asked him, "could I get a copy of your list of truths too?"

*Heavenly Father, thank You for teaching me who I am in Christ. Help me speak only the truth. Remind me to agree with You in who You say I am and who You want me to become. May I grow in Your truth each day.*

## Day 272

# A Promise Is a Promise

*Then Moses summoned the leaders of the tribes of Israel and told them, "This is what the LORD has commanded: A man who makes a vow to the LORD or makes a pledge under oath must never break it. He must do exactly what he said he would do."*

NUMBERS 30:1–2 NLT

I GOT FREE TICKETS FOR US TO SEE THE MOVIE IN 3D, Jill texted.

I CAN'T GO. I'M BABYSITTING, Susanna replied.

CAN'T YOU JUST TELL HER SOMETHING CAME UP? WE HAVE TO USE THE TICKETS TODAY.

NO! I MADE A PROMISE AND I'M KEEPING IT, Susanna texted again. I GAVE MY WORD. IF I START BREAKING PROMISES NOW, NO ONE WILL TRUST ME TO DO WHAT I SAY. I'M SURE SOMEONE ELSE WOULD LOVE TO GO WITH YOU. SORRY I HAVE TO MISS IT.

Jill replied with a sad-face emoji.

Susanna's mother had grown up with lots of promises that were seldom kept. Because of that, Susanna knew what it was like to have parents who kept their promises. She'd seen friends who hoped and expected only to have their dreams dashed by people who didn't keep their word. She had come to know Christ and found He also kept His promises. Determined to follow His example, she stayed determined to consider her commitments before making them and then, once made, keeping them no matter what.

- - - - - - - - - - - - - - - - - - - - - - - - - - - - - - - - - - - - - - - - - -

*God, You are the ultimate promise keeper. Thank You for teaching me how important it is for people to be able to trust that I keep my commitments. Give me wisdom in which promises to make and then help me keep them.*

## Day 273

# Lift Your Voice

*My dear friends, you always obeyed when I was with you.*
*Now that I am away, you should obey even more. So work with*
*fear and trembling to discover what it really means to be saved.*
*God is working in you to make you willing and able to obey him.*
PHILIPPIANS 2:12–13 CEV

"Seems like there is a lot of talk on TV about what you can and can't do at See You at the Pole," Karen commented quietly to a small group in her fifth-period class.

"Not necessarily," Chad commented. "Teachers and employees of the school district have gotten in trouble for sharing their faith, but as students, we have the freedom to plan it. SYATP is specifically designed as a student-led, student-initiated movement of prayer. It's all about us praying together."

"Right," Carlson chimed in. "It can't be left up to youth pastors or teachers. We have to plan it, let our administration know we want to do it, advertise it, and then lead it."

"It's a great opportunity to speak life into our school using the Word of God. We can really have a say in what happens as we take our place as spiritual leaders on our campus. We need to have strong spiritual student leaders who are willing to take a stand. Only then can we make a difference."

· · · · · · · · · · · · · · · · · · · · · · · · · · · · · · · · · · · · · · · · · · · · · · · · · · · · · · · · · · · ·

*Lord, give me courage to take a stand. Give me the words to*
*boldly declare Your will, Your purpose, and Your plans for*
*my school. Help each one at the pole speak Your truth and*
*love as we declare salvation and safety over our school.*

# So Very Talented

*For we are His workmanship, created in Christ Jesus for good works,*
*which God prepared beforehand that we should walk in them.*
EPHESIANS 2:10 NKJV

It seemed hard sometimes for Becca to find her place. She was neither the oldest nor the youngest—she was the middle child. She wanted to know who she was and how she could set herself apart from everyone else. *I'm the middle—average. It's so easy to get lost when everything is mediocre. I'll never be better or worse, but just okay*, she wrote in her journal.

Becca liked to escape into the little gathering of trees at the edge of her family's property. The little sliver of woods had a creek that ran through it. She liked to sit on a rock near the edge and write poetry for hours.

A teacher had taken interest in Becca's writing and encouraged her to do more. One afternoon her teacher pulled her aside. "Becca, I hope you don't mind, but I submitted a couple of your poems to a company looking for teen writing talent. I have a letter here requesting permission to print two of them in an upcoming book. Your talent for writing is really developing."

Becca's heart leaped. She had found her passion, and a gift God had given her was starting to take shape.

. . . . . . . . . . . . . . . . . . . . . . . . . . . . . . . . . . . . . . . . . . . . . . . . . . . . . . . . .

*God, You created me on purpose. You filled me with passion*
*and have given me gifts that will bring You glory. Show me*
*how to open those gifts and use them to please You.*

# Why God Has Rules

*Love the LORD your God and keep his requirements,
his decrees, his laws and his commands always.*
DEUTERONOMY 11:1 NIV

Sometimes our parents give us rules we don't understand. It may seem like they don't want us to grow up or they're keeping us from having any fun. But the truth is, parents have rules for their children because of love.

When Mom says not to play in the busy street, it's because she doesn't want her daughter to get hurt by a careless driver. When Dad won't allow his girl to see a certain movie, it's often because he wants to protect her mind from things that might steal her innocence and joy.

God is the same way. He loves His children with His whole heart. He didn't give us a bunch of strict rules to keep us from being happy. His laws do the opposite: they make it possible for us to live a truly joy-filled life. God's rules are set in place to keep us from sin's harmful effects.

If we disobey our parents and play in the busy street, our bodies could be seriously injured. If we disobey God's rules, our spirits can be badly wounded, and sometimes it takes a long time to heal. Because God cares about us so deeply, He wants to keep us safe from harm.

* * *

*Dear Father, I know Your rules are there to keep me safe. Help me
love You and obey You always, even when I don't understand.*

## Day 276
# Avoiding Setbacks

*Observe therefore all the commands I am giving you today,
so that you may have the strength to go in and take over the land
that you are crossing the Jordan to possess, and so that you may live
long in the land the LORD swore to your ancestors to give to them
and their descendants, a land flowing with milk and honey.*
DEUTERONOMY 11:8–9 NIV

Mistakes set us back. They make us tired and wear us out trying to fix them. For example, if we refuse to study for a test because we'd rather hang out with our friends, we may fail the test. Then our grade average is lower, and we have to work a long time to get the grade back to where it should be. Refusal to study was a mistake. It would have been much better to study for the test in the first place.

God wants our lives to be full of joy and peace. He wants us to move forward instead of always having to go back and clean up our messes. He knows if we don't do the right things, we'll mess up and have to work hard to fix our mistakes. But when we obey God's commands, we get things right the first time, and we avoid the hassle of cleaning up the mess we made. Our lives are better, we feel stronger, and we have more joy when we obey God.

*Dear Father, I know You are leading me to a beautiful place. Help me
follow You and not get sidetracked with things that don't please You.*

*Day* 277

# God Helps Me

*This is what the LORD says—he who made you, who formed you in the womb, and who will help you: Do not be afraid. . . . For I will pour water on the thirsty land, and streams on the dry ground.*

ISAIAH 44:2–3 NIV

Every day there are new things to worry about. No matter how old we get or how many things we live through, there will always be something new to bring us stress and anxiety. Whether it's a test in school or mean people or overwhelming bills to pay, life just brings trouble.

But there's good news! God loves us more than we can imagine. He made us, and we belong to Him. He will never let the child He loves, the one He created, go without needed help. With every breath, He adores us, and He promises to take care of us.

When we ask Him for help, He is there. He doesn't always take away our problems, but He helps us through them. He gives us wisdom and strength to know how to face each hard thing as it comes. When He pours out His wisdom, we can soak it up, like water on dry ground. Then we'll feel nourished and refreshed to face whatever may come.

*Dear Father, I'm so glad You always help me when I ask. Please give me wisdom and strength to handle the problems I face right now. I need Your help.*

## Day 278
# Fear and Hope

*"Those who hope in me will not be disappointed."*
ISAIAH 49:23 NIV

Hope and fear are direct opposites. While fear is the belief that something bad will happen, hope is the assurance that something good will happen. God wants us to have hope.

Many people allow fear to control them. They don't try new things because they're afraid of failure. They don't reach out to others to make new friends because they're afraid of rejection. But with God, we don't need to be afraid. We don't have to live that way.

God loves us more than we can ever understand, and He wants good things for us. In fact, He's already planned beautiful things for each of us, right now, today. We can enter each situation without fear. We can live each moment with hope, knowing exciting, happy things await us each and every day.

When we believe with our whole hearts that God wants good things for us, we won't be disappointed. He wants us to trust Him, and when we do, He surprises us with joy and peace and blessings we never thought possible. Next time we find ourselves feeling afraid, we can remember that fear is the opposite of hope. With God, there is always the promise of good things to come.

*Dear Father, thank You for teaching me the difference between hope and fear. Help me not be afraid. I want to live in hope, knowing You have good things in store for me.*

# Hang in There

*"When you pass through the waters, I will be with you; and when
you pass through the rivers, they will not sweep over you."*
ISAIAH 43:2 NIV

Life is full of ups and downs, highs and lows. There will be times of
intense joy. There will be times of great sorrow. And there will be many,
many in-between times.

When we go through low times, the times when the pain and tears
are more than we can handle, we can hold on to this verse. God will not
let those difficult times be the end of the story. As long as we trust Him,
He will bring us safely through to a better place.

I guess life is a little bit like a roller coaster. It dips low only to rise
high again. Our lives will have their low points, for certain. But when
we pass through those times, we can breathe deeply and cling to our
heavenly Father. He will hold us, comfort us, and keep us safe during the
most difficult times. And He will eventually bring us out of the valley to
a high place of joy and peace again.

*Dear Father, when life gets hard, sometimes it feels like it will never
get better. During those times, I cry. I get angry. I just want to run
away and hide. But I know You won't leave me alone in those times.
I know You'll stay with me, and one of these days, I'll feel happy again.
Thank You for Your love and Your promise of good things to come.*

# Pleasant Memories

*"Forget the former things; do not dwell on the past. . . .*
*Now it springs up; do you not perceive it? I am making*
*a way in the wilderness and streams in the wasteland."*
Isaiah 43:18–19 niv

It's fun to think about pleasant memories. God gave us our memories as a gift, to remind us how He's shown His love in the past. While it's good to remember the sweet things, sometimes we let our memories control our feelings in a bad way.

If we're not careful, we can remember unhappy things, and we feel sad over the past. We forget to be thankful for the good things we have today. Other times we remember good things from our past, and we think things will never be that good again. It's wrong to allow our feelings about the past, whether good or bad, to control the way we act and feel today.

The truth is, no matter how pleasant or horrible something may have been, it's gone. We can't change it, and we can't get it back. God wants to do some pretty amazing things in our lives today and every day to come. So while it's okay to smile at sweet memories, we need to spend more time living for God today and thinking about the beautiful future we have in Him.

*Dear Father, thank You for my past, for it has helped make*
*me who I am today. Remind me to focus on You, not on things*
*I can't change. Thank You for my beautiful future.*

# His Love Never Fails

*"Though the mountains be shaken and the hills be removed,*
*yet my unfailing love for you will not be shaken nor my covenant*
*of peace be removed," says the LORD, who has compassion on you.*
ISAIAH 54:10 NIV

In the course of our lives, lots of stuff happens. Wars break out. Disasters occur. People die, and people are born. Things are constantly changing. And for most of us, change can be unsettling.

But in the midst of the chaos, in the center of all the change, is one thing we can always, always count on: God's love. He is love, and He can never be anything different. He adores us, and that love will never be altered. Though our circumstances may be difficult, He loves us. Though it may feel like He's forgotten us, He hasn't. He sees everything we go through, and He is actively working to make us better people and to take us to a better place.

Remember, nothing lasts forever except God and our relationship with Him. No matter how hard things seem at the moment, our circumstances aren't permanent. We'll survive. We'll get through them. But through it all, God's love will never fail, and it will never change.

*Dear Father, thank You for Your unfailing, unchanging love. When things get crazy and it seems like You've forgotten me, remind me. Help me hold on to Your faithfulness when there's nothing else to hold on to. I love You.*

## Day 282
# Trees Applaud

*"You will go out in joy and be led forth in peace;*
*the mountains and hills will burst into song before you,*
*and all the trees of the field will clap their hands."*

ISAIAH 55:12 NIV

This verse almost sounds like an animated cartoon movie. Birds sing. Forest animals dance. Even the trees wave and clap in delight, all for you, God's child.

But what God wants for His children is even better than a make-believe movie. Every day in countless ways He pours out reminders of His love for us. He sends beautiful flowers in spring, gorgeous bright leaves in fall, snowcapped mountains in winter, and crystal cool waters in the summer. He gives us pets to love and care for, friends to laugh with, and the things we need each day.

Unfortunately, we can get distracted with things that shouldn't matter much, like wondering if we look right or if we're popular or smart enough. God doesn't want us to worry about those things; instead, He says "Slow down! Enjoy the good things I've given you that are right in front of you!"

God wants us to have hearts filled with joy, and He provides constant reminders of His love. Next time you find yourself upset or worried about something, look around. I'll bet it won't take long to find a tree clapping its hands, just for you.

*Dear Father, thank You for the reminders of Your love You send every day.*
*Help me look for them and feel the joy You want me to feel. I love You.*

## Day 283
# Like Him

*"I form the light and create darkness, I bring prosperity and
create disaster; I, the LORD, do all these things. You heavens
above, rain down my righteousness; let the clouds shower it
down. Let the earth open wide, let salvation spring up,
let righteousness flourish with it; I, the LORD, have created it."*
ISAIAH 45:7–8 NIV

Sometimes it's easy to forget just how big God is. Think about it. He
created light and darkness. He calls forth the rain and sprinkles the stars
in the heavens and sets the moon in place. That's pretty amazing stuff.

What's even more amazing is that He created you and me in His
image. Of all the things He made, He chose each of us to look and act
and think like Him. He chose us as His children.

Then He gave us free will. Although He loves us immensely and
wants to have a relationship with us, He never forces that relationship.
We have a choice to belong to Him, to act and think like Him—or not.

When we choose to have a relationship with God, He causes His
righteousness to grow in us. That means as long as we pursue a close
relationship with Him, we will continue to become more like Him. And
when we become like God, that's pretty amazing stuff.

*Dear Father, thank You for creating me to have a
relationship with You. Help me make the choice each day
to grow in that relationship. I want to be like You.*

## Day 284

# Hide-and-Seek

*"You will seek me and find me when you seek me with all your heart."*
JEREMIAH 29:13 NIV

In October people in the United States celebrate Columbus Day. This is the day we honor Christopher Columbus, who is credited for discovering America. While not everyone in the world celebrates this day, we can all learn something from Columbus. He was a discoverer. He sought out new things; he knew there were places in the world that hadn't yet been drawn into the maps, and he wanted to find them.

God wants us to be discoverers too. Only instead of discovering land, He wants us to discover Him. There are things about God we will never know; He is too great. But that shouldn't stop us from trying to know as much about Him as we can or from trying to have as close a relationship with Him as we can.

God promises that when we look for Him, we will find Him. He doesn't want to play hide-and-seek with us. But He does want to know we're interested enough to seek Him out. That shows Him we want to have a relationship with Him. When we do, He will greet us with His arms open for a big, welcoming hug.

*Dear Father, I want to know You. I long to know everything about You. I want to live in Your presence, and I want You to walk with me in everything I do. I'm looking for You, God. Please help me find You.*

# Loving and Strong

*One thing God has spoken, two things I have heard:*
*"Power belongs to you, God, and with you, Lord, is unfailing love";*
*and, "You reward everyone according to what they have done."*

PSALM 62:11–12 NIV

Sometimes we focus on only one aspect of God's character. We remember how strong He is, and we may feel afraid. We're scared to mess up because we think God will punish us.

Other times we remember how loving He is. We may be tempted to take advantage of that love by doing whatever we please. We think, "Oh, God won't punish me for that. He'll just forgive me. It will be all right."

We must always remember that God is both powerful and loving. He loves us and doesn't want anything bad to happen to us. He also loves other people and wants to protect them. He will take care of us when we trust and obey Him, and He will bless us with good things. But if we disobey or act in a way that would disrespect or hurt someone else, He will protect them too because He loves them as much as He loves each one of us.

We need to always do what is right because we respect God and His power. But as long as we are doing our best to honor Him and love other people, we can relax. We don't need to fear God, because He loves us in an amazing way.

*Dear Father, thank You for Your strength and Your love.*
*I want to love others and protect them the way You do.*

# Day 286
# Spirit Song

*Because you are my help, I sing in the shadow of your*
*wings. I cling to you; your right hand upholds me.*
PSALM 63:7–8 NIV

Sometimes life gets hard, and we feel overwhelmed. We cry or get angry or stressed. No matter how hard we try, we can't seem to relax. But God says we can feel joy to the point of singing, right in the middle of the worst trouble, because He is there to help. And with God helping us, we can always know it's going to be okay.

Next time we're worried about a test, we can study and prepare, and then our spirits can sing. He will help us do our best. And if we fail, maybe He'll use that failure to get us even more help.

Next time we're upset about the way a friend is treating us, we can continue to treat them with love and sing in our hearts. God is there, and He will help us. He'll either work in that person's heart to change their attitude, or He'll send us another friend, or He'll move in some other way to protect us.

Even when things are stressful at home, we can trust God and sing. He is always working to bring about good things in our lives, as long as we rely on Him.

If everything always went the way we wanted, we wouldn't need His assistance. Life will have trouble and hardships, but God is always there to help us.

*Dear Father, thank You for guiding me through difficult things.*
*Help me trust You so much that my spirit sings.*

# God Will Take Care of Us

*"Ask and it will be given to you; seek and you will find; knock and the door will be opened to you. For everyone who asks receives; the one who seeks finds; and to the one who knocks, the door will be opened."*

MATTHEW 7:7–8 NIV

God wants us to ask Him for the things we need. When we ask, it shows we trust Him to provide. He often uses others to meet those needs, but He doesn't want us to depend on other things or people more than we depend on Him. He wants us to trust Him completely.

That doesn't mean He'll give us everything we ask for, like a spoiled child. But when we look to Him to provide the things we need, like food, clothing, and even friendship, He will provide. He loves us, and He loves taking care of us.

When we let Him know what we need, we must step back and allow Him to take care of it in His time and in His way. It's tempting to tap our feet and cross our arms impatiently, but we must remember—He is not our servant to do what we demand. He is our caring master, our loving Father. He will take care of us, but we have to trust Him. When we place our confident hope in Him, He will give us the things we need.

*Dear Father, thank You for giving me what I need.*
*Teach me to trust You for everything.*

# Brick House

*"Therefore everyone who hears these words of mine and puts them into practice is like a wise man who built his house on the rock. The rain came down, the streams rose, and the winds blew and beat against that house; yet it did not fall, because it had its foundation on the rock."*

MATTHEW 7:24–25 NIV

Have you ever built a sandcastle? It's fun to build with sand because it gets wet and squishy and feels nice in our hands. But sand won't hold its shape. As soon as a big wave or a strong wind comes along, *splat!* All our hard work is gone.

When we live our lives based on anything other than God's Word, our lives are kind of like a sandcastle. It may feel nice for a minute. For a short time, it may look beautiful and seem great. But the first time a big wave of stress or a strong wind of trouble comes along, our lives will go *splat*.

But when we base our lives on God's Word and live according to His laws, it's like building a brick house on a cement foundation. It may take more work in the beginning. But when we put in the patience and discipline to pattern our lives after God, we will withstand the storms of trouble and difficulty. A brick house is always sturdier and will protect us better than a sandcastle.

*Dear Father, thank You for Your wisdom. Help me live for You. I want to build a strong foundation for my life.*

# Don't Be a Drama Queen

*Warn a divisive person once, and then warn them a second time.*
*After that, have nothing to do with them.*

TITUS 3:10 NIV

Some people aren't happy unless they're miserable, and they make everyone else miserable with them. While that sounds silly, it's a fact of life. There are drama queens (and drama kings) in this world, and God wants us to stay away from them. And He certainly doesn't want us to be one of them.

God loves everyone, and He wants us to be kind to everyone. But if a person in our lives wants to gossip and bully and stir up trouble, God will deal with them. He wisely instructs us to encourage them to be kind and live at peace with others. If they don't listen the first time, we can encourage them again. But if they still don't listen, God wants us to avoid that person, for they will cause nothing but misery.

Sometimes we can't avoid the person completely, but we can do our best to avoid the drama. We can refuse to take part in gossip. We can try to make peace between all parties. We can leave the room, read our Bibles, and pray. If all else fails, we can continue to say kind things to that person or about the person they're slandering. If we try to avoid the drama kings and queens of the world and try to live at peace with everyone, God will honor our commitment to Him.

. . . . . . . . . . . . . . . . . . . . . . . . . . . . . . . . . . . . . . . . . . . . . . . . . . . . . . . .

*Dear Father, help me be kind to everyone.*
*I don't want to be a divisive person.*

## *Day 290*

# **Doing My Best**

*Do your best to present yourself to God as one approved, a worker who does not need to be ashamed and who correctly handles the word of truth.*

2 TIMOTHY 2:15 NIV

God created each of us with a special purpose, and He wants us to do our best to live out that purpose. The key here is finding our purpose and doing our best. If we are lazy and do a sloppy job of things, that doesn't honor God. If we get distracted and jealous because we're not as good as someone else at something, that doesn't honor God either.

Instead of lamenting that we can't sing as well as somebody else or that we're not athletic enough or smart enough or pretty enough, we should do our best in those areas and be satisfied to let someone else shine. And instead of doing a hurry-up job at our homework or cleaning our rooms, we should do our best so we can be proud. Most importantly, we should find the things we're good at, the things God has especially equipped us to do, and become the best we can be at those things so we can point people to Him and live out our purpose in this life.

. . . . . . . . . . . . . . . . . . . . . . . . . . . . . . . . . . . . . . . . . . . . . . . . . . . . . . . .

*Dear Father, help me be the best I can be at the things You want me to do.*

# Godless Chatter

*Avoid godless chatter, because those who indulge in
it will become more and more ungodly.*

2 TIMOTHY 2:16 NIV

It's fun to talk about stuff. Conversation is an important way to build relationships. But as we talk to one another, we need to always keep our conversations godly and uplifting.

That means we shouldn't say negative things about other people. When speaking of others, it's best to only say positive, encouraging things about them. That way we don't hurt others or make them angry at us.

We should also avoid talking about things that wouldn't please God or that would make our parents unhappy. Making plans to disobey or discussing things that are sinful doesn't help us grow into the people God created us to be.

God loves us, and He wants our conversations to reflect His love and His goals for us. So it's fine to discuss a great sports team or a fun new fashion or a yummy recipe as long as we keep the tone of our words and attitudes positive, uplifting, and encouraging for all who hear.

A good rule of thumb is to talk about things, not people. And we should always let our words reflect God's love, kindness, and compassion.

. . . . . . . . . . . . . . . . . . . . . . . . . . . . . . . . . . . . . . . . . . . . . . . . . . . . . . . . . .

*Dear Father, it's easy to let my conversations get away from me.
Sometimes before I know it, I've said something negative or unkind
or I've focused on something that wouldn't please You. I want to
become the person You want me to be. Help me guard my words.*

## Day 292
# Decisions

*Flee the evil desires of youth and pursue righteousness, faith, love and peace, along with those who call on the Lord out of a pure heart.*

2 TIMOTHY 2:22 NIV

It's normal to want to do things that are wrong. It's called temptation, and even Jesus was tempted. Sometimes the things we're not supposed to do seem more exciting than the things we're allowed to do. We long for the thrill of getting away with something.

But there's a reason God sets boundaries. He loves us so very much, and He doesn't want us to get hurt. He knows that poor decisions made when we're young can affect us for the rest of our lives.

Instead of pursuing the thrill of evil, He wants us to chase after righteousness, faith, love, and peace. When we're faced with a decision, we should ask ourselves: Is it right? Does it show faith in God? Does it demonstrate love and promote peace?

He also wants us to surround ourselves with others who have pure hearts, who long to honor Him with their lives. He knows that we tend to become like those people we hang around with, so it's important to choose our friends wisely.

God doesn't want us to live for today only; that causes us to make foolish choices. Instead, He wants us to live for eternity, making wise decisions that will lead us to a life filled with love, peace, and joy.

* * *

*Dear Father, forgive me for wanting to do things that are wrong. Help me resist temptation and make choices that will honor You.*

## Day 293
# Let It Go

*Don't have anything to do with foolish and stupid arguments,*
*because you know they produce quarrels. And the Lord's servant*
*must not be quarrelsome but must be kind to everyone.*
2 TIMOTHY 2:23–24 NIV

There's a popular song titled "Let It Go." It encourages the listener not to hold back anything. While this is good advice when it comes to pursuing our goals and dreams, it's not always wise to let our tongues go when we're offended.

Instead, it's often better to let go of the offense. If someone has a different opinion about a matter, that's fine. Let them have their opinion, and we can hold on to ours. We don't always have to argue about everything. As a matter of fact, unless it's a matter of life and death, it's usually best to just keep our mouths shut.

If someone does something we don't like, it's often wise to let that go too, without making a big deal of it. The stress and anger stirred up by a heated argument is usually much worse than the original offense that caused the argument.

If someone repeatedly offends us, perhaps we can find ways to avoid that person rather than make an enemy by starting an argument. God loves us, and He doesn't want us losing sleep over some petty disagreement that could have been avoided if we'd just chosen to let the offense go.

*Dear Father, help me keep my mouth shut when I'm angry.*
*Help me let offenses go so I can live at peace with others.*

## Day 294
# A Noble Life

*In a large house there are articles not only of gold and silver,*
*but also of wood and clay; some are for special purposes and*
*some for common use. Those who cleanse themselves from the*
*latter will be instruments for special purposes, made holy,*
*useful to the Master and prepared to do any good work.*

2 Timothy 2:20–21 NIV

God's children are royalty. Since He is the King of kings, all His children are princes and princesses. He wants us to remain set apart for noble purposes.

But sometimes His children choose to get bogged down with the things of this world. We act and live more like peasants than daughters of the King. We choose to fill our minds with junk instead of things of value.

God wants us to be gold, not garbage. He wants our minds to be filled with silver, not slop. The only way that will happen is if we make a conscious effort to be choosy about how we live and what we put in our minds. When we talk, our conversations should be uplifting. When we watch television or listen to music, the subject matter should be fitting for a child of the King. God loves us, and He wants us to live noble lives, fitting for children of the King.

. . . . . . . . . . . . . . . . . . . . . . . . . . . . . . . . . . . . . . . . . . . . . . . . . . . . . . . .

*Dear Father, I want to be careful about the things I allow into*
*my life. Help me make wise decisions with my words and the*
*things I put in my mind. I want to live a life of nobility.*

## Day 295

# Addition and Subtraction

*Do not add to what I command you and do not subtract from it,*
*but keep the commands of the LORD your God that I give you.*

DEUTERONOMY 4:2 NIV

Most of us want to obey God when it's easy. But there are times when living by God's standards isn't convenient or fun. In those times it's tempting to only listen to the parts of God's Word we want to hear and ignore the rest. We'll take one verse we like and ignore another that we don't like. We might even want to add a little bit here and there to make it more comfortable for us to do what we want. We twist His words to justify our actions.

But God says not to ever do that. He wants us to be familiar with His entire Word and obey every part of it. We're not allowed to alter it or change it in any way.

That's hard because sometimes God's Word may seem to say different things in different places. In one place He encourages compassion, in another place justice. But God never contradicts Himself.

If we're confused about what God's Word says, we can ask a trusted pastor or teacher. But we must always remember that love is the overriding theme in the Bible. If we're not sure what to do, we can ask for wisdom and make certain we're acting in love.

*Dear Father, help me obey every part of Your Word. I don't want*
*to ignore or change any part of it. Help me always act in love.*

# All the Time

*"I am the LORD, and there is no other; apart from me there is no God.
I will strengthen you, though you have not acknowledged me, so that
from the rising of the sun to the place of its setting people may know
there is none besides me. I am the LORD, and there is no other."*

ISAIAH 45:5–6 NIV

When we choose to accept Christ as our Savior, we are marked as His. We belong to God. Throughout His Word, He promises He'll never leave us or turn His back on us. He's there for us all the time, and He wants us to succeed so others will know He's a great God to serve.

But we occasionally get distracted and forget to acknowledge His goodness. He knows that sometimes life gets in the way. We forget to pray, or we forget to say "thank You" to Him.

If we never pray, that's a big problem. But if we make it a habit to seek God, to honor Him in our choices, and to live for Him each day, we don't have to worry that we didn't pray at the exact moment or that we forgot to say thanks for every little thing. He knows our hearts, and when our thoughts are pure, He will strengthen us and take care of us.

God loves us more than we can comprehend, and He wants us to succeed. When His children are strong, we are happy, and that makes others want to know Him more.

. . . . . . . . . . . . . . . . . . . . . . . . . . . . . . . . . . . . . . . . . . . . . . . . . . . . . . . . . .

*Dear Father, thank You for being there for me,
even when I forget to acknowledge You.*

# Naming the Stars

*Lift up your eyes and look to the heavens: Who created all these? He who brings out the starry host one by one and calls forth each of them by name. Because of his great power and mighty strength, not one of them is missing.*

ISAIAH 40:26 NIV

God is a pretty incredible God, isn't He? He created the heavens and the earth, the moon and billions of stars to fill the galaxy. This verse tells us He gave each star a name, and He knows that not one of them is missing.

That's a lot of stars.

If God cares that much about stars, how much more must He care about people, who He made in His own image? The stars are His creation, but we are His children. He formed us to be like Him because He longs for a relationship with us. He wants to talk to us, listen to us, laugh and cry with us.

Sometimes when we feel lonely or discouraged, it can seem like God is distant. Like He's forgotten all about us, and He doesn't even know our names anymore. Nothing could be further from the truth.

Just as God knows each of the stars by name, He knows each of us intimately. He never leaves us alone for a moment. He loves us, and that love will never, ever end.

*Dear Father, thank You for knowing my name. Thank You for loving me and wanting to have a relationship with me. Forgive me for the times I forget about You, for I know You never forget about me.*

# Such Great Goodness

*How abundant are the good things that you have stored up for those who*
*fear you, that you bestow in the sight of all, on those who take refuge*
*in you. In the shelter of your presence you hide them from all human*
*intrigues; you keep them safe in your dwelling from accusing tongues.*

PSALM 31:19–20 NIV

Have you ever had a new puppy or kitten? Or better yet, maybe you have
a younger brother or sister. When another living thing loves us, obeys us,
and runs to us when afraid, something happens in our hearts. We become
very protective of that person or pet, and we want to take care of them.

If we have enough love in our hearts to care for an animal or another
person, think how great God's love for us must be. He created us. He
adores us. He wants to give us lovely blessings to make us happy, and
He longs to protect us from things that will harm us. God is nothing
but good, nothing but love.

He is so full of love for us that He wants to pour out His goodness
until we are saturated. When we run to God, we have nothing to fear,
for He will always take care of His own.

*Dear Father, thank You for Your love and Your goodness.*
*When I feel afraid, remind me to run to You. I love You, and I*
*want to stay close to You and live each day in Your presence.*

# When I Need It Most

*Praise be to the LORD, for he showed me the wonders of his love when
I was in a city under siege. In my alarm I said, "I am cut off from your
sight!" Yet you heard my cry for mercy when I called to you for help.*
PSALM 31:21–22 NIV

Do you ever feel like you're in a bad situation and there's no way out of
it? That's how David felt when King Saul and his army were chasing
him, trying to kill him. At those times, it can feel like God has forgotten
about us, like He doesn't even see us anymore.

But God always sees us. He's always aware of every detail of our lives,
and He cares deeply. Sometimes He rescues us from bad things before
they ever happen, and we don't even know to be thankful. Other times, He
leaves us on our own for a while. He wants to give us the opportunity to
stand strong, to be wise, to make good decisions. He may even let us get
a few nicks and bruises along the way, to teach us some valuable lessons.

But He is right there, all the time. He will never leave us, and He
will certainly never let us be defeated. God will always give us help when
we need it most.

*Dear Father, thank You for never leaving me alone.
Keep me strong during the hard times, and remind
me of Your presence when I need it most.*

# Hope in the Lord

*Love the LORD, all his faithful people! The LORD preserves those who are true to him, but the proud he pays back in full. Be strong and take heart, all you who hope in the LORD.*

PSALM 31:23–24 NIV

Hope is a beautiful thing. It is a confident belief that good things are coming your way. Time and again, God tells His children to have hope in Him. We can be strong. We can smile at the future as long as we are faithful to love Him and follow His commands.

Satan doesn't want us to have any hope. He wants us to be afraid of the future, afraid that bad things will happen. He throws all kinds of frustrations and hurts and heartaches our way and tries to convince us that life will always be that way. Or he tries to make us worry about things that will never even happen to us. He's a thief, and he wants to steal our joy.

When we love God and trust Him, we don't have to be afraid. We don't have to believe Satan's lies that bad things will come. Even if they do happen, most things aren't as bad as we thought they'd be. And on the other side of the hurt, God always has a happy ending planned for those who love Him with all their hearts.

*Dear Father, I love You. Help me recognize fear for what it is: Satan trying to steal my joy. Remind me to live with hope—the belief that You have good things in store for my life, each and every day.*

*Day 301*

# How to Be Strong

*The LORD thunders at the head of his army; his forces are beyond number, and mighty is the army that obeys his command.*
JOEL 2:11 NIV

This is a great big world, and each of us is just a tiny part of it. Sometimes we can get overwhelmed and feel insignificant, like we don't matter or we aren't important. But we must never forget that although we're small, our God is mighty and powerful. And when we join with others who also love and serve God, we gain strength.

Obedience to God makes us more powerful, both as individuals and as a group. When we honor Him and live to please Him, He lives in us. And though we may not be able to accomplish much on our own, with God all things are possible.

With God, we can succeed where we might have failed. With God, we can endure when we might have given up. With God, we can love even the most unlovable people. Obedience to God allows us to be more than we ever thought we could be.

God loves us, and He longs to make us strong in every way. When we live for Him, He lives through us, and everything we do is powered by His presence.

. . . . . . . . . . . . . . . . . . . . . . . . . . . . . . . . . . . . . . . . . . . . . . . . . . .

*Dear Father, I'm glad to know You're so strong and that I serve in Your army. Help me be an obedient servant. I want the kind of strength that only comes from You.*

## Day 302

# God's Secret Formula

*Live in harmony with one another. Do not be proud, but be willing to associate with people of low position. Do not be conceited. Do not repay anyone evil for evil. Be careful to do what is right in the eyes of everyone.*
ROMANS 12:16–17 NIV

Sometimes we feel that in order for people to like us, we have to associate with the cool crowd. We think if we're friends with the pretty people, the popular people, the ones with the perfectly styled hair and the trendy clothes, others will associate us with those qualities and they'll like us too.

But there's a flaw in that way of thinking. Most people are thinking more about themselves than they are about anyone else; it's human nature. So even if we're standing next to the most impressive person around, people aren't likely to notice us.

Because God loves us, He taught us a secret formula to make most people like us all the time. If we make them feel good about themselves, they'll like us. If we're nice to everyone and treat everyone with kindness no matter what they look like or how trendy their wardrobe, people will start to notice. They'll realize they have nothing to fear from us because we always treat everyone with respect. They'll know whenever they're around us that they feel safe and wanted. Pretty soon we'll be popular, not for what we look like or how much money we have, but for how we treat others.

*Dear Father, help me avoid acting like I'm better than others. Teach me to be kind to everyone, no matter what.*

## Day 303

# Always There

*May the God of hope fill you with all joy and peace as you trust in him,*
*so that you may overflow with hope by the power of the Holy Spirit.*
ROMANS 15:13 NIV

Have you ever seen a dad throw his little girl in the air and catch her? It's a delightful thing to watch because the child usually squeals with delight. Even though she's being thrown in the air and could fall and badly hurt herself, that thought never crosses her mind. She knows her daddy will catch her. In that moment, she's all about the joy, and fear is a thousand miles away.

That's how God wants us to be with Him. When we feel like life is tossing us around, we can smile and laugh and feel total peace and joy, knowing our Father will catch us. He's not going to let us fall. That's called trust.

Somewhere along the way, as we grow up and skin our knees and experience some bangs and bruises, we forget to trust our Father. Instead of squealing with joy, we cry in fear. We forget that He loves us and will always be there to catch us.

Life does carry some hurts, but we don't have to expect them. That expectation steals the joy and peace from our lives. Today and every day, think of that daddy and his little girl, and expect joy.

*Dear Father, sometimes I forget how good You are and I forget to*
*trust You. Remind me to always expect good things from You.*

# He Prays for Me

*We do not know what we ought to pray for, but the Spirit himself intercedes for us through wordless groans. And he who searches our hearts knows the mind of the Spirit, because the Spirit intercedes for God's people in accordance with the will of God.*
ROMANS 8:26–27 NIV

Sometimes we find ourselves in the middle of a confusing situation, and we don't even know how to pray. We have no idea what to even ask God for because we don't know what the right thing is. That can feel pretty frustrating.

But even in those times, we can trust that God knows what we need. He knows our hearts, and He knows everything about us. He knows what is best, even if we don't. And He is always, always working for our best.

This verse tells us the Holy Spirit prays for us, even when we don't know what to say. He prays for us, even when we can't form words to pray ourselves. As long as we're doing our best to stay close to God and please Him, we don't have to worry about the little details of forgetting to pray or not praying right. All we have to do is call out to God in our hearts. He hears, and He understands perfectly.

*Dear Father, thank You for hearing and understanding the deepest part of me, even better than I understand myself. Thank You for always caring and for always seeking my good.*

# Wisdom and Innocence

*I want you to be wise about what is good, and innocent about what*
*is evil. The God of peace will soon crush Satan under your feet.*
Romans 16:19–20 niv

Halloween, originally called "All Hallows' Eve" or "All Saints' Eve" is a
celebration dating back several centuries. Some say it originated to honor
the saints and martyrs of the Christian faith. Some say its traditions are
intended to mock the power of death because God's power is stronger.
Others say it's not a Christian celebration at all, but a pagan (godless) one.

Whether or not we choose to participate in Halloween traditions,
we'll probably see trick-or-treaters and jack-o'-lanterns and people
dressed as witches and ghosts. Some are tempted to explore dark, scary
things at this time.

God likes to see his children have fun, but He wants us to remain
innocent about what is evil. He doesn't want us to get drawn in by dark,
bloody, frightening tales of murder and the supernatural. Today if we
feel frightened, we can remember that God is overwhelmingly more
powerful than evil. And we can remember that in the midst of our fun,
our most important task is to share His love and His goodness with
everyone we meet.

*Dear Father, thank You for giving me wisdom about what*
*is good. Remind me today, and every day, not to be too*
*curious about evil things. Help me stay focused on the pure*
*love, kindness, and compassion that comes from You.*

## Day 306

# Growing Up with Jesus

*Then he returned to Nazareth with them and was obedient to them. And his mother stored all these things in her heart.*

LUKE 2:51 NLT

Can you imagine what it must have been like to grow up in the same neighborhood as Jesus? If you had been alive when He was a boy, would you have wanted to be His friend? The other kids may have thought He was a little different, but most likely they didn't know about the angels who announced His birth or the shepherds and wise men who came to worship Him.

When He was twelve years old, He went to Jerusalem with His family and their friends for the Jewish celebration of Passover. Afterward, on their way home, Joseph and Mary couldn't find Him. They were frantic and hurried back to search for Him. They finally found Him in the temple, talking to a group of teachers. He acted surprised that they worried. He said, "Didn't you know I'd be doing My Father's business?"

Until then, even though they knew He was special, they probably treated Him just like other children. What He said made it clear that He knew He was from His heavenly Father. But after they got home, He was obedient to His folks.

If the Son of God needed to obey His earthly parents, it sets a wonderful example for children everywhere. Do you suppose kids who knew Him then tried harder to obey their parents when they watched Him?

*Dear Jesus, I want to be like You. Help me obey my parents and teachers and any others who have authority over me.*

# Learn to Be Happy

*There is a time for everything, and everything
on earth has its special season.*
ECCLESIASTES 3:1 NCV

Don't you sometimes wish you were completely grown up already? People act like you're still a child who can't take care of herself. Everyone tells you what to do and how to do it. You have to remind your parents you don't need a babysitter every time they go out. But when you try to tell them to treat you differently, they say something like, "You're too young to understand. Someday you'll wish you were still a little girl."

What do you think you can do to show them you're growing up? It doesn't help when you get angry because they don't do what you wish they would.

Think about your age as a season. Whether it is summer or winter, there are fun things to do; you can't play in the snow when it's hot outside, but you can swim. Just as the seasons have different opportunities, so does each age.

You will get older. When you are twenty, some of the things you do now won't be appropriate. But there are other activities you'll be able to do then. There is a time for everything. Some days this may feel like a tough age to be, but you can choose to make it better with a happy attitude. Look forward to the years ahead while you have fun now.

. . . . . . . . . . . . . . . . . . . . . . . . . . . . . . . . . . . . . . . . . . . . . . . . . . . . . .

*Lord Jesus, help me be happy, just as I am. I don't want to get mad at people
because they treat me like a kid. Help me know I'm special right now.*

*Day 308*

# Look through God's Eyes

*But the L*ORD *said to Samuel, "Don't look at how handsome*
*Eliab is or how tall he is, because I have not chosen him.*
*God does not see the same way people see. People look at the*
*outside of a person, but the L*ORD *looks at the heart."*

1 SAMUEL 16:7 NCV

How do you suppose other people see you? Do they think you're pretty?
Kind? Funny? Smart?

This scripture from the Old Testament is about David when he was
a young teen. God sent Samuel, a prophet, to David's family to anoint
the man who would be the next king of Israel. Of course David's father
was thrilled to think one of his sons would become king. He introduced
seven of his boys, one at a time, starting with the oldest. But the prophet
knew none of them was the one the Lord had chosen.

Finally, Samuel said, "Are these all your sons?"

Their father said, "Well, the youngest is out in the pasture with the
sheep. He's just a boy—surely it's not him."

But God saw David's heart. He knew this young man would learn to
lead the people. David's family just saw a shepherd, but God saw a king.

What do you think God sees when He looks at you? He sees the
person you will become. He catches a glimpse of your heart and says,
"She's special!"

* * * * * * * * * * * * * * * * * * * * * * * * * * * * * * * * * * * * * * * * * * * * * *

*Heavenly Father, I ask You to let me see myself the way You do.*
*Even when I do something dumb, help me resist getting discouraged.*
*Remind me You are working to make me the person You have planned.*

## Day 309

# Listen to Your Words

*When you talk, you should always be kind and pleasant so you
will be able to answer everyone in the way you should.*

Colossians 4:6 ncv

✦

The tone on Emily's phone let her know she had a text. She was doing
homework and wasn't supposed to call or text till she finished, but she
peeked at the screen. Allison! She was one of the most popular girls in
their class. Emily went ahead and read the message.

She was excited at what she saw: Can u come to a party Friday
nite? Allison had never acted especially friendly to her before.

Then another text came: Don't tell Jenna. She's a pig!

Emily's excitement evaporated. Jenna was her best friend.

Just then, her mom tapped on the door and came into Emily's room.
"Everything okay?"

Emily's mom always seemed to know when something was wrong.
"What should I do," Emily said, "when a really popular girl invites me
to a party, but then says something rude about my friend?"

"Well, before we talk about the party," her mother said, "you have to
decide if you want to get closer to someone like that."

Emily and her mother talked a little longer, and Emily made up her
mind. Her friend was more important than a party with someone who
said unkind things. She felt more excited about keeping a good friend
than about the invitation to Allison's.

· · · · · · · · · · · · · · · · · · · · · · · · · · · · · · · · · · · · · · · · · · · · · · · · · · · · · · · · ·

*Dear Lord, help me remember to keep my words kind and to say things that
are positive and encouraging. I want to please You when I talk to others.*

*Day 310*

# Be a Shining Light

*Do everything without grumbling or arguing. Then you will be
the pure and innocent children of God. You live among people who
are crooked and evil, but you must not do anything they can say is
wrong. Try to shine as lights among the people of this world.*

<small>PHILIPPIANS 2:14–15 CEV</small>

Lindsey's parents were getting a divorce, and it felt like every time they talked, they argued about Lindsey and her brother, Austin. Where would the children spend holidays? How long should they be with each parent in the summer? Who had to pay for school expenses?

It made Lindsey feel guilty, and that made her grumpy. She seemed to get angry with Austin, no matter what he did. One day when she lashed out, he said, "I wish you wouldn't be mad at me all the time. You're no fun anymore."

Instead of her usual fury, Lindsey started to cry. "I don't know what's wrong with me! I hate feeling this way. I'm sorry."

They sat down on the family room floor and talked about what was happening in their family. Lindsey realized her brother was hurting as much as she was. That made her want to protect him. "I'll try my best to be nicer, Austin. It's not your fault that I'm mad."

"I know. And it's not your fault Mom and Dad are getting a divorce," he said.

*Dear Jesus, even when things go wrong and other people don't do
what I like, help me avoid grumbling or arguing. I want to be like
a bright light that shines in dark places to help people see You.*

## Day 311

# God's Protection

*The LORD is good. He protects those who trust him in times of trouble.*
NAHUM 1:7 CEV

Sydney was friendly with almost everyone at school, but one boy, Zach, seemed creepy. There was something about his eyes. He wasn't in any of her classes, so she only saw him in the hallways, but every time she noticed him, he seemed to be staring at her.

One day after school, Zach was standing by the door Sydney went through. When she passed him, he followed her. She lived near the school and usually walked home alone. When she realized Zach was behind her, she went faster and pulled her phone from her pocket. Her hands were shaking. She didn't want her parents to freak out, but she was getting scared.

She punched in her dad's number. When he picked up, she whispered what was going on. Zach was still there, staying about half a block away. Her father tried to calm her down and told her he would pray for God to take care of her. He also said, "Stay on the line. I'll call for help from a different phone."

Within a few minutes, a police car drove by, slowly. Sydney glanced behind her and saw Zach turn around and run the other way. When the police got near him, one of the cops jumped out and ran to stop him. Sydney began to relax. She believed God showed her what to do and who to call.

. . . . . . . . . . . . . . . . . . . . . . . . . . . . . . . . . . . . . . . . . . . . . . . . . . . .

*Heavenly Father, thank You that You promise to protect me. I want to always trust You to watch over me and keep me from being afraid.*

## Day 312

# Trust in the Lord

*You love him even though you have never seen him. Though you do not see him now, you trust him; and you rejoice with a glorious, inexpressible joy. The reward for trusting him will be the salvation of your souls.*

1 PETER 1:8–9 NLT

Have you ever heard someone say, "I'm a Christian," but act hateful or say mean things? You may know other people who are really nice, but they don't claim to believe in Jesus.

So what is a Christian? Just thinking God is real or even that Jesus actually lived here on earth isn't enough. Christianity is so much more than how we behave or just believing He's real without faith that makes a difference in our actions. True believers ask Jesus Christ to forgive them and take control of everything. They know He died to take away their sins, and they are filled with joy because of His amazing love.

Christians aren't always super sweet and don't necessarily do everything right. Sometimes we really mess up and aren't proud of what we do, but we know Jesus loves us no matter what. Our actions don't make us Christians, but because people notice how we act, our lives should show that we belong to Him.

When we learn to trust Him, He gives us joy that's more than mere happiness. In this verse, Peter calls it glorious and inexpressible. And when we experience that kind of joy, people around us are going to see something special.

*I love You, Jesus, and want people who are with me to know You are in control of my life.*

## Day 313

# Don't Grumble—Pray

*Try to do good, not evil, so that you will live, and the LORD
God All-Powerful will be with you just as you say he is.*

AMOS 5:14 NCV

When elections are coming up, every time we turn on the TV, candidates tell us why they're the best. Signs about who is running for what are posted in yards and all along streets. It's hard to know who is telling the truth and who isn't. Even though you aren't quite old enough to vote, you may have an opinion. Do your parents talk about who they hope will win? Maybe you have an idea about the best candidates just from seeing the ads.

We're very fortunate to live in a free country where the people choose their leaders. Even though the ones we like might not always win elections, it's decided by the majority of the citizens. That's not true in a lot of nations.

The Bible tells us to pray for our leaders (see 1 Timothy 2:2) and to obey and honor them (see 1 Peter 2:13, 17). Unless a government forces people to do things that go against what the Bible teaches, we are to submit to elected officials. Sometimes we grumble and complain about our leaders, but that doesn't please God. If we want to do good and not evil, we need to have the right attitude about people in authority.

*Lord Jesus, help me remember these things as I grow up. I want to understand how important it is to elect godly people and to honor those who are in office. Give me opportunities to show others that You are in control.*

## Day 314
# Direct My Heart

*Now may the Lord direct your hearts into the love*
*of God and into the patience of Christ.*
2 THESSALONIANS 3:5 NKJV

What do you think of when you hear the word *direct*? Sometimes people direct traffic around construction sites. Musicians learn to pay close attention to their director so all the voices or instruments stay together. Political leaders direct the government, teachers direct students, and parents direct their children.

So how does the Lord direct our hearts? He doesn't hold a big stop sign or a conductor's wand, but He gets our attention. He is gentle, is persistent, and always knows the best way to get us where we need to go. He'll direct us to avoid dangerous situations and will take us straight into the heart of God's love.

Sometimes God uses a scripture from the Bible to speak to us and show us what we should do. Other times a preacher, teacher, or good friend tells us something, and we know it's the Lord. He has a wonderful imagination and will use whatever works best to show us what we need at that time.

When we listen to Him, we can feel safe and secure. Even then, sometimes it takes a long time to see where He's taking us. That's when we need the patience of Christ. It's really hard to wait patiently for anything. We want to see results quickly. But when we learn to wait on Him, we grow more like Jesus.

. . . . . . . . . . . . . . . . . . . . . . . . . . . . . . . . . . . . . . . . . . . . . . . . . . . . . . .

*Lord, I really want to understand You more. I want You to lead*
*my heart into Your love and teach me to be patient—like Jesus.*

# Discipline Shows Love

*My dear child, don't shrug off God's discipline, but don't
be crushed by it either. It's the child he loves that he
disciplines; the child he embraces, he also corrects.*

HEBREWS 12:5–6 MSG

"This place is so boring," Lauren said. "How do you stand it?" Emma lived in a very small town, and her cousin was visiting for a weekend from the city. To Emma this was normal. She hadn't thought much about it.

That night Lauren said, "Let's do something fun, like a movie."

"How? We'd need a ride."

Lauren just said, "Watch."

After Emma's parents were in bed, Lauren tiptoed to the back door, with Emma following. They hurried to the highway, and Lauren stuck out her thumb when a car came along. The driver stopped to let the girls in.

"Where in the world are you two headed at this time of night?" the driver asked. Oh no! The driver was Emma's teacher.

Both girls scrunched down in their seats as Mrs. Maxwell headed toward Emma's house.

Emma's parents were upset and disappointed. They told Emma they'd have to decide what to do, but she knew she deserved to be punished. Before they all headed for bed, her folks hugged both girls and said, "We love you. We'll discuss this tomorrow."

* * *

*Dear heavenly Father, thank You for parents who show their love by
discipline as well as hugs. I want to learn from the discipline I receive.*

# Heroes

*GOD's Message: "Don't let the wise brag of their wisdom.*
*Don't let heroes brag of their exploits. Don't let the rich brag*
*of their riches. If you brag, brag of this and this only: That you*
*understand and know me. I'm GOD, and I act in loyal love."*
JEREMIAH 9:23–24 MSG

Destiny's whole family waited at the airport for Justin's plane. She was so excited! He was coming home after a year in Afghanistan, just in time for Veterans Day. Her school had invited him to speak at a special assembly.

When Destiny spotted him, she jumped up and down like a little kid. And when he saw them all waiting, a huge grin spread across his face. The next few minutes were filled with hugs and laughter.

One of their uncles said, "Glad you came home in one piece." But at his words, something seemed to change in Justin.

Destiny didn't understand until the next day at the school assembly. Justin talked about his friends who were real heroes. Some of them were badly injured or killed. He said, "I can't brag about anything I did over there. Every victory was God's doing, and He's the one who kept me alive. I got to know the Lord better than I ever had, and I experienced His love when I was scared and far from home."

It was a sober time. The kids seemed to be thinking about God's loyal love.

* * * * *

*Dear Lord, thank You for all the men and women who*
*serve in the military to keep us free. Show each of them*
*how much You love them. Let them really know You.*

## Day 317

# Be an Example

*Don't let anyone think less of you because you are young.
Be an example to all believers in what you say, in the way
you live, in your love, your faith, and your purity.*

1 TIMOTHY 4:12 NLT

✦

Lexi was cute and perky—the one who said funny things to make her friends laugh. Even though she was smart, people who didn't really know her thought she was an airhead.

One day she overheard some girls at school and realized she was the topic of their conversation. "She's so ditzy! How has she been able to get this far?"

Lexi didn't want people to think she was dumb. She just liked to have fun and make others happy. After hearing the girls, she decided she'd better get serious. So she tried, but she had to work hard to hide her naturally bubbly personality.

One of her close friends asked, "What's wrong? You always act like you're mad now."

"People think I'm stupid when I'm happy, so I have to change."

"Your friends know how smart you are. You act goofy because you want us to feel good. Look at your grades—you make straight As!"

"So what can I do?"

"Just be you! Don't try to change from the person God made you. You're a good example of how someone can be fun and still have faith and integrity. We all know you care about us."

. . . . . . . . . . . . . . . . . . . . . . . . . . . . . . . . . . . . . . . . . . . . . . . . .

*Lord Jesus, thank You for making me the person I am. Let me enjoy
life and show others You are with me, keeping me pure and faithful.*

*Day 318*

# Growing Up

*But grow in the grace and knowledge of our Lord and Savior
Jesus Christ. To him be glory both now and forever! Amen.*

2 PETER 3:18 NIV

It's hard to imagine our parents, our grandparents, or other adults when they were children. Even if we see pictures and hear stories of things they did, they'll always be older than us. Their lives are different. They've experienced and learned from a lot of things that take time.

When we accept Jesus as our Savior, we're like babies all over again. We need to grow up by talking to God and reading the scriptures to learn more. That was even true for Jesus! Luke 2:52 says that Jesus grew in wisdom and stature. It's easy to imagine Him as a baby in a manger, like we see at Christmas. And we know about miracles and all the wonderful things He did when He was an adult. But none of that came automatically. He grew from an infant to a toddler to a teenager to an adult, just like everyone else.

Christians "grow up" by learning about Jesus, our Lord and Savior. As we study the Bible and pray, His grace and love will show in our own lives. We'll gain knowledge of what He is like and how He treats people. Then whatever we do, we can imagine what He would do. That doesn't make us proud or act like we're special. Actually, we have to be humble to depend on Him.

*Dear Jesus, I'm so glad You came to earth so we can picture
how You lived. Teach me how to glorify You by my life.*

# Don't Take the Bait

*Don't let me so much as dream of evil or thoughtlessly fall
into bad company. And these people who only do wrong—
don't let them lure me with their sweet talk!*

Psalm 141:4 msg

Leah was fascinated by a couple of girls on the bus. They wore lots of makeup and dressed in clothes barely within the school's dress code. They were always laughing.

When she got home that afternoon, she tried some dark eyeliner, heavy mascara, and bright lipstick just to see what she looked like. She fiddled with her hair till it looked kind of sexy. Then she pinned up one of her skirts so it was shorter than anything she ever wore. She stood in front of the mirror, swishing this way and that.

Right then, she heard her mother at the front door and felt like she'd been caught doing something wrong. She ran to the bathroom to scrub her face but wasn't fast enough.

"Good grief, honey—what are you doing?"

"Just playing around with some makeup."

"You're much prettier without it, but I understand. I did the same thing when I was your age."

"Really? Some girls at school use lots of makeup, and all the boys watch them. I just wanted to see what I'd look like."

"Don't be fooled by looks. Maybe that's the only way some girls know to get attention. Don't let them lure you away from what's right."

* * *

*Lord, I ask You to make me happy with the way I look. I trust You
to keep me from getting involved with anything I shouldn't.*

*Day 320*

# Keep Your Eyes Clear

*Your eyes are a window for your body.*
*When they are good, you have all the light you need.*
MATTHEW 6:22 CEV

A pop-up appeared on Alyssa's screen while she checked out Facebook. It had a picture of a gorgeous guy and said, "Meet a hunk!" She was intrigued and clicked on the window. What came up was shocking. Even though it was offensive, for some reason she kept scrolling through the photos.

Suddenly, she stopped herself and clicked off the site. Hardly thinking about what she was doing, she'd spent several minutes staring at those images. She felt dirty simply from looking at them. So why did she go there? It was really disgusting! She was at home by herself, but she looked around feeling guilty, glad no one saw her.

Alyssa realized how easy it is to get caught up in such things without even trying. Fascinated by that little bit of temptation, she had taken a wrong step. Her pastor said being tempted isn't evil—even Jesus was tempted—but giving in to temptation was sin.

Alyssa had accepted Jesus as her Savior a few years earlier. She knew He loved her and would forgive her. She prayed right then but hated how simple it was to fall into something that made her feel so cruddy.

*Dear Jesus, thank You for dying for me, erasing my sin with Your blood.*
*Forgive me any time I fall for the stupid things that seem appealing*
*when I see them. Keep my eyes clear so Your light shines through me.*

# Be Kind, Even to Your Enemies

*"But to you who are listening I say: Love your enemies, do good to those
who hate you, bless those who curse you, pray for those who mistreat you."*
Luke 6:27–28 niv

"I hate those girls!" Alexis could hardly believe the words she read. "Why
would anybody act so mean?" She just saw a post about Bailey, a new girl
in her class who had moved from Texas. "She's shy and having a hard
time making friends, but she seems really nice," Alexis said.

Some girls from her class made ugly comments about Bailey's drawl
and said, "She sounds like she belongs on a farm. Somebody should rope
her like a cow and put her in a barn where she belongs."

Alexis started to type a reply, but her little sister, who heard her fume,
said, "I'm glad you aren't mean. You treat everyone nice."

Alexis stopped. She realized the words she was about to write weren't
nice. She wanted to blast those hateful girls, but hearing her sister made
her feel uncomfortable. Her Sunday school teacher had just been talking
about how God wants us to treat others—even our enemies. Firing back
a hateful response wouldn't be right. In fact, it would probably make
things worse.

Instead, she prayed for God to bless those girls and show them how
to be kind.

. . . . . . . . . . . . . . . . . . . . . . . . . . . . . . . . . . . . . . . . . . . . . . . . . . . . . . .

*Dear Father in heaven, it's easy to get mad and say mean things, but I
ask You to keep me from just doing what's easy. I want to make You happy
by doing something good for those who act hateful to me or to others.*

## Day 322
# God Is Love

*Beloved, let us love one another, for love is of God; and
everyone who loves is born of God and knows God. He who
does not love does not know God, for God is love.*

1 JOHN 4:7–8 NKJV

God isn't just loving. He *is* love. It's more than merely one of His special traits—love defines who He is. And it's pretty scary to think that if we don't show love to others, we don't really know God. Not only that, but we don't get to choose who we love. It's not just people who treat us special. We're to love everyone.

God sent Jesus to earth to show us what love looks like. We can hardly imagine anyone loving so much He'd even forgive the people who spit on Him and called Him names and jammed a thorny crown on His head. He loved those who beat Him and drove spikes into His hands and feet.

Because of His tremendous love, He can expect us to love those in our lives. Most people will never experience anything as horrible as Jesus did. We may know bullies and people who say mean things, but nothing like what Jesus suffered.

Can you love the people in your life? All of them? You can if you ask Jesus to give you the grace you need to be a loving person. We have to depend on Him for everything—even the love we need to show.

*Dear Father, on my own I can't love the way You want me to.
I ask for grace to let me love others the way You do.*

## Day 323

# True Love

*Love is patient and kind, never jealous, boastful,*
*proud, or rude. Love isn't selfish or quick tempered.*
*It doesn't keep a record of wrongs that others do.*

1 CORINTHIANS 13:4–5 CEV

On their way home from church, Olivia thought about something the pastor said: "God's kind of love involves emotions, but isn't ruled by them."

Later while she and her older sister changed clothes, she asked Hailey, "So, do you love Jason the way Pastor Bradley talked about?"

Hailey giggled. "Probably not! We just have fun together, and I feel good when I'm with him."

"Do you think you're going to marry him?"

"I don't know. I don't think the pastor meant the love we're supposed to have for everyone—not just boyfriends."

"But if it's for everyone, that includes boyfriends."

"Okay, you're probably right, but for now we're not that serious." They were quiet for a while, then Hailey said, "You know, Jason does treat me like that scripture says. God probably wants us to love everyone that way, but I guess if I was dating somebody that was selfish and proud and impatient, I wouldn't like him very much."

"Maybe God means it for everyone, but especially for the people we spend the most time with. Even sisters," Olivia said and threw her sock at Hailey.

"Stop it!"

"Remember, don't keep track of wrongs," Olivia teased.

* * *

*Thank You, Lord, for showing us what true love is.*

## Day 324

# Real Peace Comes from Jesus

*Therefore, since we have been made right in God's sight by faith, we have peace with God because of what Jesus Christ our Lord has done for us.*
Romans 5:1 NLT

Whether people realize it or not, everyone needs to live in peace. That doesn't mean we're boring and don't ever do exciting things—even things that can be risky sometimes.

The word for peace in the Bible is *shalom*. That's still a greeting in Israel—instead of saying "Hello," people say, "Shalom." It's sort of like passing on a blessing.

When we have a close relationship with God because of our faith in Jesus, we feel complete and peaceful. Shalom doesn't just mean there's no fighting or trouble. In fact, we can have the kind of peace God wants even in the midst of problems if we know Jesus.

When angels announced to some shepherds that Jesus, the Savior, was born, they said, "Glory to God in highest heaven, and peace on earth to those with whom God is pleased" (Luke 2:14 NLT). Genuine peace only comes from God.

Hundreds of years earlier, Isaiah prophesied about the Messiah who would come. One of His titles was to be Prince of Peace. The prophet even said, "His government and its peace will never end" (Isaiah 9:7 NLT). Wars and huge problems have always been issues people have to deal with, but when we depend on Jesus, we can have peace even then. Isn't that awesome?

*Dear Lord Jesus, I want to always experience the peace You promise. I trust You to give me real peace no matter what's happening around me. Thank You!*

# Humility

*Now Moses was a very humble man, more humble*
*than anyone else on the face of the earth.*
NUMBERS 12:3 NIV

Do you know the story of Moses? When he was born, the Egyptian king was worried about the Hebrews in his country becoming too strong. So he did something horrible. He ordered the Hebrew women to kill their sons when they were born.

Moses' mother couldn't do anything that awful and hid her baby for a few months. Eventually she placed him in a watertight basket, and Moses' sister took him to a place near the river where the king's daughter would find him. She was tenderhearted and raised Moses as her son.

When he grew up, Moses saw an Egyptian beating a Hebrew. Moses killed the Egyptian but realized he'd been seen. So he left town! Years later when he was old, God called him back to rescue the Hebrews from slavery.

Can you imagine leading hundreds of thousands of people, along with lots and lots of livestock, through the wilderness? The people grumbled and complained and faced one problem after another for forty years. It would take an incredibly powerful leader to accomplish what Moses had to do. He was capable and strong, but—what was most important—he was more humble than anyone else. God knew exactly what sort of man could do the job—and humility was one of the essential traits.

We probably won't lead a multitude, but whatever we do, humility is vital. And it takes strength to be humble.

*Lord, I want to be humble. Please show me how to*
*be strong enough to live with humility.*

## Day 326

# Bear Delicious Fruit

*"I am the vine, you are the branches. He who abides in Me, and I in him, bears much fruit; for without Me you can do nothing."*
John 15:5 NKJV

Autumn loved to visit her grandparents when grapes ripened in late summer. Plump purple grapes grew along a fence in their backyard. She helped her grandpa pick them and popped some in her mouth as she moved along. They were sweet and juicy, warm from the sunshine. Her mother would probably have said to wash them first, but her grandpa didn't worry about it. They carried baskets of grapes to the kitchen, where her grandma was making jelly.

One day Autumn's grandpa said, "Do you know what would happen if I cut the vines down to the ground?"

"You wouldn't get any grapes," she said.

"Right. Even if I left branches dangling from the fence, without the vines they would wither and die. The vine carries nutrients and water from the soil so the plants thrive and bear grapes."

Grandpa went on to talk about how Jesus called Himself the vine and His followers the branches. "If we separate ourselves from Jesus," Grandpa said, "we won't produce a good crop of fruit."

God wants us to share good fruit with others—love, joy, peace, kindness, and other good traits—but without Jesus' life-giving power, we can't do it. The more time we spend with Him, the better our fruit will taste to others.

*Dear Lord, I know I can't produce good fruit on my own. Show me, every day, how to stay connected to You so I bear good fruit.*

## Day 327

# What God Wants

*But he's already made it plain how to live, what to do, what GOD
is looking for in men and women. It's quite simple: Do what is
fair and just to your neighbor, be compassionate and loyal in your
love, and don't take yourself too seriously—take God seriously.*

MICAH 6:8 MSG

Jessica was usually serious. She obeyed the rules, both at school and home. She did her homework and turned everything in on time. She kept her room neat and read her Bible most days. Her friend Jordan sometimes laughed at her. "Loosen up, Jess! Do you think the world would fall apart if you didn't do what you're supposed to once in a while?"

"What do you mean? I want God to like me."

Jordan gave her a strange look. "You think He won't like you if you relax?"

The girls went to the same church, but Jordan wasn't as disciplined as Jessica and didn't see anything wrong with the way she did things. "Look, I'm not saying to be bad, but you worry too much about whether you're doing things right. I don't think God's love depends on how we act. He just expects us to love Him and treat others the way we want to be treated. You make it too hard."

Jessica thought about it. "But I wouldn't be comfortable if I didn't do things the way I do."

"Okay, but remember you can't earn God's love by being strict with yourself. His rules are simple."

. . . . . . . . . . . . . . . . . . . . . . . . . . . . . . . . . . . . . . . . . . . . . . . . . . . . .

*Dear heavenly Father, show me what matters to You.
I don't want to expect more from myself than You do.*

*Day 328*

# Most Important Commandment

*"And you shall love the LORD your God with all your heart, with all your soul, with all your mind, and with all your strength.' This is the first commandment."*

MARK 12:30 NKJV

What do you suppose the Bible means when it says we're to love the Lord with all our heart, soul, mind, and strength? When we commit our lives to Jesus, every part of us belongs to Him, but that doesn't explain what it means to love Him with our total being. The kind of love God has for us, and what He wants from us, doesn't have any edges—no boundaries.

If you stood (or sat) on a tiny life raft in the middle of an ocean, you could look all around and not notice anything that breaks the expanse of sky and sea. It's blended together endlessly.

The Bible says God's love is endless like that, and higher than the heavens. Imagine floating in space, and all you see is. . .space. That might feel scary, but think of that space being filled with God's love. His arms surround you. His strength protects you. His heart adores you. His love can't be measured. That's the kind of love He wants us to return to Him.

Boundless love frees us to trust God completely. We're willing to take risks when we know He is telling us to do something. We totally surrender to Him.

*Dear Jesus, I want my love for You not to have any edges. Keep me safe in Your loving embrace, and overwhelm me with a desire to give You everything, not holding anything back.*

# Celebrate What God Does

*I trust your love, and I feel like celebrating because you rescued me.*
*You have been good to me, LORD, and I will sing about you.*
PSALM 13:5–6 CEV

It had been a tough year for Erin. She struggled in a couple of classes, a girl in the neighborhood bullied her, and she felt fat. It seemed like everything was going wrong.

School was out for Thanksgiving break, and her cousins were coming. Usually she loved that, but now she just wanted to be alone. Her mom yelled, "Erin, come on down and help. Our company will be here soon, and we have a lot to do."

She wanted to pretend she didn't hear but knew that wouldn't work, so she headed downstairs. Outside her bedroom, the aroma of turkey and something sweet brightened her attitude a little.

Suddenly the front door burst open for her cousins and their parents to spill into the living room. Jade ran toward her and wrapped Erin in a huge hug. "I'm so glad to see you!" They both automatically headed toward the kitchen and started helping as they chattered about everything imaginable.

Everyone pitched in, and the Thanksgiving feast was ready in no time. They sat down and followed their tradition of letting everyone tell something they were thankful for. When it was her turn, Erin realized she needed to stop concentrating on problems. "I'm thankful that God rescued me from feeling sorry for myself and showed me what a great family we have. He's so good!"

*Dear Lord, help me always celebrate Your goodness*
*instead of letting negative thoughts drag me down.*

## Day 330
# Stay Righteous

*"Yet the righteous will hold to his way, and he who has clean hands will be stronger and stronger."*

JOB 17:9 NKJV

That's an amazing statement because it came from Job when he was in the pits. He was the richest man in town and the father of ten children. But in one day his life fell apart. Job's children died in a terrible storm while they were celebrating together. All his servants were killed, and his huge herd of livestock was stolen by an enemy.

Some people would have given up on God. But the first thing Job did was fall to his knees and worship the Lord.

Satan did his best to turn Job against God, but he didn't succeed. Job was covered with boils and sat among ashes, scraping the sores with shards of pottery. His wife put him down for clinging to God's promises. So-called friends said they knew he must be sinning for all that disastrous stuff to happen.

But through it all, Job's faith never failed. He spoke the words of this scripture even though his heart was breaking. In spite of everything, he knew he was righteous and believed he would grow stronger if he kept holding on.

Eventually God honored Job for staying faithful. He became rich again and had more children. But the lesson for us is that he trusted God even when he couldn't see anything positive happening.

. . . . . . . . . . . . . . . . . . . . . . . . . . . . . . . . . . . . . . . . . . . . . . . . . . . . . . . . . .

*Almighty God, I don't ever want to go through horrible things like Job, but I do want to stay strong and trust in You to take care of all my needs, no matter what.*

## Day 331

# Guard Your Heart

*Guard your heart above all else, for it determines the course of your life.*
PROVERBS 4:23 NLT

✦

Cheerleader tryouts were coming up, and even though Faith was good, she wasn't positive she could make it.

As she was walking to class one morning, a cute guy from the football team caught up with her. "Hey, you going out for cheerleader? I can make it happen if you're interested."

"What do you mean?"

"My mom is one of the judges. She'll make sure the girls I want are on the squad."

Faith was flattered to think he would do that for her, even though she felt a tug at her conscience. All she could think to say was, "That's nice of you."

"So, when can we go out?"

She didn't know a lot about guys, but her guard went up immediately. "My parents won't let me date yet."

"Oh come on. You can figure out a way."

"Sorry. I'll figure out a way to do my best at the tryouts and not depend on your help."

· · · · · · · · · · · · · · · · · · · · · · · · · · · · · · · · · · · · · · · · · · · · · · · · · · · ·

*Lord Jesus, please protect my heart from getting involved in any relationship or scheme that isn't what You want for me.*

## Day 332

# Light in Shadows

*"If you are generous with the hungry and start giving yourselves
to the down-and-out, your lives will begin to glow in the
darkness, your shadowed lives will be bathed in sunlight."*
ISAIAH 58:10 MSG

Shelly was excited about going on a mission trip to Honduras with her youth group. Her dad was a chaperone, so the idea of a foreign country didn't seem scary. They went to a few classes to give them an idea of what to expect and how to be a blessing to the people. They would work with a church to help build a house for a needy family and have Vacation Bible School for the children.

When the plane touched down, the pastor greeted them. They climbed into his beat-up van for a bumpy ride to the church. Shelly was stunned by what she saw along the way. Everything seemed desolate and dirty. People lived in huts with grubby-looking children playing outside. Even though she knew what to expect, actually seeing it touched her heart. She blinked back tears.

After they dropped their bags in the church basement, the group headed out to meet people. They had trinkets for the children, who came running to them with expectant grins. The days zipped past quickly, and Shelly loved everything they did for these people, who were so appreciative.

After ten days, they boarded the van to leave. Shelly's face glowed with joy, even as tears streamed down her cheeks when the kids ran for one last hug.

*Heavenly Father, thank You for showing Your heart through the
joy we get from helping others. Give me a generous spirit.*

*Day 333*

# God Reigns

*How great are His signs, and how mighty His wonders!*
*His kingdom is an everlasting kingdom, and His*
*dominion is from generation to generation.*
DANIEL 4:3 NKJV

That scripture is powerful no matter what, but even more so because of who said it. Do you know? It was Nebuchadnezzar, king of Babylon. He loved to be praised by people and believed in multiple gods. . .until Shadrach, Meshach, and Abednego, Daniel's companions, survived a trip through the fire.

That happened after the king made a gold statue, about ninety feet tall. It was so huge, people couldn't miss it. And he ordered everyone to bow down to the statue at certain times. Shadrach, Meshach, and Abednego refused. That made the king furious. He watched as his servants tied them up and threw them into a furnace.

But what he saw astonished him. They were walking around in the flames, along with a fourth man who looked "like the Son of God" (see Daniel 3:25). Nebuchadnezzar called for them to come out, and when they did, they weren't burned and didn't even smell like smoke. The king was amazed by God's mighty wonders and His everlasting kingdom.

God honored Daniel's friends because they wouldn't worship things of this world. We probably won't be forced to bow down to a statue, but sometimes other things can get in the way of us worshipping the one true God. He blesses those who refuse to compromise their faith.

* * * * * * * * * * * * * * * * * * * * * * * * * * * * * * * * * * * * * * * * * *

*Heavenly Father, help me always stay faithful to You,*
*no matter what might tempt me to turn away.*

# Be One Who Honors God

*Just as water fills the sea, the land will be filled
with people who know and honor the LORD.*
HABAKKUK 2:14 CEV

✦

Taylor and her family were in the great room watching Monday night football. Their dad sat in his favorite recliner. Mom was on the couch, more interested in her magazine than men who got paid big bucks to run around a field.

Seats at the stadium were packed with screaming fans. When Taylor's mother glanced at the screen, she said, "Wow! Look at that crowd!"

"See, Mom, lots of people really love football," Taylor said.

Their mother got quiet again but wasn't really paying attention to her magazine. At halftime she headed to the kitchen and returned with popcorn and Cokes. "Just imagine," she said, "what it would be like if Christians were that excited about God. What if we loved the Lord so much we packed stadiums all around the country every week to hear more about Jesus?"

Dad muted the sound. Somehow what she said made an impact on each of them, and they started talking about how awesome it would be. "Can you picture people screaming and yelling and cheering because they're so excited about their faith?" Taylor said.

"What if there were so many excited Christians, we spilled out of churches and even stadiums. Think of a sea of people who can't stand not to shout for joy because they've been saved."

The game started again but wasn't quite as exciting.

· · · · · · · · · · · · · · · · · · · · · · · · · · · · · · · · · · · · · · · · · · · · · ·

*Lord God, I want to join a sea of people who shout praises to You.*

# Clothed in Christ

*For you are all children of God through faith in Christ Jesus.*
*And all who have been united with Christ in baptism*
*have put on Christ, like putting on new clothes.*
GALATIANS 3:26–27 NLT

✦

Do you like to shop for new clothes? When we "put on Christ," we don't need to go to a fitting room and try various styles or sizes. He's a perfect fit for each of us as soon as we trust Him to be our Savior.

Jesus wants us to abide in Him, like we read in John 15. Then people will see Him when they are with us. They'll be aware of His amazing grace and love. Everywhere we go, we take Him—or maybe He takes us where He goes.

Do your friends see Jesus in you? Picture wearing garments that gleam from your love-filled words, sparkle as particles of joy shimmer in you, and feel velvety smooth with peace. Jesus' patience and kindness leave a sweet fragrance when you pass by. Traces of His goodness shine from you like diamonds.

When we go to heaven and stand before God, if we've devoted our lives to Jesus, we will be completely covered in Christ's glorious righteousness. The Father will be so pleased! When we're clothed in Jesus, our mistakes are all washed away, totally forgiven and forgotten. We are sparkling clean, completely pure, not because of who we are, but because of who Jesus is.

. . . . . . . . . . . . . . . . . . . . . . . . . . . . . . . . . . . . . . . . . . . . . . . . . . . . .

*Precious Jesus, I don't know the right words to tell You how much I love*
*You. Thank You for what You've done for me that no one else could do.*

## Day 336
# Having Dreams

*"For I know the plans I have for you," declares the LORD, "plans to prosper you and not to harm you, plans to give you hope and a future."*
JEREMIAH 29:11 NIV

Think really hard. In your heart of hearts, what is your deepest desire? Everyone has different hopes and dreams. Do you want to write a book one day? Be an engineer? Be a mother? Perhaps even president of the United States? People are naturally inquisitive and curious, so it should be no surprise that you have plenty of plans and goals for your life.

God has given you these dreams, and they are truly good and wonderful. God knows how the story of your life will play out, and He will guide you along the journey. He will hold your hand the entire way. Even if it seems like your plans will change, don't worry. God has the very best plan in mind for you. Just as you have the courage to follow your dreams, also have the courage to let God change them. You have a bright future! Trust in God, and you will accomplish great things.

*Dear Lord, please give me the courage to chase my dreams. Also give me the patience to wait on Your timing. You have planned out all of my days. Thank You for Your wisdom and for taking care of my every step.*

## Day 337

# Your Worth Is in Christ

*[Jesus] said to me, "My grace is sufficient for you, for my power is made perfect in weakness." Therefore I will boast all the more gladly about my weaknesses, so that Christ's power may rest on me.*

2 CORINTHIANS 12:9 NIV

It can seem like every day brings a new person to tell you that you are not good enough. You don't make the team. You don't get the grade. You don't look like the girls on television. No matter how hard you try, sometimes you just don't measure up to the pressures of being a modern girl. However, as long as you pull your worth from the world around you, you will always come up short. There will always be someone "better."

Thankfully, because you are loved by Christ, you have been made a new creation! In God's eyes, you are His child. He takes your weaknesses and turns them into opportunities to show His strength through you. It doesn't matter what people think about you. You are a child of God, and that is the most powerful identity there is. Whenever you feel like you aren't good enough, remember that the God of the universe loves you, and there is nothing greater than that.

*Dear Lord, whenever I feel less-than or inadequate, I will remember that I have been filled with Your power and love. Nothing can bring me down when I have You on my side!*

# Maybe Don't Post That. . .

*But the LORD said to Samuel, "Do not consider his appearance*
*or his height, for I have rejected him. The LORD does not*
*look at the things people look at. People look at the outward*
*appearance, but the LORD looks at the heart."*

1 SAMUEL 16:7 NIV

Between Instagram, Twitter, Snapchat, and countless other social media sites, it seems like everyone is focused on documenting every single aspect of their day. It can be fun to post pictures of your friends, the occasional joke, or even a selfie online, but people are becoming more and more undiscerning with what they post.

Instead of just living life and letting things happen, people often act like if they don't Instagram it, it didn't actually happen. Also, people can very carefully control the image that they project through their social media. They can only post the amazing moments, the beautiful things. It is easy to forget that even though it looks like your friends and acquaintances have perfect lives free from pain and frustration, that just isn't true. They have the same struggles and sadness that you do. Maybe instead of just following friends and liking their pictures, hang out with them in real life. Ask them how they're really doing and get to know them in a real and tangible way. This will be even better than that eleventh like on Instagram.

*Dear Lord, help me remember that friendships call for work and*
*interaction. Show me how to be real and vulnerable with those that I love.*

# The Difference between Happiness and Joy

*Then I will go to the altar of God, to God, my joy and my delight. I will praise you with the lyre, O God, my God.*
PSALM 43:4 NIV

Think about your best day ever. The day where everything went your way and everything was beautiful. How did that day make you feel? Were you so happy that it felt like your heart would crack open to make more room for happiness? Did it stay that way? Probably not. Eventually, the sunshine went away or your friends went home or you broke your new phone. This is because happiness is a temporary feeling. It is impossible to be happy every moment of every day. However, this does not mean that you can't live a life of joy.

Joy is a little different from happiness. Happiness is a fleeting emotion in the moment, while joy refers to living a lifestyle of contentment. If you have been given true joy in the Lord, you will still find reasons to rejoice, even when life is at its bleakest. Happiness won't stay, but true joy lasts a lifetime.

*Dear Lord, thank You for making joy possible.*
*Without Your loving kindness, life would be a*
*much gloomier thing. Remind me that even when*
*I am not happy, I still have reason for joy.*

*Day 340*

# Bullies Hurt

*"Be strong and courageous. Do not be afraid or terrified because of them, for the LORD your God goes with you; he will never leave you nor forsake you."*

<small>DEUTERONOMY 31:6 NIV</small>

You know that feeling. That feeling in the pit of your stomach when you see that person who goes out of the way to be cruel to you. Whether it is with mocking words or actual physical abuse, this person is a bully and you are the victim. It can be a truly hopeless feeling. Or maybe you aren't the one who is actually bullied, but some other kid in your class is. Maybe they are a little weird or different, and that is why they have been made a target.

Being bullied is very hard, but it is important to remember that God is on your side. The key is being kind to everyone around you. If you see a kid in your class being bullied, invite them to sit with you and your friends at lunch. If you are the kid being bullied, don't let fear drive you to silence. Talk to your teacher, but remember to be forgiving. While bullies are awful, their cruelty often comes from a place of insecurity and fear. God called us to love our enemies, even the bullies.

*Dear Lord, give me the courage to stand up to the bullies of the world, but also give me the courage to forgive them.*

## Day 341

# Memorizing Scripture

*"Keep this Book of the Law always on your lips; meditate on it day and night, so that you may be careful to do everything written in it. Then you will be prosperous and successful."*

JOSHUA 1:8 NIV

On your way to school, your mom turns on the radio. As you are riding down the road, your favorite song comes on. You light up—this is your jam! You sing along at the top of your lungs, and you know every word. The next song comes on, and you still know all the words. You even know all the words to the songs that you don't like! Music is such a part of your life that your brain has stored endless lyrics away. Wouldn't it be wonderful if you knew scripture like that?

Oftentimes, Christians don't even know what is inside their Bible. However, you are called to meditate on scripture day and night, never letting it depart from your lips. By reading the Bible every day, you will always have God's Word in the back of your mind. Consequently, it will be much easier to reference it as a guide for your life. Make it a goal to memorize scripture regularly as a part of your spiritual growth.

*Dear Lord, Your Word is a lamp to guide my feet! Help me meditate on scripture daily so that I can better understand Your plan for me.*

*Day 342*

# The Importance of Friendship

*One who has unreliable friends soon comes to ruin,*
*but there is a friend who sticks closer than a brother.*
PROVERBS 18:24 NIV

Do you remember your first friend? You ran around outside and played with your dolls together, sharing secrets and watching movies. From an early age, humans are hardwired to seek out friends and build relationships. It is important to be discerning when you make friends because while a good friend can build you up, a bad one can tear you down. While people all differ in how many friends they want, everyone needs a good friend to rely on. Whether you prefer to be friends with everyone or have a small, close-knit group on your side, friendship is truly one of God's greatest gifts.

With that in mind, be thankful every day for the friends that you have! Sometimes they will hurt you and you will hurt them, but a true friend apologizes, forgives, and works out their issues. Friendship is worth all the hard stuff. Good friends support you and help you become the best version of yourself, and you do the same for them. Friendship is a two-way street—make sure that it is a safe one.

*Dear Lord, thank You for my friends! You have truly blessed me with awesome people in my life. Help me be the best friend that I can be!*

# Being a Better Sister

*Be kind and compassionate to one another, forgiving
each other, just as in Christ God forgave you.*
EPHESIANS 4:32 NIV

You were just trying to get your homework done. You would think that
you could get a little privacy in your own room, but no. You can hear the
small hands scrabbling at the door. You roll your eyes and begin to scream.
Either that or you are the younger sister. You know that your brother is
hanging out with his friends, but you want to be the center of attention.
You bang on the door until they open it, and then you run away cackling.

Sometimes it isn't easy being a sibling. Sometimes it even seems like
it is just easier to be unkind and annoy your siblings instead of trying to
build good relationships with them. However, patience and kindness can
get you a long way. Being siblings is a truly special relationship, and you
shouldn't let petty disagreements come between you. Instead, work together
to keep these disagreements to a minimum. You may even become friends
too instead of just siblings. Even if they still drive you a little bit crazy.

*Dear Lord, thank You so much for my family. Even if they can be
frustrating and insane, I know that they are always on my side.*

## Day 344

# Your Parents Are Smarter Than You Think

*"Honor your father and your mother, so that you may live long in the land the LORD your God is giving you."*

EXODUS 20:12 NIV

It happens to everyone: you get invited to your first teenage party. You desperately want to go, but your parents don't think it will be a safe environment for you. Because of their concerns, they tell you that you can't go. Because of this, your world is seemingly ending. They are dumb idiots who don't understand you. How could they be so mean?

However, with a little age and experience, you start to realize that maybe your parents knew a little more than you thought. They have your best interests at heart and just want to help you flourish and be safe. So maybe you should cut them a little slack. Instead of fighting them on every choice, learn to accept their wisdom. This doesn't mean to accept blindly—instead, try talking through your issues with your parents so you can fully understand each other's perspectives. Open communication and respect will help these relationships flourish! Your parents have so much love in their hearts for you, and you for them. Take some time to tell them.

*Dear Lord, thank You for giving me great parents! I am so blessed to have such a supportive home! Thank You for this crazy bunch of people I call my family.*

# Hard Work Will Get You Far

*I can do all this through him who gives me strength.*
PHILIPPIANS 4:13 NIV

It is good to have goals! Whether it is improving your grades, learning a new skill, or joining a sports team, all truly good things require work. You can't get As without studying. You can't learn a new piano piece if you don't practice. You can't score the winning goal without training with your team. If you really want to succeed, you have to put in the time. There is no shortcut to improvement.

Instead of just waiting around and slacking off, do the work. Even when it seems impossible, remember that God has given you the strength to succeed. However, you have to meet Him halfway. Good things come to those who try, and fail, and then try again. Even if it's hard, improving your skills and meeting your goals are great! Next time you are tempted to be lazy, think about what you could be doing instead. Success comes to those who put their talents to good use. Don't hide what God has given you under a basket!

. . . . . . . . . . . . . . . . . . . . . . . . . . . . . . . . . . . . . . . . . . . . . . . . . . .

*Dear Lord, thank You for all the talents that You have given me! Keep me humble, but also give me the drive to set goals and work hard to meet them.*

# Put Down Your Phone!

*When I consider your heavens, the work of your fingers, the moon*
*and the stars, which you have set in place, what is mankind that*
*you are mindful of them, human beings that you care for them?*
PSALM 8:3–4 NIV

Modern technology is great. On a device that fits in the palm of your hand, you can call anyone you know or get endless information on any topic you want. With all of that power at your disposal, it is easy to get drawn in and forget to engage in the world around you. It is great to be able to learn more about the world through your phone, but it is important not to forget to actually look at the beautiful world around you.

Put down your phone. Go outside. God has created a masterpiece with His creation, and you were made to care for it. Remember to spend some time out in nature and enjoy what God has made. Look for ways that you can spend a little time outside. Help your mom in her garden or plant a tree with your dad. Don't get so caught up in the digital world that you forget the beauty of the natural one.

*Dear Lord, thank You for creating such a beautiful*
*world! You didn't have to have such wonderful variety*
*in nature, and yet Your world is magnificent.*

# Everyone Deserves Respect

*Be devoted to one another in love. Honor one another above yourselves.*
Romans 12:10 niv

It is easy to forget to think of others. You get so wrapped up in your own stuff: school, friends, sports, clubs. You start to think that your stuff is more important than anyone else's, that the sun orbits you and your life. Because of this, you forget to treat the people around you with the respect that they deserve. Be understanding and realize that everyone has a lot going on, not just you. Their stuff is important as well, and you should treat them accordingly.

Everyone deserves respect. Everyone. From the teacher in your classroom to the kid down the street, it is important to treat others the way that you would like to be treated. Instead of just respecting the people who are in charge of you, try also to be compassionate to everyone, even those who can give you nothing. You may be surprised at how good you feel when you're kind to others. Everyone has been made in God's image, so everyone has value.

*Dear Lord, help me be kind and respectful to others, even if it isn't easy. Jesus cared for everyone He met. Help me follow His example.*

*Day 348*

# Be Patient

*My dear brothers and sisters, take note of this: Everyone should
be quick to listen, slow to speak and slow to become angry.*
JAMES 1:19 NIV

"Patience is a virtue!" Every time something goes wrong, your mom reminds you of this old adage: "Patience is a virtue." You know this is true, but why do you have to wait so long? You're a pretty good person—why can't you get what you want when you want it? Unfortunately, that is not how the Christian life works. God's goal for our lives is not necessarily to be happy but to be made into a more perfect image of Him. This often requires a lot of work and a lot of patience.

Instead of always frothing at the bit, try to practice being quiet or being still. Instead of always speaking first and loudly, work on your listening skills. God is molding you into a more beautiful creation every day, much like the blacksmith forges metal into a stronger, smoother shape. It may be painful, and sometimes even tedious, but having patience in the face of the Lord's molding will produce truly incredible results.

*Dear Lord, give me the patience to be molded. You are forming me
into a being that reflects You in all things, but that doesn't happen
overnight. Teach me to be patient and to wait for Your steady hands.*

Day 349

# It's Not the End of the World...or Is It?

*Therefore, since we are surrounded by such a great cloud of witnesses, let us throw off everything that hinders and the sin that so easily entangles. And let us run with perseverance the race marked out for us, fixing our eyes on Jesus, the pioneer and perfecter of faith.*
HEBREWS 12:1–2 NIV

When you're young, everything can feel like the end of the world. If you don't get to see your favorite band on tour, your life is meaningless. If you don't get to go to that party, everything is terrible. If you make a bad grade, the cosmos is crumbling around you. However, life still goes on. The band will come back, there will be an even better party, and you can study harder for the next test. By being patient, you will realize that everything happens not on your timing but on God's.

Instead of getting upset and breaking down when things don't go your way, focus on God's timing. He has a glorious plan for your life; you just have to learn to wait on His plan. When it looks like your plans won't pan out, the world is not ending. It is just shifting, and you are shifting with it. When you learn to go where God's plan leads you, you will experience true success.

*Dear Lord, I am so excited to see the plan You have for my life! I am ready for truly great things.*

# Everyone Is Lonely (Sometimes)

*Cast all your anxiety on him because he cares for you.*
1 PETER 5:7 NIV

Somehow you can be surrounded by people but still be desperately lonely. Whether your friend group changes or your parents divorce, numerous factors can lead to you spending a lot of time on your own. You might feel inadequate or that it is somehow your fault. Anxiety and self-doubt plague your thoughts, and you withdraw deeper into a dark hole.

Everyone has felt "less than" at one point or another. But even when it feels like everyone you know has abandoned you, God hasn't. He is always there for you, no matter how alone you feel. He will carry you through these darker times of your life, even if you don't realize it at the time. Either through His Word or by putting people into your orbit to help you through the lonely times, God is always on your side. He cares for you and wants you to be surrounded by people who bring you joy and help you grow. He will never, ever abandon you, even when it seems that everyone else has. It is good to know that God's love for you will never waver.

*Dear Lord, thank You for Your steadfast love. You are my rock in the difficult times. Thank You for helping me find my way out of the dark.*

# Honesty Is the Best Policy

*"Then you will know the truth, and the truth will set you free."*
JOHN 8:32 NIV

Well, it's happened. You've been caught in a lie. You didn't study for the quiz, and you tried to read the answers off of your best friend's paper. Your teacher catches you. She knows you cheated. You know you cheated, and yet you try to deny it. This only makes the deceit even stickier. Now you not only lied on your quiz but you lied to your teacher's face. She is disappointed in you, and you are disappointed in yourself. A lying tongue is an affront to God.

In most situations, honesty is truly the best policy. By lying, you are distancing yourself from the people around you, building up walls on the foundation of lies. However, God doesn't stand for that. It is said that the truth will set you free, and the truth will always find you out. Instead of waiting for that terrible moment when you are caught in your lie, save yourself the stress and just tell the truth. Being transparent with your choices is a great way to live and grow in Christ.

. . . . . . . . . . . . . . . . . . . . . . . . . . . . . . . . . . . . . . . . . . . . . . . . . . . .

*Dear Lord, I am sorry for the lies that I have told,*
*but thank You for always guiding me back to the truth.*

# Just Be Yourself

*I praise you because I am fearfully and wonderfully made;*
*your works are wonderful, I know that full well.*

PSALM 139:14 NIV

Sometimes it can feel like no one understands you. No one else loves your hobbies, or they don't like to spend their time like you do. Sometimes it can feel like it is you against the world, and no one around you gets what makes you tick. It's okay. Read your books. Listen to your music. Like what you like, and just be yourself. Eventually you will find people who are filled with the same fire, and glorious friendships will be born.

Even if it seems like you'll never fit in or find people like you, God made you to be just who you are. There is not a hair out of place. He didn't make a mistake. Instead of wishing that God had made you differently, celebrate who you are! Work on becoming the best version of yourself, the best version of who God has made. There is a peace that comes with just being yourself, and everyone deserves to have that peace.

*Dear Lord, thank You for creating me. Even when I feel weird or like the odd girl out, I know that I am a part of Your wonderful creation!*

## Day 353

# A World in Winter

*There is a time for everything, and a season for
every activity under the heavens.*
ECCLESIASTES 3:1 NIV

In the winter, you probably deal with some pretty cold climates. Whether it is just plunging temperatures or if you even have some snow and ice, it seems like the world is going into a deep sleep. Most plants are dormant, and many animals are going into hibernation. People stay home more to avoid the elements. While winter is nice for a while, it eventually begins to feel like spring will never come again. But every year, spring does come forth again, gloriously alive.

In a similar way, many years ago the world was waiting for a Savior. The hearts of men had grown cold and despondent. It felt like an endless spiritual winter, and it seemed as though the promised child would never come. However, that child did come, and His name is Jesus. This spiritual renewal was like spring had sprung in the hearts of God's people. Now, many years later, it can feel again like a winter without Jesus. Thankfully, there is still the promise of a new spring when Jesus returns.

*Dear Lord, thank You for the promise of spring. When I am stuck in
the bleakness of winter, all I have to do is remember that You will
always bring back the warmth and sunshine. You are faithful.*

# It Is Okay Not to Be Cool

*For we are God's handiwork, created in Christ Jesus to do*
*good works, which God prepared in advance for us to do.*
EPHESIANS 2:10 NIV

Being cool is hard. It takes a lot of work to stay on top, and what is considered "cool" is always changing. New music becomes popular every day. New clothing styles come into fashion as quickly as they go out. Staying on trend requires an extraordinary amount of time—and money. Is it worth it?

Instead of focusing on how to be popular, focus on how you can become a greater vessel for God's love. Show people kindness instead of just showing off designer jeans. It is okay to not be cool. That's not why you were created. You were created to do good works, to show Christ's love to the world. It is easy to get caught up in a popularity contest, but remember that isn't what life is about. Jesus hung out with the lepers, the tax collectors, and the people with the least amount of power in society. He didn't worry about being cool; He worried about being kind and about loving others well.

* * * * * * * * * * * * * * * * * * * * * * * * * * * * * * * * * * * * * *

*Dear Lord, I am sorry that I have gotten so wrapped up*
*in wanting to be popular. That isn't what life is about.*
*Instead, help me reach out to people with kindness.*

## Day 355

# Being a Better Daughter

*But the fruit of the Spirit is love, joy, peace, forbearance,
kindness, goodness, faithfulness, gentleness and self-
control. Against such things there is no law.*
GALATIANS 5:22–23 NIV

You have pretty great parents, right? They work hard every single day to provide a safe and loving home for their children, never asking for anything in return. How often do you thank them? Every day? On Sundays? On your birthday? Because it is such a natural thing, you often forget how much your parents sacrifice to provide for you.

There are many ways that you can show your gratitude. First of all, remembering to say thank you is a very simple place to start. This pair of small words can go a long way when paired with a sincere attitude. You can also help out with different things around your house without complaint. Bonus points if you do the task before you are even asked. Also, your general attitude can be either beneficial or detrimental to letting your parents know you care. Instead of emulating the teens on many television shows and being surly and insulting to your elders, try to let your thankfulness manifest itself in an outpouring of good humor. This isn't always possible, but making a conscious effort is a step in the right direction.

*Dear Lord, thank You for my loving parents. They provide so much for me that I don't even know where to begin to thank them. Show me how to be a good daughter and to grow in a spirit of thankfulness and respect.*

# Gossip Helps No One

*Keep your tongue from evil and your lips from telling lies.*
PSALM 34:13 NIV

Whether you have started a rumor, shared a rumor, or had a rumor spread about you, you have definitely been exposed to gossip. When you hear a new secret, it can be a bit of a thrill. You hold the information that could make or break a person, and with that comes the feeling of power. However, it is only hollow. Instead of helping to encourage and build up the people around you, gossip only tears down. Gossip is often the product of someone trying to feel better about themselves by making another person feel worse. However, in the long run, making someone feel worse will not make you feel any better.

While it is sometimes quite difficult, it is important to take a stand against gossip. Decline in taking part, and encourage your friends to do the same. Instead of spreading malice, focus on encouraging the people around you. A kind word can go a long way. Work on building up instead of tearing down. Gossip often does irreparable harm, and it is not how God would want you to spend your time.

*Dear Lord, let the words that come out of my mouth only be words of encouragement. Help me as I attempt to build up my friends and classmates instead of tearing them down with hateful words.*

*Day* 357

# Worry Wastes Time

*Now may the Lord of peace himself give you peace at all*
*times and in every way. The Lord be with all of you.*

2 THESSALONIANS 3:16 NIV

It is hard not being in control. You can plan out every step of your life, but there is no way to really know what will happen in the future. This worry can cause a great deal of inner turmoil and anxiety. What if I don't have any friends? What if I don't do well in school? What if something happens to my family? Worrying can be truly toxic and can have a crippling effect on your life. If you are so worried about every outcome, how will you ever actually make a choice?

Instead of worrying, trust God. He has promised countless times in the Bible that He will always take care of His people. It isn't always easy to do, but your life will be better for it. Instead of worrying about what *can* happen, look forward instead to what *will* happen. God has a great plan for you! Whatever He has in mind is infinitely more awesome than anything that you can come up with.

*Dear Lord, I am so excited to see the plans that*
*You have for me! Please ease my worried mind and*
*remind me to trust Your timing, not my own.*

## Day 358

# Facing Temptation

*"Watch and pray so that you will not fall into temptation.
The spirit is willing, but the flesh is weak."*
MATTHEW 26:41 NIV

You are faced with temptation every single day. You can be tempted to be unkind to your little sister or disrespectful to your parents. You may be tempted to cheat on a test or post a tweet making fun of your teacher. You may have even been tempted to go too far with boys. Unfortunately, the constant allure of temptation never goes away. Staying on the straight and narrow path never gets easier. Every day, the devil will try to tempt God's people to stray.

Luckily, you serve a God who can handle the pressure. He will give you all the strength and tools that you need to stand up in the face of temptation; you only need to call on Him for help. By constantly being in God's Word and filling your mind with His teachings, you will have everything you need to resist temptation. Never give up! Always keep fighting! The righteous path is never easy, but it always reaps the greatest rewards in the end.

*Dear Lord, I look to You for guidance. Even though it is hard to resist the temptations of the world, the flesh, and the devil, I know that with You on my side, I can stand strong against anything.*

## Day 359

# Anticipating the Savior

*For to us a child is born, to us a son is given, and the government will be on his shoulders. And he will be called Wonderful Counselor, Mighty God, Everlasting Father, Prince of Peace.*
ISAIAH 9:6 NIV

Christmas is coming! There are so many delightful things to do! It is time to chop down that tree and hang some twinkling lights on the front porch. Caroling, wrapping presents, baking cookies—it is truly the most wonderful time of the year. However, there is so much more to Christmas than all that. When it becomes all about the experience and material gain, people lose sight of the real meaning of Christmas: the birth of Jesus.

While all of the trees and trimmings are fun, it is important to remember that Jesus is the true reason for the season. He came down into a sinful world as an innocent baby and saved the world while sacrificing His life. He brought with Him the promise of peace, freedom, and eternal life. So instead of waiting for Santa this Christmas Eve, wait for Jesus. Wait for the Savior. He is coming. Will you hear His call? Will you answer?

*Dear Lord, as we approach Christmas, help me remember that it isn't about the superficial things; it is about the Savior. You sent Your only Son to save the world, and because of that, my relationship with You has been restored.*

## *Day 360*
# The Ultimate Gift

*But the angel said to them, "Do not be afraid. I bring you good news*
*that will cause great joy for all the people. Today in the town of*
*David a Savior has been born to you; he is the Messiah, the Lord."*

LUKE 2:10–11 NIV

You have been waiting forever, and the day is finally here: Christmas! You run downstairs, full of anticipation, and you are greeted by your family and a mountain of presents under the Christmas tree. Everyone is smiling and content. Your parents got you exactly what you wanted, but still you wonder: *Is this it?* Is this what you have been waiting for all year? There is still a bit of emptiness because ultimately, these gifts are just things.

There is only one Christmas present that can bring true contentment: the gift of salvation. God looked down on a weak and weary world, and instead of leaving them to their own sinful devices, He sent His only Son to free the world from the bonds of sin and death and to rebuild the communion between God and man. This is truly the greatest gift that you have ever been given.

*Dear Lord, thank You for giving the world the gift of*
*Your Son! You are truly merciful, and You have filled*
*us with gladness and tidings of great joy!*

## Day 361
# Real Freedom

*"So if the Son sets you free, you will be free indeed."*
JOHN 8:36 NIV

When you're young, you are always waiting on someone else. Waiting for your mom to get your little brother into the car so you can make it to your soccer game. Waiting for your teacher to let your class out at the end of the day. Waiting for your friend to come over so you can hang out. Waiting, waiting, waiting. You can't wait to be older and be able to live by your own time and be free to live your life. However, even then, you won't truly be "free." With this newfound freedom, you will also find yourself with a new, long list of responsibilities.

The only real freedom is when you put your life in God's hands. It may seem wrong to hand over control of your life to experience true freedom. However, the only way to be free from the worries of the world is to trust in God. Trusting in God on earth will also prepare you for the ultimate freedom: freedom in heaven to worship Christ endlessly.

*Dear Lord, You alone provide real freedom! I will focus on the help that You provide instead of looking for fleeting forms of freedom. Thank You for removing the shackles of sin and death from my ankles.*

## Day 362
# Helping Others

*"In the same way, let your light shine before others, that they may see your good deeds and glorify your Father in heaven."*
MATTHEW 5:16 NIV

As you get older, you start to get busier and busier. Instead of just playing with your friends all day, you go to school, you go to clubs, you join teams, you make more friends. Slowly but surely, your life is incredibly full, and it is easy to lose sight of the people who need you. You get wrapped up in your own busyness, and you forget that it isn't all about you. Life with Christ is about helping others.

You can start out with small steps. Offer to help your mom take care of the house—or at least do your chores without her having to ask twice. Help your dad do some yard work on Saturday morning. Help your little sister build that fort that's been collapsing on her all week. You can even think beyond the walls of your home. Talk to your youth leader about getting your youth group involved with local organizations that help those who really need it, like the Red Cross or Habitat for Humanity. When you are filled with the love of Christ, there is no limit to how much you can help!

*Dear Lord, You have poured out so much love into me that it is overflowing into the hearts of others! Thank You for helping me cultivate a compassionate spirit. Give me opportunities to help in every situation.*

## Day 363

# Being Grateful

*Enter his gates with thanksgiving and his courts with praise;*
*give thanks to him and praise his name. For the LORD is good and his*
*love endures forever; his faithfulness continues through all generations.*

PSALM 100:4–5 NIV

Sometimes you don't get what you want. You don't get the latest and greatest smartphone for your birthday. You don't get to hang out with your friends on Friday night. You have to share a room with your sister, and you may even have to wear some of her hand-me-down clothes. In such a consumerist culture, it is easy to get bogged down in what you don't have. "Life would be easier if I just had. . ." is often a common response. But would it really? Would your life really be easier if you had more stuff?

No, it wouldn't. There is always that next new, cool thing that you just have to have. If your life becomes one endless quest for what's next, you will just end up exhausted and grouchy. Instead of focusing on what you don't have, look at all the wonderful things God has given you! A loving family, a roof over your head, your good health—these are all gifts from God! His grace truly abounds.

*Dear Lord, You have given me so much more than I deserve!*
*Thank You for all the treasures of Your grace! I am so very grateful.*

## Day 364
# Pray, Pray, Pray!

*The LORD is near to all who call on him, to all who call on him in truth.*
PSALM 145:18 NIV

+

Think about how often you talk to your best friend. Between smartphones, the internet, and actual face-to-face time, it is possible to talk to your best friend constantly throughout the day. You can tell a joke that you just heard or talk about your bad day to a willing ear. It is great to have someone to talk to all the time. Now imagine if you treated your relationship with God like you did your best friend.

God is always listening. If you bring your troubles and praises to Him daily, imagine how much your relationship will flourish! People get so caught up with trying to live a Christian life that they forget the relational aspect. God doesn't want you to just read and obey; He wants you to talk to Him like a child talks to her Father. While it may feel a little weird at first, try to institute an attitude of continuous prayer. You may be surprised by the results.

. . . . . . . . . . . . . . . . . . . . . . . . . . . . . . . . . . . . . . . . . . . . . . . . . . . .

*Dear Lord, thank You for always lending a willing ear. You truly care about my life and desire that I approach You as a Father and friend. Even with all the universe at Your command, You still want to hear from me. Thank You for this beautiful gift.*

# Being a Better Friend

*Two are better than one, because they have a good return for*
*their labor: If either of them falls down, one can help the other*
*up. But pity anyone who falls and has no one to help them up.*

ECCLESIASTES 4:9–10 NIV

Have you ever let a friend down? It's a terrible feeling, isn't it? A friend should always be there to help, but you missed your opportunity. You got caught up in your own life and forgot to ask them about theirs. Being a friend means putting others first, but selfishness is a weed that can often choke out the blossom of friendship. Instead of focusing on what a friend can do for you, set some concrete goals to strengthen your friendships.

For example, instead of just unloading all your drama after a hard day, ask them how they are doing first. And don't just ask without engagement. Really listen to what they have to say. Also, a big part of being a good friend is just showing up. If they are having a bad day, bake some cookies with your mom and deliver them with an encouraging note. If they have a big game, cheer them on from the stands. If their grandparent is in the hospital, visit them. By putting their needs above your own, you will prove yourself to be a really stellar friend.

*Dear Lord, thank You for all my wonderful friends! You have truly blessed me with a great group of people. Help me strive to be the best friend I can be, always looking for what I can contribute instead of what I can gain.*

## Day 366
# Looking Ahead

*Therefore, if anyone is in Christ, the new creation
has come: The old has gone, the new is here!*

2 CORINTHIANS 5:17 NIV

Woo-hoo! Another year older, another year wiser. It was surely a year of growth in the Holy Spirit. Over this past year, you have truly become the new creation that God has called you to be. You have continued to scrape off the old, sinful self while pulling on the new robes of righteousness that God has given you. The new year also presents a great opportunity to cast off lingering bad habits. How can you keep this up in the new year?

The main thing to remember is to stay in the Word. Set a goal to read through the Bible in a year! It may seem daunting when you look at it all in one giant book, but by breaking it down into small goals, it is a totally manageable goal. Maybe encourage your entire family to take part. Also, as you approach the new year, remember to be thankful. You have been given the gift of life. What a blessing! Don't forget to shine your light in the new year!

*Dear Lord, thank You for a great year. It has truly been a time
of growth, and I have been blessed beyond measure. Give me
the fortitude to continue to follow You in the coming days.*

# Contributors

**Alyssa Fikse** lives and works in West Georgia but is planning to continue her education at Drexel University with a graduate degree in Library and Information Sciences. Alyssa's devotions appear on days 336–366.

**Renae Brumbaugh Green** lives in Texas with her handsome country-boy husband, her noisy children, a rowdy dog, and a bunch of chickens and ducks. She's published more than twenty-five books and a whole bunch of articles. Her favorite color is blue, unless you're talking about nail polish, in which case her favorite color is bubblegum pink. Renae's devotions appear on days 275–305.

As an author, speaker, mentor to authors, ghostwriter, editor, and product developer, **Shanna D. Gregor** has served various ministries and publishers for more than twenty years to develop more than eighty books that express God's voice for today. Through her company, Gregor Connections, she offers editorial services and author mentorship and helps others create, write, and develop products. She and her husband, Blaine, are empty nesters, enjoying thirty-plus years of marriage. Shanna's devotions appear on days 245–274.

**Carol Hill** is the author of *100 Days Until Forever* and *Steps Toward the Shepherd*. A mother of five and grandmother of four, Carol and her husband of over forty years are enjoying their empty nest. Carol's devotions appear on days 32–60.

**Ardythe Kolb** is a wife, mother, and freelance writer with three books and devotions or stories in over a dozen compilations. She serves on the board of Heart of America Christian Writers' Network as editor of its monthly newsletter. Besides writing, she volunteers as a CASA for abused children. Ardythe's devotions appear on days 306–335.

**Shelley R. Lee** is the author of *When Jesus Speaks a Mother's Heart* (Barbour), *Before I Knew You*, *Mat Madness*, and numerous magazine and book contributions, most recently to both *3-Minute Devotions for a Cat Lover's Soul* and *3-Minute Devotions for a Dog Lover's Soul* (Barbour). She resides in the rural Bowling Green area with her husband of thirty years, David. Their four adult sons, daughter-in-law, and two grandchildren continue to provide humorous adventure stories posted on her blog at shelleyrlee.com. Shelley's devotions appear on days 153–182.

**Emily Marsh** lives in Virginia with her husband, Seth. She works at a downtown real estate firm, at a local dance studio, and as a Pilates instructor. Emily's devotions appear on days 1–31.

The three things that inspire **Lydia Mindling**'s writing are God's love, Christ's sacrifice, and creation. When not writing, Lydia enjoys horseback riding, hikes, and attempts at baking the world's best brownies. Lydia's devotions appear on days 92–121.

**MariLee Parrish** lives in Colorado with her husband, Eric, and their young children. She's a freelance musician and writer who desires to paint a picture of God with her life, talents, and ministries. MariLee's devotions appear on days 214–244.

**Karon Phillips** of Alabama is an inspiration to the tens of thousands of women who've read her books (*You're Late Again, Lord!*, *Grab a Broom, Lord...*, and *You Still Here, Lord?*). She has also written for many magazines, including *Woman's Day* and *Writer's Digest*. Karon's devotions appear on days 122–152.

**Shana Schutte** is an author and speaker. She is the author of several books including *30 Days of Hope*. You can learn more about Shana by visiting shanaschutte.com. Shana's devotions appear on days 61–91.

**Karin Dahl Silver** lives in Colorado Springs, Colorado, with her husband, Scott. When she's not writing or editing, she loves to hike, bake, and have long talks about art. Karin's devotions appear on days 183–213.

# Scripture Index

## OLD TESTAMENT

## Proverbs

# NEW TESTAMENT

# More Encouragement for Your Beautiful Spirit!

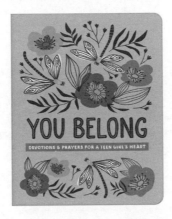

### You Were Created with Purpose by a Loving, Heavenly Creator. . .*You Belong!*

This delightful devotional is a lovely reminder of that you were created with purpose by a heavenly Creator. . .and that you belong—right here and now—in this world. 180 encouraging readings and inspiring prayers, rooted in biblical truth, will reassure your uncertain heart, helping you to understand that you're never alone and always loved. In each devotional reading, you will encounter the bountiful blessings and grace of your Creator, while coming to trust His purposeful plan for you in this world.

Flexible Casebound / 978-1-63609-169-3